Doing VISUAL ETHNOGRAPHY

3RD EDITION

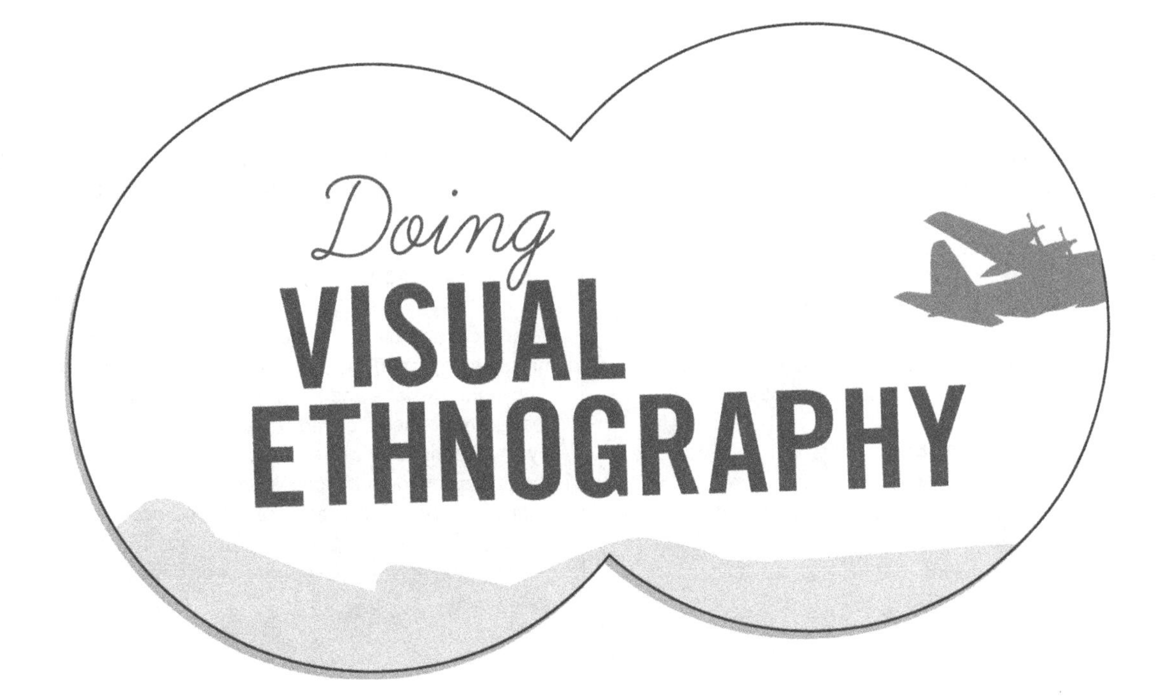

SARAH PINK

Los Angeles | London | New Delhi
Singapore | Washington DC

Los Angeles | London | New Delhi
Singapore | Washington DC

SAGE Publications Ltd
1 Oliver's Yard
55 City Road
London EC1Y 1SP

SAGE Publications Inc.
2455 Teller Road
Thousand Oaks, California 91320

SAGE Publications India Pvt Ltd
B 1/I 1 Mohan Cooperative Industrial Area
Mathura Road
New Delhi 110 044

SAGE Publications Asia-Pacific Pte Ltd
3 Church Street
#10-04 Samsung Hub
Singapore 049483

Editor: Jai Seaman
Assistant editor: Anna Horvai
Production editor: Ian Antcliff
Copyeditor: Jennifer Hinchliffe
Proofreader: Anna Gilding
Indexer: Silvia Benvenuto
Marketing manager: Ben Griffin-Sherwood
Cover design: Francis Kenney
Typeset by: C&M Digitals (P) Ltd, Chennai, India

First published 2001, reprinted 2002, 2003, 2004, 2005.
Second edition published 2006, reprinted 2007, 2009, twice 2010 and 2012.

First published 2013

Library of Congress Control Number: 2012955561

British Library Cataloguing in Publication data

A catalogue record for this book is available from the British Library

ISBN 978-1-4462-1116-8
ISBN 978-1-4462-1117-5 (pbk)

Contents

Acknowledgements vii
About the author ix

Introduction 1

Part 1 Thinking About Visual Ethnography: Historical, Theoretical And Practical Perspectives 13

1 Visual Ethnography across Disciplines 15
2 Ways of Seeing, Knowing and Showing 33
3 Planning and Practising Visual Ethnography 49

Part 2 Producing Knowledge 71

4 Photography in Ethnographic Research 73
5 Video in Ethnographic Research 103
6 Doing Visual Ethnography with the Web 123
7 Making Meanings in Visual Ethnography 141

Part 3 Representing Visual Ethnography 161

8 Photography and Ethnographic Writing 165
9 Video in Ethnographic Representation 183
10 Making Visual Ethnography Public Online/Digitally 203

References 215
Index 233

Acknowledgements

When I wrote the first edition of *Doing Visual Ethnography* in the late 1990s I did so with the conviction that a visual approach to ethnographic research was emerging as a key methodological strand. The book's title, which was proposed by SAGE, sums up very well my intentions. In preparing it I drew together my own and other researchers' experiences along with theoretical and substantive interests in visual cultures and visual representations to propose a visual ethnographic methodology. In its original form this book was inspired greatly by my readings and viewings of and conversations about the work of visual anthropologists, sociologists and artists and since the publication of the first edition I have corresponded with and met many more ethnographers who share an enthusiasm for the visual – across disciplines and interdisciplinary fields, and internationally. Some of the research and images introduced in the second edition and in this third edition draw on the work of visual ethnographers who have dialogued with *Doing Visual Ethnography* in their publications and practice. I am greatly indebted to them for both appreciating my initial text and for providing, through their own practice, a new body of work that this new edition is, in turn, created to dialogue with.

The ideas and examples discussed in this book also draw extensively on my own theoretical and methodological research around visual and digital methods and media in recent years. Such reflections and discussions form part of my ongoing participation in fields including visual studies, media studies and everyday life research. Therefore while I do not directly re-publish any existing texts in this book, I do refer often to the ideas and arguments that have formed part of my research trajectory over the last ten or so years. In this sense most of the arguments and some of the examples given here are developed and discussed in more depth and detail or from different perspectives in other publications. On the one hand my purpose in mentioning this is to acknowledge the relationship between this book and existing work. However on the other it is to highlight that, where relevant, these existing works are always referenced so that readers can follow up theoretical discussions and methodological developments in more depth where needed. *Doing Visual Ethnography* is of course intended to make a clear statement about visual ethnography in its own right. However, it is by nature a book that seeks to do so by reviewing and analysing the wider field of practice in question, therefore within it I have endeavoured to maintain a balance between its intellectual and practical engagement.

The book also draws extensively from my own experiences and would not have been possible without the support of the many people who have collaborated in my research, allowing me to photograph or video them over the last 20 or so years. A special thanks is due to all those who are mentioned in this particular book, but my appreciation goes beyond that. I cannot name here everyone in person, but I would like to extend these thanks to all those who have worked with me, for showing me aspects of their lives and, in doing so, allowing me to learn how to be an ethnographer. For the combination of visual and ethnographic training that has informed this work, and technical support in producing images for this book, I am indebted to the staff of the Granada Centre for Visual Anthropology at the University of Manchester, where I trained as a masters student, the Centre for Anthropology and Computing at the University of Kent, the Department of Social Sciences at Loughborough University, and multimedia developers at the University of Derby, all in the UK. At Loughborough, the IN3 in Barcelona (Spain), and RMIT University in Melbourne (Australia) where the ideas for this third edition began to form and have developed, I have benefitted from academic environments and the time needed to complete this work. For the intellectual inspiration to continue to work on *Doing Visual Ethnography* over the years leading to this third edition I would like to thank the many people who have invited me to speak about visual ethnography at workshops and conferences, the researchers and students who have attended these events, shown me their work, discussed ideas and asked inspiring questions. Finally, for the opportunity to keep developing visual ethnography in practice over the last years I would like to thank both the colleagues who have collaborated with me and believed that visual ethnography will deepen our understandings, and the various organisations who have funded my research: the ESRC which funded my PhD research into women and bullfighting in Spain; Unilever who funded my video ethnography work on the home; the Nuffield Foundation who funded my work on Slow cities; Construction Skills who funded the interdisciplinary work of my colleagues and myself into migrant workers in the construction industry; and the interdisciplinary LEEDR project, based at Loughborough University, which is jointly funded by the UK Research Councils' Digital Economy and Energy Programmes (grant number EP/I000267/1). For further information about LEEDR collaborating research groups and industrial partners, please visit www.leedr-project.co.uk.

About the author

Sarah Pink is Professor of Design and Media Ethnography at RMIT University, Australia, Professor of Social Sciences at Loughborough University, UK and Honorary Professor at the Centre for Public Culture and Ideas at Griffith University, Australia. She is known internationally for her work relating to digital visual methodology. Her books in this area include *Advances in Visual Methodology* (ed. 2012), *Visual Interventions* (ed. 2007), *The Future of Visual Anthropology* (2006) and *Working Images* (co-ed., 2004), as well as *Doing Sensory Ethnography* (2009) and *Ethnographic Research in the Construction Industry* (co-ed., 2013). Her methodological work is often developed in the context of research projects that seek to connect theoretical scholarship with applied research, which explores questions including digital media, everyday life, sustainability and ways of knowing.

Introduction

Images are 'everywhere'. They permeate our academic work and everyday lives. They inhabit and inspire our imaginations, technologies, texts and conversations. As mobile media become increasingly ubiquitous images are embedded in the digital architectures of the environments we move through in our everyday routes. The visual is therefore inextricably interwoven with our personal identities, narratives, lifestyles, cultures and societies, as well as with definitions of history, time, space, place, reality and truth. Ethnographic research is likewise intertwined with visual technologies, images, metaphors and ways of seeing. When ethnographers produce photographs or video, these images, as well as the experience of producing and discussing them, become part of their ethnographic knowledge. Images are indeed part of how we experience, learn and know as well as how we communicate and represent knowledge. In research contexts images may inspire conversations, conversation might invoke images; conversation and performances visualise and draw absent printed or digital images into their narratives through verbal descriptions and references to them. Likewise just as an image might invoke a memory of an embodied affective experience, experiences also inspire images. Images are thus an inevitable part of the experiential environments we live and research in; *Doing Visual Ethnography* is an invitation to engage with images, technologies and ways of seeing and experiencing as part of the ethnographic process.

Why do we need Visual Ethnography?

Photography, video and web-based media are increasingly integral elements of the work of ethnographers. It could in fact be argued that it would be difficult to be a contemporary ethnographer without engaging with these media forms and environments and the practices associated with them. We use (increasingly digital) media in doing ethnographic research, we seek to develop understandings of the meanings and experiences that images and visual and media practices have in other people's lives, and our very fieldwork sites may cross online and offline contexts. In these roles visual and digital media are part of the ways we constitute ethnographic knowledge, as well as being used to create representations of ethnographic knowledge. As such, visual ethnographic media and materials offer us forms of continuity between fieldwork in academic and applied research contexts that other media cannot. It is now almost inevitable that as ethnographers we will encounter and benefit from digital visual technologies and images in the course of our research and scholarly practice. We therefore need to understand how they become implicated in the production and dissemination of the ways of knowing that are part of the ethnographic process.

Along with their growing prevalence in ethnographic practice, visual methods and media are also part of the way many of us learn to become ethnographers. For instance, visual methods are taught as topics of university courses in subdisciplines such as visual anthropology and visual sociology, as well as in advanced research training workshops.There is additionally an increasingly global spread of conferences and seminars that focus on visual methods. Yet while visual ethnography might be said to have grown from the disciplines of anthropology and sociology, it is by now definitely not restricted to them. The benefits of a visually oriented ethnographic approach are increasingly recognised in other disciplines including geography as well as in interdisciplinary fields such as consumer research, health studies, education studies, media studies, organisation studies, design research, buildings research and in schools of art. I find myself writing this third edition of *Doing Visual Ethnography* in a context where there is now a wealth of existing literature about visual methods, selected elements of which I discuss in the following chapters of this book. This literature is increasingly spread across academic disciplines and informed by a range of methodological approaches. This context is a stark contrast to the late 1990s when I set about creating the first edition of this book. At that time I believed that visual ethnography was an emergent field that needed to be brought somehow into vision. I did not then have the sense that I do now of this being part of a growing and dynamic international and interdisciplinary field of practice.

This book is primarily for researchers from across 'ethnographic' disciplines and interdisciplinary fields who wish to incorporate audiovisual media into their research practice. It would be impossible to list the range of disciplines such practices would appeal to but, for instance, I would include researchers locating themselves in disciplines as seemingly diverse as those mentioned above. The book is also for visual media practitioners who seek a deeper understanding of how ethnographic research may inform their work. This includes on the one hand photographers, video makers and digital artists. On the other, it refers to scholars and practitioners for whom the visual forms a central element of their work, for instance in fields such as art therapy and phototherapy. My interest in engaging with practitioners and scholars from these fields is not simply based on the idea that they might benefit from the approach of visual ethnography. Rather, these are also disciplines from whose scholarship and practices I have learned since I began to write about visual ethnography.

A shifting context for *Doing Visual Ethnography*

To understand what doing visual ethnography means today, we need to understand something of where it has come from. To contextualise this here I account for its recent history. During the last two decades I have worked with photography, video and web-based media in my own ethnographic work, through periods of technological and theoretical innovations and 'turns'. In the late 1980s proponents of the then 'new ethnography' introduced ideas of ethnography as fiction and emphasised the centrality of subjectivity to the production of knowledge. Anthropology, the discipline in which my work began, experienced a 'crisis' through which positivist arguments and realist approaches to knowledge, truth and objectivity were challenged (see Clifford and Marcus 1986). These ideas paved the way for the visual to be increasingly acceptable in ethnography as it was recognised that ethnographic film or photography were essentially no more subjective or objective than written texts and thus gradually became acceptable to (if not actively engaged with by) most mainstream researchers. During the 1990s new innovations in visual technology, critical postmodern theoretical approaches to subjectivity, experience, knowledge and representation, a reflexive approach to ethnographic fieldwork methodology, and an emphasis on interdisciplinarity invited exciting new possibilities for the use of photographic technologies and images in ethnography. Emerging from that context, at the beginning of the twentieth century, there was a flurry of new literature about and practical work involving visual methodologies. Traversing the social sciences and humanities these developments grew from social anthropology (Ruby 2000a; Banks 2001; Grimshaw 2001; Pink, Kürti and Afonso 2004; Grimshaw and Ravetz 2004; El Guindi 2004; MacDougall 2005; Pink 2006), sociology (Emmison and Smith 2000; O'Neill 2002; Pole 2004; Knowles and Sweetman 2004; Halford and Knowles 2005), and geography (Rose 2001), (see Pink 2006, Chapter 2). Collectively these texts set a new scene for visual methods in an intellectual climate where the impact of the postmodern turn had been assessed and put to rest leaving as its legacy, amongst other things, the reflexive approach to ethnographic and visual research that these works insist on. It was from that context that the second edition of *Doing Visual Ethnography* emerged, through three key influences. First, an enthusiasm for exploring new interdisciplinary themes, connecting ethnography and arts practice (e.g. da Silva and Pink 2004; Grimshaw and Ravetz 2004; Schneider and Wright 2005; Bowman, Grasseni, Hughes-Freeland and Pink 2007) and recognising that visual research must also accommodate embodiment and the senses (e.g. O'Neill 2002; Grimshaw and Ravetz 2004; MacDougall 2005; Pink 2006, 2009). Second, a new emphasis on research about and training in methodology and ethical scrutiny emanating from the institutional requirements now made by funding bodies and universities. This context on the one hand encouraged innovative methodologies. On the other it emphasised the importance of ensuring ethical practice through external scrutiny, and as such in ways often seemingly quite different from those suggested by the self-scrutiny of the reflexive ethnographer. In this environment visual ethnographers needed to be not just self-reflexive about their methods, but also conversant about them in institutional languages (Prosser et al. 2008; Clarke 2012). Finally, visual ethnography began to emerge as an applied as well as an academic practice (Pink 2006, 2007a). These shifts continue to frame the writing of this third edition of *Doing Visual Ethnography*. Yet they are also re-shaped by the further changes and 'turns' of the latter part of the first decade of the twenty-first century. When I was writing the second edition of this book, it was clear that a *visual* ethnography was fast encompassing a digital and web-based form of doing ethnography. Yet, there was still much that could be said about the doing of visual ethnography that did not need to be understood as digital practices. This remains the case to some extent today as we embark on the second decade of the twenty-first century, but with some important differences. Visual ethnography is now a practice which, in my experience, rarely involves the use of analogue cameras, that in some way or other nearly always involves the use of computing equipment and web-based media, and is practised in a context where sometimes ethnographers and research participants have access to very similar technologies. While of course this latter point needs to be qualified by the acknowledgement that global and national inequalities and other forms of difference mean that of course we do not all have equal access to the same media and technologies, the equipment that is needed to do a visual ethnography is no longer incredibly specialised (although some visual ethnographers innovate with highly specialised equipment). On the other hand, using visual methods in ethnographic practice does not have to involve new media, as even recent examples (e.g. Grasseni 2012; Hogan and Pink 2012) show that using printed maps, paper, pens, pencils and other 'old' technologies also make for visual ethnographic methods. Those readers who are holding this very book in its printed form as they read will be experiencing an 'old' materiality that persists in the present. While other readers will be accessing these words and images through digital technologies, perhaps a laptop, tablet computer or smart phone, and developing a different relationship to its written and visual elements as well as the web-based materials it provides links to.

Contemporary ways of doing visual ethnography are also framed by a series of wider shifts that I have argued elsewhere (Pink 2012b) create the context in which visual research methodologies are more generally being shaped. In the introduction to my edited book *Advances in Visual Methodology* (Pink 2012a, 2012b) I discuss these themes, which include the new technological context noted above as well as a series of theoretical turns, leading to a focus on concepts of practice, place and the senses (all themes that I also write about in relation to sensory ethnography (Pink 2009)). Indeed the focus on the senses that became consolidated during the early twenty-first century, necessitates a re-situating of 'visual ethnography' in relation to its arguments and priorities – a question I begin to address in terms of how sensory scholars might engage visual methods in my book *Doing Sensory Ethnography* (Pink 2009) and take up from the perspective of visual ethnography in Chapter 2 of this book. The increasing importance of non-representational (see e.g. Thrift 2008) and 'more-than-representational' (Lorimer 2005) approaches in human geography and in anthropology (see Ingold 2011) demands that we re-conceptualise the ways that we think of the role of images in the world and invites an approach to the visual that departs from conventional cultural studies treatments (see Ingold 2010a; Pink 2011a). Simultaneously, we have seen a further shift towards public and applied visual research and scholarship. Visual methods and media are increasingly engaged in applied research in anthropology and cognate disciplines (Pink 2007b, 2011b, 2012a; Mitchell 2011). As is evident in the examples of recent work I draw on in the discussions in the following chapters, an increasing amount of recent visual ethnography practice is part of this move towards a more engaged, participatory, collaborative and public form of visual scholarship.

Visual ethnography as practiced is therefore shaped by a range of interrelated influences, including disciplinary trajectories and commitments (which are discussed in Chapter 1), theoretical understandings of the meaning and potentials of images and media, technological possibilities, researcher's skills, biographies, subjectivity and reflexivity, and relations of power (see Chapter 2), the research question being addressed and ethical issues (Chapter 3). They are moreover framed by the ways that we define our research contexts and environments, the ways these change and how these are attended to by other scholars and researchers. As demonstrated by Figures 0.1, 0.2 and 0.3, these different elements come together in different ways in relation to different localities, identities, temporalities and technologies. Yet, in making this point I also wish to emphasise that earlier examples of visual ethnography practice do not become redundant as new technologies emerge. Indeed, as we see in Figure 0.1, in the year 2000 themes of identity, technologies, texts and locality are equally important as they are in 2005 in Figure 0.2, and in 2011 in Figure 0.3. The temporality of these images progressively encompasses the digital materialities that are now part of many people's everyday lives. Yet Figure 0.1 remains equally relevant today as it was in 2000.

As these examples suggest, contemporary fieldwork domains, however we construct them, are saturated with visual images, practices of image making and of looking. Of course none of these are closed research environments, but constructed as research sites. They show how visual ethnography methods are applicable across a range of interconnected domains of human experience. Moreover, much of the visual ethnography research I show in the following chapters, happens in movement crossing such domains in multiple ways (see also Pink 2009, 2012d; Pink and Leder Mackley 2012).

As this brief overview makes clear, the field of visual methods and methodology is burgeoning in a number of directions. While in 2001 when the first edition of *Doing Visual Ethnography* was published it was one of a handful of books about visual research, it now offers one among a set of related and contrasting approaches

Master Caravela. © Olivia da Silva 2000

Figure 0.1 Master Caravela is a member of the fishing community in Matosinhos (Portugal) represented in Olivia da Silva's photographic project, *In the Net* (2000). Da Silva uses anthropological methods to inform her photographic practice, writing how 'As a participant observer I worked closely with the subjects of my portraits as they lived out their everyday lives to access the personal and domestic arenas of fishing communities and to record individual histories and narratives' (see da Silva and Pink 2004). The relationship between arts practice and visual ethnography is a two-way process, while visual ethnographic practices can inform photographic representations, the visual practices of documentary artists also provide new and inspiring examples for visual ethnographers.

to encountering the visual in our social, material and sensory worlds. In Chapter 1, I outline this context as it has emerged across disciplines and methodologies and as such situate visual ethnography within a growing field of visual research practice. In the remainder of this Introduction I set out my agenda, through a discussion of the relationship of theory, methodology and method in this book. As should become clear, *Doing Visual Ethnography* is not a methods text. Rather it is a methodology book: my aim is to bring together the theoretical and practical elements of visual approaches to learning and knowing about and in the world, and communicating these to others.

'David and Anne show me a print of their plans for the community garden'. © *Sarah Pink 2005*

Figure 0.2 As part of my research about a community garden project in a UK Slow City (Cittaslow town) I photographed research participants in ways that were significant for them and their projects. In this photograph David and Anne show a print of some digital photographs of the type of path that they and other committee members wished to have in the community garden they were developing.

Theory, methodology and method in *Doing Visual Ethnography*

The relationship between theory and method is important for understanding any research project. Similarly, an awareness of the theoretical underpinnings of visual research methods is crucial for understanding how those images and the processes through which they are created are used to produce ethnographic knowledge. Such questions have long since been debated in the literature on visual research methods. Earlier texts were criticised for being 'centred on how-to manuals of method and analysis working within a largely unmeditated realist frame (e.g. Collier and Collier 1986)' (Edwards 1997a: 33). Such works, like Prosser's notions of 'an image-based research methodology' (1996), tended to propose prescriptive frameworks that aimed to distance, objectify and generalise, and therefore detract from the very qualities and potentials that the ambiguity and expressivity (see Edwards 1997a) of visual images offers ethnography. In its first edition *Doing Visual Ethnography* along with other new volumes published at the beginning of the twenty-first century (e.g. Banks 2001; Pink, Kürti and Afonso 2004) signified a departure from this scientific and realist paradigm towards a new approach to making and understanding

Figure 0.3a The boat in the port

Figure 0.3b The virtual boat in the lighthouse

Figure 0.3c The Lighthouse

In 2011, Lisa Servon and I toured the Spanish town of Lekeitio with our hosts as part of our research into Slow Cities (Pink and Servon forthcoming). As we toured the port, and then later the lighthouse I photographed as we went, using my iPhone as a research tool that would both digitally make images as I walked through the environment of the town and geo-tag these images on a virtual map (see Pink and Hjorth 2012 for a discussion of this in relation to camera-phone photography). When we entered the lighthouse, which had been established as a maritime heritage centre, my mobile ethnographic image-making intersected with local audio-visual digital culture. Within one of the centre's installations we got into a boat and sailed out through a digital projection into the sea, passing the same lighthouse we were viewing as part of our journey (Pink and Servon forthcoming). Photographs © Sarah Pink 2011.

Figure 0.3d The lighthouse from the sea, as we journeyed through the digital projection

ethnographic images. Therefore the first edition of *Doing Visual Ethnography* was written as against the arguments of those visual sociologists who sought to incorporate a visual dimension into an already established methodology based on a 'scientific' approach to sociology (e.g. Grady 1996; Prosser 1996; Prosser and Schwartz 1998) and elements of those arguments linger in this third edition. Their proposal that visual images should support the project of a scientific sociology, I argued, suffered from the problems of perspectives like equality feminism: it must subscribe to the dominant discourse in order to be incorporated. The advocates of this conservative strategy were thus obliged to prove the value of the visual to a scientific sociology that is dominated by the written word, thus effectively evaluating the worth of images to research on the terms of a sociological agenda that has rejected the significance of visual meanings and the potential of images to represent and generate new types of ethnographic knowledge.

At that time, in the late 1990s, the contrasting view I took was that to incorporate the visual appropriately, social science should, as MacDougall has suggested, 'develop alternative objectives and methodologies' (1997: 293). This meant abandoning the possibility of a purely objective social science and rejecting the idea that the written word is essentially a superior medium of ethnographic representation. I argued that images should be regarded as an equally meaningful element of ethnographic work and therefore visual images, objects or descriptions should be incorporated when it is appropriate, opportune or enlightening to do so. In some projects the visual may become more important than the spoken or written word, in others it will not. In this book I continue to argue that there is no essential hierarchy of knowledge or media for ethnographic representation. Rather, different epistemologies and technologies complement each other as different types of ethnographic knowledge that may be experienced and represented in a range of different textual, visual and other sensory ways. This, however, is not to say that images and words can or should have to play the same role in academic, applied or public scholarship. As I insist in the final chapters of this book, visual representations bear an important relationship to, but cannot replace, words in conventional theoretical discussion.

In a current theoretical and practice-based climate, where visual methods have proliferated widely across disciplinary and interdisciplinary fields the approach I advocate in this book equally needs to be situated. My own approach to ethnography is informed by phenomenological anthropology, spatial theory in geography and to some extent theories of practice, as I outline in relation to sensory ethnography (Pink 2009) and everyday life (Pink 2012b). These theoretical commitments are not necessarily compatible with others. For instance while visual ethnography methods can be used in relation to multi-modality approaches, my own approach does not share the theoretical commitments of multimodality scholars (Pink 2011c) or of visual culture studies where it takes a semiotic approach to treat the visual as text to be 'read' (Pink 2012b).

However, since the outset *Doing Visual Ethnography* was not intended as a recipe book for successful visual research, and I continue to insist on this point. This book rather suggests an approach, invites readers to engage with this approach, to assess if or how it might work in their own projects, and to appropriate and change it as they wish. As regards the status of methods and methodology, many points made during the 1990s – a period when there was intense discussion of ethnographic fieldwork methodologies – still hold. In the words of the cultural studies scholar Jim McGuigan 'as most good researchers know, it is not unusual to make up the methods as you go along' indeed, '[t]he methods should serve the aims of the research, not the research serve the aims of the method' (McGuigan 1997: 2). Methodologies tend to be developed for/with particular projects, they are interwoven with theory, with our own biographies as researchers and as the anthropologist Lizette Josephides stressed 'our ethnographic strategies are also shaped by the subjects' situations, their global as well as local perceptions, and their demands and expectations of us'. Therefore, she wrote, 'There can be no blueprint for how to do fieldwork. It really depends on the local people, and for this reason we have to construct our theories of how to do fieldwork *in the field*' (Josephides 1997: 32, original italics). The same point still applies to using visual images and technologies in fieldwork; specific uses should be creatively developed within individual projects. Visual methods are not simply transferred from one project to be used again on another. Rather, methods themselves have biographies (Pink and Leder Mackley 2012) they evolve through different projects, bringing with them, inviting and inspiring new methodologies through their practice and findings. Therefore, rather than prescribing *how to do* visual research I draw from my own and other ethnographers' experiences of using images in research and representation to present a range of examples and possibilities. These are intended as a basis, or even point of contrast, from which new practices may be developed. In doing so I draw on examples from across analogue and digital media and material and electronic texts. However as I show, the important differences do not necessarily always lie in the medium one is using, but in the contexts in which they are being developed, and the theoretical ideas that inform their use.

The book

Chapter 1 situates visual ethnography in its wider historical and disciplinary context. It is chronologically placed in that because it is a chapter about the 'background' of the methodology that I discuss, it comes before the more contemporary discussions of the practice and theory of visual ethnography. However, books are not necessarily to be read directly from start to finish, and it will depend on the reader to decide whether to read this chapter first or last. For the reader who takes it as a first chapter, it will offer a historical and disciplinary narrative of how the visual ethnography approach discussed in later chapters came about. In it I tell the stories of the different disciplines through which visual ethnography practices and principles emerged, and the debates that were had in them since the 1990s. We still find some of the traces of these debates and arguments in contemporary texts on visual methods, and Chapter 1 will help readers to recognise them.

Chapter 2 outlines an approach, situating visual images and technologies in relation to a reflexive ethnography that focuses on subjectivity, creativity and self-consciousness. It combines anthropological ideas about the individual in society with theories of the visual and an exploration of consumption and material culture, to consider how visual images and technologies are interwoven with both the cultures that ethnographers study and the academic cultures they work in. In Chapter 3 this discussion is followed by a focus on the more practical aspects of preparing for visual fieldwork. Here I reflect on questions of project design, ethical considerations and questions of identity through the example of the gendered relations of fieldwork.

The following three chapters begin the second part of the book by examining visual ethnography methodology and methods through a focus on the different visual and digital technologies that have conventionally been used in its practice. In Chapter 4, I focus on uses of photography in ethnographic research practice. Building on its roots in visual sociology and anthropology I show how it may be engaged across a range of fields and in different ways. In Chapter 5, I discuss how video might be used in visual ethnography research. Here, departing from the focus on ethnographic film, which has dominated the practice and literature of visual anthropology, I consider the different ways in which recording video might become part of the ways we know in ethnographic contexts. In Chapter 6, which has been written especially for this new edition of the book, I focus on the implications of web-based practices for visual ethnography, exploring how new visual ethnography research practices that incorporate this context are emerging. Chapter 7 follows from these preceding three chapters to focus on the organisation and interpretation of visual materials in the ethnographic process.

In the final part of the book I turn to the use of digital and visual images in the dissemination of our work as ethnographers. Chapters 8 and 9 discuss the production of different types of text and how visual, written and other materials may be combined and interlinked in different representations, focusing respectively on photography and video. Digital media have opened up new and fascinating possibilities for the use of visual images in research and representation. However, these new potentials also raise a series of issues of representation, interpretation and the authoring of knowledge discussed in Chapter 10.

PART 1

Thinking about Visual Ethnography: Historical, Theoretical and Practical Perspectives

Our uses of visual and digital media in ethnographic research might be developed according to disciplinary agendas or within an interdisciplinary project. They might be meticulously planned in advance, or may unexpectedly become part of a project that is already in progress. Ethnographers would always be well advised to expect the unexpected, and this includes the possibility of new visual ethnographic innovations and/or interdisciplinary encounters along the way. It is always important to be well prepared in the theoretical and practical possibilities raised by visual and digital research methods. Part 1 of this book offers a grounding in the historical disciplinary, theoretical, practical and ethical issues that can inform a researcher whose uses of the visual and digital in ethnography are either planned or (like many moments in ethnography) serendipitous.

1

Visual Ethnography across Disciplines

Over the last ten or so years since the publication of the first edition of *Doing Visual Ethnography* I have met and communicated offline and online with many people from across the world about this field of practice. From them I have learnt much and I have developed my own approach to visual ethnography through new research collaborations with colleagues from across diverse fields. One of the most interesting and exciting elements of this process is that it has taken me far beyond my first discipline – I trained originally as a social and visual anthropologist. Working closely with scholars and researchers from other disciplines and giving lectures, seminars and workshops in departments and research groups beyond anthropology has offered me opportunities to learn about the priorities and needs of these related fields and to understand better how visual ethnography might be meaningful to their practices and scholarship. This has included directly collaborating with scholars and researchers whose work is based in for instance, design, engineering, the construction industry, urban planning, media studies, education studies and the arts. It has led me to dialogues with scholars in fields including geography, health studies, sports studies, ethnology, tourism studies, organisation studies, and art therapy. Moreover I am always left with the feeling that there are more collaborative possibilities to develop. In this chapter I map out the key influences and developments in visual ethnography as it crosses a series of central disciplinary and interdisciplinary fields. On the one hand this demonstrates the interdisciplinary situatedness of visual ethnography practice. On the other I hope to offer points of connection for researchers who might feel that in some ways their work belongs to one particular discipline or field of study, but who are open to others, and who seek to learn and innovate in their own practice. There are many connections yet to be made, and this book follows the same approach that generally characterises my writing on methodology in that it stands as an invitation to make new connections and relationships, rather than simply setting out to define those that are already there. Below I outline the disciplinary pasts and possibilities of visual ethnography. In doing so I trace its development, how the theoretical and practical elements of this trajectory have shifted and changed across and within disciplines, and how disciplinary influences and interdisciplinary theoretical 'turns' and debates have shaped the development of this trajectory.

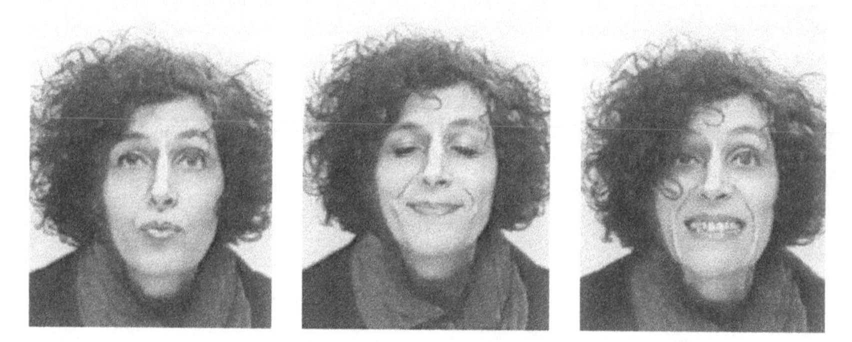

Figure 1.1 Visual Ethnography in Interdisciplinary Encounters
Christina Lammer develops visual ethnography methods alongside and in relation to her work with surgeons, artists, documentary filmmakers and photographers. Her blog and web site show how she combines these different perspectives and media in her research and arts practice. In her blog entry Lammer uses her own face and a very traditional medium – photo-booth photography – to explore patient experiences.

In her blog post of the 10 January 2012, Christina Lammer writes a short text and includes some images that she has taken of herself in a photo cabin at the Westbahnhof (train station) in Vienna. The photographs with her text below are a selection from 21 self portraits in which Lammer goes through a series of facial exercises designed for patients she is doing research with to do after they have been through surgery. Here we can see how using photography can enable us as researchers to develop and communicate about empathetic understandings of what we imagine other people's experiences to be.

As Christina Lammer explains:

'human expressiveness is not limited to a smiling or angry face. The whole body is included in how a person expresses him- or herself. Making faces is very much like dancing. However we automatically read in the faces of other people. Feelings are shared. A smile can be contagious ... I am working together with facially paralyzed persons who are treated in plastic and reconstructive surgery. After surgery the patients need to do exercises in front of a mirror on a daily basis. They get a list with schematic drawings of a human face and explanations of particular movements they shall do every day.'

Disciplinary concerns and visual ethnography research

There are two ways to consider the relationship of visual ethnography to academic disciplines and interdisciplinary fields. One is to ask to which disciplines might visual ethnography practice be relevant, and from that perspective to consider how the theoretical tenets of those disciplines and fields might inform the way it is practiced. The other is to consider which disciplines have overlapping concerns in seeking to understand visual images, audiovisual media, mobile technologies and the internet. Following this route we can ask more than just how visual ethnography might serve the intellectual and research agendas of these disciplines and how their theories might be used to engage it. Rather we might also investigate how the understandings of images, technologies and media that are developed in these fields will enable us to understand visual ethnography practice itself. The result of treating the interdisciplinarity of visual ethnography from these two perspectives is that it allows us to go beyond simply seeing visual ethnography as a practical device that can be used to produce knowledge, to understand it further as a practice and way of knowing and learning in the world that might be equally analysed. Following this approach therefore the visual ethnographer plays a dual role – she or he seeks to understand the visual practices and images that participate in other people's worlds, while also casting a reflexive focus on her or his own visual practices and images and the ways of knowing associated with them. Thus following arguments I have made elsewhere (Pink 2009, 2012b, 2012d) it provides us with a way to apply a theoretical approach that is coherent across the ways we understand research practice, and the findings of our research.

To develop the understandings of visual ethnography practice I apply in my own work I draw, sometimes critically, on a range of disciplines and fields, including: visual anthropology, media anthropology, visual sociology, media and internet studies, visual studies/visual culture studies and art history and geography. This is a shift from the approach I took in the first edition of *Doing Visual Ethnography* in the 1990s. I was then much more concerned with the emergent relationship between anthropological ethnography and cultural studies (e.g. as developed in the work of the anthropologist Penny Harvey (1996)). As Harvey pointed out at the time anthropologists hostile to cultural studies approaches focused 'on the differences between studying texts and studying people, between representation and situated practice' (1996: 14). Instead, a visual ethnography approach, as I developed it, explicitly acknowledged the need to attend to representation and text, as part of ethnographic practice. I continue to call for an approach to ethnography that attends to representations (see also Pink 2012d), yet I now distinguish a visual ethnography approach more sharply from the semiotic approaches to text that often inform cultural studies analysis, along with the Geertzian (see Geertz 1973) notion that culture, like text might be 'read' (see Pink 2011c).

Therefore while in earlier editions of this book I identified anthropology, sociology and cultural studies as the core disciplines informing visual ethnography, in this third edition I call for a visual ethnography that is informed by recent theoretical turns to theories of place and space, practice, movement and the senses. This follows my other methodological and substantive writings, relating to sensory ethnography (Pink 2009), advances in visual methodology more generally (Pink 2012a) and ways of researching and theorising everyday life (Pink 2012d), thus reframing the ways that culture and representations are understood in and as relevant to visual ethnography through an approach that seeks to recognise the interwovenness of socialities, objects, texts, images and technologies in people's everyday lives and identities and as part of the wider environments in which they live, move through and sense.

The idea of an interdisciplinary approach to visual ethnography is close to its roots in visual anthropology where disciplinary boundary crossing has brought together, for instance, the theories and practices of art and photography with anthropological theory and practice (e.g. Edwards 1997a; da Silva and Pink 2004; Grimshaw and Ravetz 2004; Schneider and Wright 2005). The interdisciplinary focus in visual methods has also been represented in Theo van Leeuwen and Carey Jewitt's *Handbook of Social Research* (2000) and Chris Pole's *Seeing is Believing* (2004) both of which combine case studies in visual research from across disciplines. The idea that visual research as a field of interdisciplinary practice is also central to *Advances in Visual Methodology* (Pink 2012a) and is demonstrated by the work of the volume's contributors, as well as by the recent *SAGE Handbook of Visual Research Methods* (Margolis and Pauwels 2011). Likewise the interdisciplinary journal *Visual Studies* (formerly *Visual Sociology*) provides an excellent series of examples of visual research, practice, theory and methodology.

A final point concerning the situating of visual ethnography within a context of interdisciplinarity relates to the status of ethnography as a field of practice. Ethnography itself, although its development has historically been associated with anthropology and sociology (see O'Reilly 2011), is not owned by any one discipline. Ethnography as practiced is shaped and formed by the disciplinary theories and priorities that inform the work it is required to undertake. Yet, this seems a necessary condition of its use. Ethnography itself is not an academic discipline, but a methodology (see Chapter 2). It is an *aspect* of research and representation not the totality of a research project in itself and is rarely the sole means or end of a research project; different disciplinary uses of ethnography are likely to situate it differently within their processes of research and representation by drawing from ethnographic and other approaches to varying extents (e.g. with textual, historical, narrative, statistical or a whole range of other research practices that intertwine and overlap or link conceptually as the research proceeds). This therefore enables ethnographic knowledge to develop in new relations to the types of knowledge produced by other approaches and methods. Moreover, other methods can enable deeper understandings of the contexts in which we do visual ethnography. For example, in Chapters 4, 5 and 6, I discuss how studying local photographic, media and internet practices, cultures and histories can inform our understanding of how to practice visual ethnography in given contexts. Statistical sources or analysis of existing visual texts can likewise inform the design and interpretation of visual research. In Chapters 8, 9 and 10, I emphasise the importance of understanding the media we use for ethnographic representation in relation to possible audiences and users of photography, video and the internet.

Therefore while scholars from across the social sciences and humanities study and analyse and use photography, film, video and web-based images in research and representation, historically and in different disciplines they have done so with varying degrees of acceptance and continuity. Moreover, both between and within disciplines the development of visual research methods has been informed by different theoretical approaches. In the following sections I review key historical and contemporary contributions to this field.

Visual and media anthropology: from anthropological film to phenomenological anthropology

Historically, ethnographic uses of the visual in anthropological research were a debated area (Pink 2006, Chapter 1). From the 1960s to the early 1980s debates focused on whether visual images and recordings could usefully support the observational project of social science (e.g. Collier and Collier 1986; Hockings 1975, 1995; and Rollwagen 1988). During this period some social scientists claimed that as a data collection method visual recording was too subjective, unrepresentative and unsystematic. Ethnographers like Margaret Mead, John Collier Jnr. and Howard Becker set out to prove otherwise, in both their theoretical arguments and practical applications of photography and film. Visual ethnographers were forced to confront the accusation that their visual images lacked objectivity and scientific rigour. Mead's response was that cameras left to film continuously without human intervention produced 'objective materials' (Mead 1995 [1975]: 9–10). Others, suggesting that the specificity of the photographed moment rendered it scientifically invalid (see, for example, Collier 1995 [1975]: 247), endeavoured to compensate for this. For instance, Becker (following Jay Ruby) proposed that the photographs anthropologists and sociologists might take during field-work 'are really only vacation pictures' (Becker 1986: 244), indistinguishable from those of the anthropologist's – or anyone else's – vacation. He advocated a systematic approach to photography as the social scientists' key to success (Becker 1986: 245–50) in an echo of Collier, who warned that '[t]he photographic record can remain wholly impressionistic UNLESS it undergoes disciplined computing' (1995 [1975]: 248). Thus some disputed the validity of the visual on the grounds of its subjectivity, bias and specificity. Others responded that, under the right controls, the visual could make a contribution as an objective recording method.

One of the most influential publications of this era was Collier's (1967) *Visual Anthropology: Photography as Research Method* (revised with Malcolm Collier and reprinted in 1986), a comprehensive textbook on the use of photography and video in ethnographic research and representation. Collier and Collier advocated a systematic method of observation whereby the researcher is supported by visual technology. They asserted that 'good video and film records for research are ultimately the product of observation that is organised and consistent. The equipment, except in specialized circumstances, cannot replace the observer' (1986: 149). This approach depended on a realist interpretation of still and moving images and was later criticised on that basis (for example, by

Edwards 1997a). For Collier and Collier, the research plan was key to the ethnographer's project of recording an appropriate version of the reality he or she could observe. Therefore they distinguished between the fiction of the '"shooting scripts" often used in the photographic and film world' and research plans that purport to record reality. On their terms ethnography was an observation of reality, as opposed to the constructedness of the narrative-based communication 'stories' of scripted films (Collier and Collier 1986: 162). Their visual anthropology presented an alternative to the existing text-based ways of doing anthropological ethnography, which had an important and enduring influence in visual anthropology and visual sociology. Yet alongside this, also in 1986, in the now landmark collection, *Writing Culture*, James Clifford made the rather different suggestion that in fact ethnographies themselves are constructed narratives: in a word, 'fictions'. Clifford used the term 'fiction', not to claim that ethnographies are 'opposed to the truth' or are 'false', but to emphasise how ethnographies cannot reveal or report on complete or whole accounts of reality; that they only ever tell part of the story (1986: 6). For Clifford, not only was ethnography a constructed version of truth, but 'Ethnographic truths are ... inherently *partial* – committed and incomplete' (1986: 7, original italics). This can be applied to both research and representation. Clifford's ideas thus questioned Collier and Collier's claim that research shooting guides differ from 'fictional' shooting scripts because the 'systematic selectivity' of 'field shooting or observation guides' is concerned 'with defining procedure, structure, and categories for recording that produce data on which later research analysis and summations are built' (Collier and Collier 1986: 162). Clifford's very point was that 'cultural fictions are built on systematic, and contestable, exclusions' (1986: 6). The selectivity, predetermined categories and precautions that Collier and Collier assumed would prevent ethnography from being a 'fiction' rather than a realist observation were in fact the very cornerstones upon which Clifford's ethnographic 'fictions' were constructed. For example, while Collier and Collier of course recognised that the 'whole' view of a situation cannot be recorded on video, they urged the research photographer to confront 'the challenge of gathering a semblance of the whole circumstance in a compressed sample of items and events observed in time and space' (1986: 163). In doing so, however, their work was inconsistent with the 'postmodern turn' in ethnography since they did not account for the possibility that any attempt to represent a 'whole view' itself would constitute a 'partial truth' or, in Clifford's terms, a 'fiction' based on 'systematic exclusions'. Collier and Collier's (1986) work remains a very important guide to visual ethnographic methods, and John Collier's visual ethnographic practice has left an enduring legacy. However, as a methodology it was a response to the demands of a scientific realist twentieth century anthropology, which was surpassed by theoretical shifts during the 1980s and 1990s.

From the 1980s Clifford's ideas helped to create a favourable environment for the visual representation of ethnography. The emphasis on specificity and experience, and a recognition of the similarities between the constructedness and 'fiction' (in Clifford's sense of the term) of film and written text, created a context where ethnographic film became a more acceptable form of ethnographic representation (Ruby 1982: 130; Henley 1998: 51). During this period the focus on the mediation of meaning between anthropologists and informants was developed in the reflexive ethnographic film style of David and Judith MacDougall and their contemporaries (Loizos 1993).

In the 1990s a new literature emerged around the historical debates and developments concerning the relationship between photography, film and the observational approaches of both anthropology and sociology (e.g. Edwards 1992; Chaplin 1994; Harper 1998a, 1998b; Henley 1998; Loizos 1993; Banks and Morphy 1997; Pink 1996, 1998). Edwards's (1992) and Marcus Banks and Howard Morphy's (1997) volumes signified an intentional departure from the scientific-realist paradigm but recognised that the contemporary context was one in which '[m]any anthropologists still feel caught between the possibility of conceptual advances from visual anthropology and the more conservative paradigms of a positivist scientific tradition' (MacDougall 1997: 192). Rather than attempting to fit visual anthropology into a scientific paradigm, whereby visual research methods could support and enhance an objective anthropology, David MacDougall proposed a significantly different approach that would 'look at the principles that emerge when fieldworkers actually try to rethink anthropology through use of a visual medium' (1997: 192). This implied a radical transformation of anthropology itself that would 'involve putting in temporary suspension anthropology's dominant orientation as a discipline of words and rethinking certain categories of anthropological knowledge in the light of understandings that may be accessible only by non-verbal means' and 'a shift from word-and-sentence-based anthropological thought to image-and-sequence-based anthropological thought' (1997: 292). Therefore, rather than attempting to incorporate images into a word-based social science, MacDougall advocated that since '[v]isual anthropology can never be either a copy of written anthropology or a substitute for it ... [f]or that very reason it must develop alternative objectives and methodologies that will benefit anthropology as a whole' (1997: 292–3).

When I wrote the first edition of *Doing Visual Ethnography* in the late 1990s MacDougall's analysis seemed an accurate characterisation of the academic climate. There was increasing curiosity about visual methods as technology became more available and the visual more acceptable, along with a growing number of examples of visual research practice in ethnographic fieldwork contexts. By 2006 when I revised *Doing Visual Ethnography* for its second (2007) edition anthropologists had written and edited several books on visual anthropology practices (Banks 2001; Pink, Kürti and Afonso 2004; El Guindi 2004) and were exploring the relationship between visual anthropological and arts practice (da Silva and Pink 2004; Grimshaw and Ravetz 2004; Schneider and Wright 2005). The representational practices of visual anthropologists had taken new directions as further critiques of ethnographic documentary filmmaking (e.g. Ruby 2000a; Chalfen and Rich 2007) inspired both new forms of ethnographic documentary video (e.g. MacDougall 2005), the production of anthropological hypermedia representations (e.g. Kirkpatrick 2003; Ruby 2000b; and see Pink 2006) art and drawing (Ramos 2004), and applied visual anthropology practice (Pink 2006, 2007a). The challenge for visual anthropology as it re-established itself in the twentieth century was no longer the question of how it would be accepted by the mainstream, but how to connect with and contribute to mainstream anthropological debates. As I elaborated in *The Future of Visual Anthropology* (Pink 2006) the sub-discipline faced a series of opportunities and challenges that meant its practitioners needed to engage with a context framed by: interdisciplinary engagements of visual ethnography methods; the theoretical shifts in mainstream anthropology that had made the visual more acceptable; a focus on experience and the senses; technological developments in digital and hypermedia possibilities; and uses of visual methods and media in applied anthropology (Pink 2006: 3). This framing influenced the writing of the second edition of *Doing Visual Ethnography* as complementary to that wider project. Yet it also meant that the second edition was specific to its moment, created at a point in the early twenty-first century when a new focus on anthropology of the senses was emerging, and in a web 1.0 technological context when DVD hypermedia publishing was an emergent practice. The focus on the senses indeed developed further (Pink 2009), and I will account for this in Chapter 2. It is always, however, more dangerous to speculate about the emergence of technological contexts, and the short rise of DVD hypermedia publications is a good example of an emergent media form that initially appeared to offer exciting new possibilities but was quickly surpassed as a web 2.0 context emerged. This is not to say that web 2.0 should be coined as 'the' context for digital visual ethnography publications; web 2.0 itself might be considered to be a transient form in that predictions for the qualities and possibilities of web 3.0 already exist. Yet as Veronica Barassi and Emiliano Treré demonstrate these web forms are defined by the ways that practitioners engage with them as much as by their technological possibilities and might better be understood as 'cultural constructs' (Barassi and Treré 2012: 1283). The same of course applies to how we might use them as researchers. As we will see in Chapters 4, 5 and 6 contemporary media theory can inform our understandings of the digital and web-based media contexts for the doing and representation of visual ethnography research, yet it cannot necessarily tell us how this will be lived out in another five or ten years into the future.

During and after this first decade of the twenty-first century visual anthropology has thus re-emerged in renewed form. Banks's and Ruby's (2011) volume *Made to be Seen* charts this context and its history through a series of chapters that represent the key strands in the historical and contemporary development of the sub-discipline, making it a point of reference for readers wanting to engage with visual ethnography through a visual anthropology perspective. Cristina Grasseni's work on what she calls the 'skilled visions' approach (Grasseni 2007, 2011) focuses on vision as 'situated practice' (see Grasseni 2011: 21–32). Grasseni argues that 'from the point of view of an ecological approach to visual practice, it is important that we consider our visual inscriptions as *artifacts* and that we assess the way in which they contribute to structuring a material, cognitive and social environment for situated action' (2011: 42–3). This perspective might urge visual ethnographers to likewise consider both their own disciplinary and scholarly visions through this lens in addition to understanding the ways that other people see as equally skilled and situated. Grasseni's approach draws on the work of the anthropologist Ingold, whose ideas are increasingly influential across the disciplines I discuss in this book. Ingold's is a phenomenological approach to anthropology in which, as he puts it, his 'overriding aim is to understand how people perceive the world around them, and how and why these perceptions differ' (Ingold 2011: 323). Ingold's work offers insights that enable us to better understand the senses in visual ethnographic research, as well as the environments in which we do ethnography. I refer to these at different points throughout this book. Of particular interest for visual ethnographers however are his works that attend to the place of images in the worlds we inhabit (e.g. Ingold 2010a), along with his edited volume *Redrawing Anthropology: Materials, Movements, Lines* (2011b). There Ingold's focus is on drawing, as a way to develop what he calls a '*graphic anthropology*' (2011: 2, original italics). The book's agenda to 'consider the potential of drawing, as a method or technique much neglected in recent scholarship, to reconnect observation and description within the movements of improvisory practice' (2011: 2) is especially interesting for visual ethnographers. As Ingold explains, 'This is to think of drawing not just as a means to illustrate an otherwise written text, but as an inscriptive practice in its own right, and of the lines of drawing as weaving the very text and texture of our work' (2011: 2). This indeed offers inspiring and novel ways for re-thinking elements of the visual ethnography methods discussed in earlier editions of *Doing Visual Ethnography* (and see Pink 2011d).

An impulse towards a more engaged, applied and public form of visual anthropology has also had an inevitable impact on the way it is practised. This includes the use of visual anthropology methods and practices in applied research on the one hand and on the other a move towards the making of ethnographic films that are directed towards a more participatory and public anthropology: that seek to address questions relating to change in the world. I have explored this context in earlier publications (Pink 2007a, 2011b). The contributors to my *Visual Interventions* volume (Pink 2007a) collectively show how visual methods and media have been used in anthropological projects that seek to inform processes of change across public, NGO and industry sectors. Such work is also increasingly being developed in ways that incorporate online and offline contexts (see Pink 2011b) and examples from this field of practice also feature in the following chapters.

These works reflect therefore a context not only framed by shifts to digital and web 2.0 technologies and platforms, but where there is an increasing emphasis in visual anthropology, towards the experiential, the phenomenological, a focus on practice (e.g. Grasseni 2007; Pink 2009; Ingold 2011), an urge towards applied and public scholarship (Pink 2007a) and a focus on the connections between anthropological ethnography and arts practice (Schneider and Wright 2010).

Visual Sociology: changing approaches to images and society

While from the late 1970s visual anthropologists, turning their attention to ethnographic film and video, began to question the notion of visual realism, visual sociologists (e.g. Wagner 1979) continued to develop their use of photography within the realist paradigm (Harper 1998a: 27). When I wrote the first edition of *Doing Visual Ethnography* in the late 1990s my agenda to develop visual ethnography through an increasingly reflexive and subjective visual anthropology was partially a response to the visual sociology of the 1990s where scholars were slower to incorporate ideas from outside, tending to look inwards to sociological measurements for approval. Concepts of 'validity', sampling and triangulation (still important in some approaches to qualitative research in sociology) were stressed in sociological ethnography texts (see, for example, Hammersley and Atkinson 1995: 227–32; Walsh 1998: 231) and often visual sociologists attempted to incorporate these conditions into their use of visual images, making their visual ethnographic 'data' succumb to the agenda of a scientific and experimental sociology (e.g. Grady 1996; Prosser 1996; Prosser and Schwartz 1998). During this period some sociologists responded to feminist and postmodern critiques, for instance to develop interdisciplinary approaches to the sociology of visual culture (e.g. Crawshaw and Urry 1997) or to examine the implications of photography for sociological understandings of the individual and self-identity (Lury 1998). However visual sociologists themselves engaged little with social theory or debates over reflexivity and subjectivity in research. For instance, in the 1990s Jon Prosser and Donna Schwartz considered how photography could be incorporated into 'a traditional qualitative framework rather than adopt ideas emanating from postmodern critique' (1998: 115). Stephen Gold maintained a similarly close alliance with existing sociological methods. He saw visual sociology as divided into two camps that deal with either the interpretation or the creation of visual images. He defined this as a 'theory/method split' – and 'a major obstacle in the further development of visual sociology' and proposed that theory and method may be brought together through the established 'grounded theory' approach (Gold 1997: 4).

However, some visual sociologists began to account for the critique of ethnography. Douglas Harper called for a redefinition of the relationship between researcher and informant through the collaborative approach developed in the 'new ethnography' and a postmodern approach to documentary photography that 'begins with the idea that the meaning of the photograph is constructed by the maker and the viewer, both of whom carry their social positions and interests to the photographic act' (1998a: 34–5, 1998b: 140). Nevertheless Harper did not propose a radical departure from existing sociological approaches to the visual. He recommended that visual sociology should 'begin with traditional assumptions and practices of sociological fieldwork and sociology analysis' that treat the photograph as 'data', and that it should open up to integrate the demands of the 'new ethnography' (1998a: 35). A key critic of traditional approaches to the visual in sociology during this period was Elizabeth Chaplin. In her book *Sociology and Visual Representations* (1994) Chaplin engaged with post-feminist, and post-positivist agendas to advocate a collaborative approach that would reduce the distance between the discipline and its subject of study. Rather than treating the visual as being 'data' that is subjected to a verbal analysis, she argued the potential of the visual as sociological knowledge and critical text should be explored (1994: 16), thus going further than most visual sociologists by engaging with the visual not simply as a mode of recording data or illustrating text, but as a medium through which new knowledge and critiques may be created. Some visual sociologists explored this potential in their practice in the 1990s (e.g. Barndt 1997; Barnes et al. 1997).

In the early twenty-first century further departures developed. Emmison and Smith criticised visual sociology as 'an isolated self-sufficient and somewhat eccentric specialism' that was unable to connect with social scientific theory (2000: ix). Their own response was, however, to develop visual methods as part of an approach that treated observable human behaviour and material forms as visual data, finding interviewing often unnecessary. Other sociologists developed more participatory approaches, placing collaboration between researcher and participants at the centre of the visual research. For example, linking sociological theory with performance art, Maggie O'Neill suggested that 'by representing ethnographic data ... in artistic form we can access a richer understanding of the complexities of lived experience which can throw light on broader social structures and processes' (2002: 70). Indeed these works stressed collaboration, not solely between researcher and research participants, but also between the visual, textual and performative and the producers of images and words. Such developments, combined with two edited volumes by Caroline Knowles and Paul Sweetman (2004) and Susan Halford and Caroline Knowles (2005), signified new territory for visual sociology through methodological innovation, linking it more closely with the concerns of mainstream sociologists.

Since the early twenty-first century visual sociology has indeed moved on. In the following chapters I will discuss further the innovative works of sociologists such as: Dawn Lyon (2013), who has collaborated with a photographer to research and represent a refurbishment project; Christina Lammer (2012) who draws together sociology with other disciplines in visual and research practice; and Maggie O'Neill's continuing work (2012). As is evident in the work of both Lammer and O'Neill, a visual approach to sociology is also one that attends to the senses. This makes stronger connections between visual sociology practice and the sensory turn in ethnographic scholarship (see Pink 2009). Simultaneously, others are working with an agenda to re-focus the subdiscipline of visual sociology by exploring questions relating to the image in a digital context. For instance, Francesco Lapenta seeks to re-frame the ways that we understand photography in the context of digital cartography (Lapenta 2011) and in doing so offers new ways of conceptualising how visual ethnography might be undertaken (Lapenta 2012). Yet, visual sociology remains part of a discipline that is in many ways diverse, which in turn means that its applications of visual ethnographic methods will not always ascribe to the same intellectual agenda.

Geography: a 'visual' discipline

My original development of *Doing Visual Ethnography* in the 1990s was based on the gathering together and reviewing of the existing literature that offered either theoretical or practical discussions and examples of how ethnography might be or had been practiced through the use of visual methods and media. While, as recent discussions by geographers make it clear, there is a strong argument for understanding geography as a 'visual discipline' (e.g. Rose 2003; Garrett 2011), in my earlier reviews the idea of geography as a 'visual ethnographic' discipline did not come to the fore. Indeed, neither did the first edition of the geographer Gillian Rose's book *Visual Methodologies* (2000) cover ethnographic practice beyond discussing its potential for the study of the audiences of images. Yet, in her third edition (2011) Rose (with reference to the 2007 edition of *Doing Visual Ethnography*) notes how now 'Many social science scholars are experimenting with making images in order to explore the nonrepresentational aspects of the social' (2011: 11). In her own book she thus brings together the use of images in qualitative social research, with the analysis of images, redressing what she sees as a context where 'there has been remarkably little dialogue between social scientists using visual research methods as a way of answering research questions, and visual culture scholars who study found images' (2011: 11). Likewise, in recent years I have found myself increasingly encountering uses of visual methods and media in the research practice of geographers at conferences and meetings and in publications discussing research practice that seems to me to be a form of visual ethnography (and indeed is sometimes identified with it through references to earlier editions of *Doing Visual Ethnography*). A 2003 discussion of the visual in geography published in the journal *Antipode* to some extent explains these developments. Here Rose suggested that while there is an underlying assumption that geography is a 'visual discipline' (with the exception of the work of (David Matless) '"the visual" hasn't been analyzed in any sustained way in relation to geography as an academic discipline' (2003: 212). Visualisation, as Rose's examples show, is an important to how geography might be thought of as a visual discipline (she mentions 'maps, videos, sketches, photographs, slides, diagrams, graphs'). But, she argues that more important are 'the ways in which particular visualities structure certain kind of geographical knowledges' along with the power relations of these (2003: 213). Rose proposes that geographers might approach their interrogations of the visual in geography through a focus on the relationship between 'image, audience and space' (2003: 219) thus setting an agenda for an acknowledgement of geography as a 'visual discipline'. Other articles in the same journal issue respond to Rose's comments, through a focus on the use of slides in presentations in geography (e.g. Matless 2003; Driver 2003) rather than on fieldwork practices. Moreover James Ryan's response to Rose is informative. He writes that 'geographers need to think more deeply and imaginatively about the methods they employ in both teaching and research' (Ryan 2003: 233), noting the possibilities that might develop when geographers engage with visual artists, photography or digital media. More recently the geographer Bradley Garrett suggested that 'while geography as a discipline has seen the potential in film analysis and critique to enhance cultural understanding, and has produced some notable "landscape" films, the discipline has yet to realize the full potential of video as a research methodology' (2011: 521). By the end of the first decade of the twenty-first century, according to Garrett, photography had fared rather better as a method in geography, with some of the uses he cites being those associated with visual ethnography – he writes:

> Photography is now practiced in numerous forms including photography as experiential record, participant portrait photography, architectural photography, archival analysis and photo elicitation, with geographers showing little reluctance to become photographers in the course of work on their projects. But even 'visual geographers' seem to harbour some reservations about photography's ability to be singularly situated as a method, usually viewing it as supplementary to text (Garrett 2011: 522).

Garrett makes an argument for what he calls 'videographic geographies' (2011: 522) – an approach that he connects to visual ethnography. These new geographical considerations of the visual have emerged alongside the increasing interest in the (non-visual) senses across academic disciplines (I discuss this further in Chapter 2). Indeed Garrett notes the multisensoriality that visual methods can attend to – as he puts it 'It might of course be argued that video is a useful geographic research tool because it captures movement; video tracks the multisensual fluidity and rhythms of everyday life' (2011: 522). Other recent uses of video in ethnography by geographers also show such attention to movement and the senses (discussed in Pink 2009) – for instance the work of Justin Spinney who used video to research cycling in the city (e.g. Spinney 2009). Therefore, while it might be said that anthropology and geography have both shifted towards an increasingly visual/digital (and sensory) form of ethnographic practice during the twenty-first century, they have arrived at this through different routes.

These debates and discussions of the visual in geography demonstrate that its practice has something important to contribute to both the ways images are analysed and how they are used in ethnographic practice. Yet I believe that the relevance of critical and practical work in geography to visual ethnography goes beyond these questions of interrogating the status of the visual and the image in the discipline and in the development of innovative experiential forms of research practice. First, the attention to questions of place and space in geography offers ethnographers useful frameworks for understanding the contingencies and temporalities and power configurations of the everyday contexts in which we research (see Pink 2009, 2012d). This point might be applied to ethnographic practice in general, and I have developed this elsewhere in relation to sensory ethnography practice (Pink 2009).

Second, as a 'visual' discipline, geography has had a long-term engagement with maps and mapping. Critical geographical writing on mapping offers important insights for visual ethnographers in a context where digital and mobile media mean that everyday and other spatialities are increasingly understood and experienced through digital mapping (see Lapenta 2011). Therefore, for instance while the geographer Doreen Massey points out that not all maps are necessarily problematic (2005: 107), her critical stance on the idea of the map as a 'technology of power' and the idea that maps can 'give the impression that space is a surface' (2005: 107) has much to contribute to the ways we understand contemporary digital mapping and the ways that digital maps are constituted through the melding of 'contiguous images' (Lapenta 2011). Indeed, the power relations of digital maps are ambiguous and contingent. The platforms, software and corporations with which they are implicated imply one form of power, while their potential for participatory ventures (and research) makes them a potential tool for resistance or self-definition (see Farman 2010; Lapenta 2011). This of course is the case for paper mapping and its use in visual ethnography too (see Grasseni 2012). Given that digital maps shape a part of the way that many visual ethnographers and research participants experience and navigate everyday environments – through our laptops, smart phones and other digital mapping technologies – it seems important for us to turn to the work of geographers who have already developed a critical perspective on mapping as a way to inform our understandings of the 'visual' research contexts in which we engage.

Third, the development of and commitment to non-representational (e.g. Thrift 2008) or more-than-representational (e.g. Lorimer 2005) theory in geography offers us ways to engage with the visual, and with images themselves that go beyond the cultural studies interest in the image as representation and as text that henceforth dominated this field. Such approaches go beyond representation to focus on the tacit, sensory, habitual and sometimes seemingly mundane elements of everyday life, they give an emphasis to flow and movement and invite us to explore the unspoken and ongoingness of activity in the world as it is performed and experienced. Moreover, this move to non-representational theory, as I discuss towards the end of this chapter, enables us to make connections between developments across anthropology, geography and art history/visual culture studies which support the interweaving, or at least the establishment of interdependencies between these disciplines in the doing of visual ethnography. This move also facilitates new developments in the long-term geographical interest in the senses (discussed also in Pink 2009), and therefore likewise helps to inform the way that visual ethnographic practice along with visual media and images are situated in relation to the 'sensory turn' outlined in Chapter 2.

Therefore, along with a growing commitment to the interrogation of the visual that Rose (e.g. 2003) argued for (and has developed herself e.g. 2011), geography is increasingly becoming a discipline that offers convincing theoretical propositions concerning how we might comprehend the visual and the power relations in which it is embedded, as well as a growing body of literature that demonstrates how geographers are using visual methods and media in ethnography. It is, I suggest, a discipline that those aspiring to undertake visual ethnographic research might turn to for inspiration and examples of theoretical and practical steps that may serve to inform their work.

Visual Culture Studies: a critical departure

In the first edition of *Doing Visual Ethnography,* I turned to Visual Culture studies as a way to begin to understand the place of images in society. This interdisciplinary area of research offered an established mode of thinking about the ways that images were produced, disseminated/circulated and consumed, and how visual meanings were made. In this edition I depart somewhat from this earlier commitment to Visual Culture Studies. While the approaches in this discipline certainly offer some viable methods of understanding and analysing images in ways that are socially and culturally situated, I believe that new interdisciplinary theory offers a route to understanding the image that is more coherent with the approach I develop to visual ethnography.

Earlier cultural studies approaches to photography and video developed established ways of studying visual representation and visual cultures. For example, Stuart Hall's influential text *Representations* used 'a wide range of examples from different cultural media and discourses, mainly concentrating on *visual* language' (1997: 9, original italics). It considered issues related to the negotiation of visual meanings, emphasising the contested nature of meaning and 'the practices of representation' (1997: 9–10). Indeed the focus in cultural studies is on interpreting existing images and objects and the social and cultural conditions within which they are produced (see also, for example, Cooke and Wollen 1995; Jenks 1995; Evans and Hall 1999). Martin Lister and Liz Wells formulated what they call 'Visual Cultural Studies'. Mirroring the eclecticism of its parent discipline a *visual* cultural studies 'allows the analyst to attend to the many moments within the cycle of production, circulation and consumption of the image through which meanings accumulate, slip and shift' (2000: 90). As such, Lister and Wells would analyse photographs 'without separating them from social processes' (2000: 64). This approach differed from that of a visual ethnography in that rather than using images to produce knowledge, they focus on the analysis of images and the contexts in which they become meaningful. Yet, their methodology made a welcome contribution to my earlier development of visual ethnography in that it suggested ways that a visual ethnographer might attend to visual aspects of culture and to the embeddedness of images in society. Moreover, although cultural studies was not a key site for the emergence of visual ethnography practice, visual cultural studies brought to the fore an emphasis that indicated the relevance of studying visual culture as a part of visual ethnography practice.

More recently, in parallel with the focus on the non-visual senses in anthropology, sociology and geography, scholars have begun to re-think the study of visual culture in relation to the senses. As I outline elsewhere (Pink 2011a), W. J. T. Mitchell defined the focus of the field of visual culture as being beyond simply the visual, writing of its interest in 'ratios between different sensory and semiotic modes' (2002: 90) and that 'Visual Culture entails a meditation on blindness, the invisible, the unseen, the unseeable, and the overlooked; also on deafness and the visible language of gesture; it also compels attention to the tactile, the auditory, the haptic, and the phenomenon of synaesthesia' (2002: 90). Likewise Elizabeth Edwards and Kaushik Bhaumik's approach to the visual sense is one that 'explores vision and sight as something sensorially integrated, embodied and experienced' (2009: 3) – an approach that I have suggested marks an 'explicit shift in the "visual culture" literature' (Pink 2011a).

These developments in the visual culture literature offer one alternative way of thinking about the images beyond the visual. Yet, from the perspective of a phenomenological anthropology, the visual culture approach is limited precisely by its focus on the image. As Ingold has put it 'For students of visual culture, seeing apparently has nothing to do with observation, with looking around in the environment or watching what is going on. Nor does it have anything to do with the experience of illumination that makes these activities possible. It rather has to do, narrowly and exclusively, with the perusal of images (Elkins 2003: 7)' (Ingold 2011: 316). Although, as I noted above, the senses have become part of the agenda of visual culture studies, for Ingold, 'they have simply added worlds of sounds, of feelings and of smells' and this has led to the study of '"scapes"' of every possible kind. If the eyes return the world to us in its visual image, conceived in art-historical terms as landscape, then likewise the ears reveal a soundscape, the skin a touchscape, the nose a smellscape, and so on. In reality, of course, the environment that people inhabit is not sliced up along the lines of the sensory pathways by which they access it. It is the *same* world, whatever paths they take' (Ingold 2011: 316).

The work of the art historian Barbara Maria Stafford offers one way to resolve some of these issues in the context of an exploration of the relationship between art and the neurosciences. Stafford's work goes far beyond the task of re-thinking the concept of visual culture, her proposal is that 'the neurosciences, cognitive science, and the new philosophy of mind need to come together with the variegated historical, humanistic, or cultural-based studies of images' (2006: 207). Her book develops a complex and crafted argument, which it would be impossible to summarise here. Instead I wish to draw readers' attention to Stafford's departure from the use of 'linguistic models of representation' to what she calls 'visual models of presentation'. She suggests that rather than being representations that 'hang around in our heads' instead we 'reperform and 'reinvent' visual compositions when we see them. Drawing on the work of J. J. Gibson (as does Ingold) and Kevin O'Regan, she writes that 'when you open your eyes and actively interrogate the visual scene, what you see is that aspect, or the physical fragments, of the environment that you perform' (Stafford 2006: 215).

If, as visual ethnographers we are to attend to the place of media and representations in the worlds we work in – that is to what have been called 'visual cultures' – then we need to attend to the theoretical shifts and turns. I believe that this current theoretical environment, characterised by the work of Stafford, and by Ingold's critique of conventional visual culture studies opens up new opportunities. This, with the growing appreciation of non-representational theory, allows us to refocus this interest in the question of the roles that images and representations play in people's lives in ways that are more coherent with the idea of visual ethnography itself as a process of learning and experiencing, rather than as a form of 'data collecting'. Indeed, this point in a sense brings me back to the starting point of the arguments I made in the first edition of *Doing Visual Ethnography*. There I sought to develop a visual ethnography approach that stood as a critical response to the scientific realist influence in the social sciences of the twentieth century. This was precisely against the idea of visual methods as modes of data collection and in favour of visual ethnography as a process of producing knowledge.

Visual Ethnography Now and in the Future

The moves towards phenomenological, sensory and non-representational approaches across anthropology, geography and visual culture studies, along with a sociology that appreciates the sensory and digital dimensions of the worlds we inhabit, offer a theoretical climate which invites the practice of visual ethnography as a way of being, knowing and learning. In a context where across the ethnographic disciplines the use of visual images in research and representation is becoming more frequently written about and more rigorously theorised, visual ethnography no longer needs to be supported by arguments that counter the twentieth century objections that they might be too subjective.

Indeed the camera and the digital image, as an increasingly constant presence in our pockets, our hands and our computers is part of our contemporary reality. As I write this book I am facing the web cam in my laptop, and my camera-phone is next to me. In contemporary technological and theoretical contexts there are still debates and arguments to be made, for example to distinguish between an approach to ethnography informed by phenomenological anthropology on the one hand and one informed by the semiotic analysis of the multimodality paradigm on the other (see Pink 2011c). Yet, perhaps more important to focus on are questions concerning how attention to the digital and technological contexts where we now do visual ethnography is creating not only new possibilities in terms of the methods we can use, but in terms of the way we can understand the visual and vision theoretically (see also Pink 2012a; Coover 2012; Lapenta 2012).

Second, as I have stressed throughout this review, the new focus on the senses, which I have taken up elsewhere in my own conceptualisation of a sensory ethnography (Pink 2009), is influential across disciplines. However, the relationship between visual and sensory ethnography is not, as it might initially appear, one of contradiction but one where visual methods and media and a sensory approach are supportive of each other. Finally the urge towards public and applied scholarship in the visual ethnographic disciplines is an important move (see Pink 2006, 2007b, 2012a). Due to their proliferation in recent years, such practices will be evident in examples discussed in the following chapters.

Further reading

Banks, M. and Ruby, J. (2011) *Made to Be Seen: Perspectives on the History of Visual Anthropology*. Chicago: University of Chicago Press.

Garrett, B. L. (2011) 'Videographic geographies: using digital video for geographic research'. *Progress in Human Geography*, 35(4): 521–541.

Ingold, T. (2010a) 'Ways of mind-walking: reading, writing, painting', *Visual Studies*, 25:1, 15–23.

Knowles, C. and Sweetman, P. (2004) (eds) *Picturing the Social Landscape: visual methods and the sociological imagination*. London: Routledge. (An edited volume of essays that demonstrate uses of visual methods in sociology.)

Margolis, E. and Pauwels, L. (2011) *The SAGE Handbook of Visual Methods*. London: SAGE.

Pink, S. (2012a) (ed.) *Advances in Visual Methodology*. London: SAGE.

Stafford, B. M. (2006) *Echo Objects: the Cognitive Work of Images*. Chicago: University of Chicago Press.

Additional material is available on the book's companion website: www.uk.sagepub.com/pink3e

2

Ways of Seeing, Knowing and Showing

Visual images, practices and ways of knowing are figuring increasingly in the critical and practical work of scholars from across the social sciences and humanities. As I outlined in Chapter 1, scholars and practitioners from outside the fields of visual culture, art history or media are also defining their disciplines as somehow 'visual'. Visualisation and images, moreover, play important roles in disciplines outside the social sciences and humanities, including medicine, design and engineering, and in later chapters I discuss examples in which visual ethnography has intersected with these fields. That the visual and vision are somehow part of contemporary scholarship and research practice is therefore clear. Yet, what exactly do we mean by these categories? As Chapter 1 has shown, the idea that something might be purely visual is problematic. It is now commonly recognised that, as the visual anthropologist Peter Crawford (1992: 66) wrote in the early 1990s, notions of 'pure image' and 'pure word' are not viable. Such points were echoed in visual culture studies in W. T. J. Mitchell's argument that 'there are no visual media' (2005), and have also been expressed (albeit differently) in phenomenological accounts of human perception (see Ingold 2000; Stafford 2006).

Therefore to do visual ethnography we need to attend to the constructedness of this distinction between the visual and other categories of experience, materiality or text. While we have come to commonly speak of 'visual research methods', this does not refer to anything that is purely visual. Rather, what are termed visual methods pay particular attention to the visual aspects of the worlds we inhabit, the cultural forms and the technologies we have categorised as visual. They also involve the experiences and practices we call vision. Vision similarly cannot be understood as a pure sensory channel of experiencing or knowing (see Ingold 2000; Pink 2009). Such challenges to the categories of the visual and of vision similarly have ramifications for the way we do visual research. Visual methods cannot be used independently of 'non-visual methods'. It would be just as hard to identify a method that was totally non-visual as it would be to find one that was exclusively visual. Similarly there cannot be a purely visual ethnography, or an exclusively visual approach to culture, society, experience or environments. The visual is thus a category that might be on the one hand easily recognised in modern western cultures, and on the other hand it is deeply problematised. Given this ambiguity, this chapter focuses on how we might understand the practice of doing ethnography that engages visual images, media and methods as routes to researching the individuals, cultures, societies and environments we seek to understand. These four categories themselves are also constructed, contested and debated in the existing literature. Here, I use them broadly to develop a discussion that is relevant across disciplines, yet stress that when used in specific research projects they become units of analysis that invite particular routes to knowing about and understanding the worlds that we seek to research.

Ethnography and ethnographic images

What is ethnography? How does one 'do' ethnography? What makes a text, photograph or video ethnographic? Handbooks of traditional research methods, which remain influential, tended to represent ethnography as a mixture of participant observation and interviewing. For example, Martin Hammersley and Paul Atkinson defined ethnography as 'a particular method or set of methods' that:

> ... involves the ethnographer participating, overtly or covertly, in people's daily lives for an extended period of time, watching what happens, listening to what is said, asking questions – in fact, collecting whatever data are available to throw light on the issues that are the focus of the research. (1995: 1)

Such descriptions are limited on two counts. First, they restrict the range of things ethnographers may actually do. Secondly, their representations of ethnography as just another method or set of methods of data collection wrongly assume that ethnography entails a simple process of going to another place or culture, staying there for a period of time, collecting pieces of information and knowledge and then taking them away. Instead, I shall define ethnography as a methodology (see Crotty 1998: 7); as an approach to experiencing, interpreting and representing experience, culture, society and material and sensory environments that informs and is informed by sets of different disciplinary agendas and theoretical principles. In my book *Doing Sensory Ethnography* (Pink 2009) I have argued for an understanding of ethnographic practice and methodology that draws on contemporary theoretical strands and acknowledges the need to innovate beyond traditional approaches. Contemporary visual ethnography likewise, through its engagement with digital and emergent technologies and media, offers more than just a set of methods to be employed. Rather it is itself a process of continuous innovation.

While I believe that my approach to visual ethnography is coherent with the work of a number of other ethnographic scholars (see for example Pink 2012a), it remains necessary to stress that a fundamental assumption of visual ethnography is that it is concerned with the production of knowledge and ways of knowing rather than with the collection of data. I understand ethnography as a process of creating and representing knowledge or ways of knowing that are based on ethnographers' own experiences and the ways these intersect with the persons, places and things encountered during that process. Therefore visual ethnography, as I interpret it, does not claim to produce an objective or truthful account of reality, but should aim to offer versions of ethnographers' experiences of reality that are as loyal as possible to the context, the embodied, sensory and affective experiences, and the negotiations and intersubjectivities through which the knowledge was produced. This may entail reflexive, collaborative or participatory methods. It may involve participants in the research in a variety of ways at different points of the research and representational stages of the project. It should account not only for the observable, recordable realities that may be translated into written notes and texts, but also for objects, visual images, the immaterial, the invisible and the sensory nature of human experience and knowledge. Finally, it should engage with issues of representation that question the right of the researcher to represent other people, recognise the impossibility of 'knowing other minds' (Fernandez 1995: 25) and acknowledge that the sense we make of research participants' words and actions is 'an expression of our own consciousness' (Cohen and Rapport 1995: 12).

There is no simple answer or definition of what it is that makes an activity, image, text, idea, or piece of knowledge ethnographic. No single action, experience, artefact or representation is essentially, in itself, ethnographic, but instead these will be defined as such through interpretation and context. Anthropologists have long since noted the absence of concrete boundaries between ethnographic and fictional texts (see Clifford and Marcus 1986), and between ethnographic, documentary and fictional film (see Loizos 1993: 7–8). Similarly, there is no clear-cut way of defining an individual photograph as, for example, a tourist, documentary or journalistic photograph (see Chapter 4), or of deciding whether a piece of video footage is a home movie or an ethnographic video (see Chapter 5). The same applies to the sometimes arbitrary nature of our distinctions between personal experience and ethnographic experience, autobiography and anthropology – all of which were discussed in depth in the 1990s (see Okley and Callaway 1992; Okley 1996) and fieldwork and everyday life (Pink 1999a). When researching everyday life as ethnographers, we do this from inside, we become immersed in its flow and, indeed, our own actions and feelings become part of the very contexts that we are researching (Pink 2009, 2012b). Any experience, action, artefact, image or idea is never definitively *just one thing* but may be redefined differently in different situations, by different individuals and in terms of different discourses. It is therefore impossible to measure the ethnographicness of an image in terms of its form, content or potential as an observational document, visual record or piece of data. Instead, the ethnographicness of any image or representation is contingent on how it is situated, interpreted and used to invoke meanings, imaginings and knowledge that are of ethnographic interest.

Visual ethnography as a reflexive practice

Since the 1980s, in their critique of natural science approaches, authors of traditional research methods texts emphasised the constructedness of ethnographic knowledge (e.g. Burgess 1984; Ellen 1984), increasingly coupled with a stress on the central importance of reflexivity (see also Fortier 1998; Walsh 1998). It is by now generally accepted that reflexivity forms an important part of ethnographic practice. A reflexive approach recognises the centrality of the subjectivity of the researcher to the production and representation of ethnographic knowledge. Reflexivity goes beyond the researcher's concern with questions of bias and is not simply a mechanism that neutralises ethnographers' subjectivity as collectors of data through an engagement with how their presence may have affected the reality observed and the data collected. The assumption that a reflexive approach will aid ethnographers to produce objective data represents only a token and cosmetic engagement with reflexivity that wrongly supposes subjectivity could (or should) be avoided or eradicated. Instead, subjectivity should be engaged with as a central aspect of ethnographic knowledge, interpretation and representation.

To understand reflexivity in the social sciences we need to turn again for a moment to the 1990s, when the reflexive approach to ethnography became consolidated. During this period postmodern thinkers argued that ethnographic knowledge and text can only ever be a subjective construction, a 'fiction' (Clifford 1986) that represents only the ethnographer's version of a reality, rather than an empirical truth. Some proposed that such approaches take reflexivity too far. For instance David Walsh insisted the 'social and cultural world must be the ground and reference for ethnographic writing', that 'reflexive ethnography should involve a keen awareness of the interpenetration of reality and representation', and researchers should not 'abandon all forms of realism as the basis for doing ethnography' (1998: 220). His argument presented a tempting and balanced way of thinking about the experienced reality people live in and the texts that ethnographers construct to represent this reality. Nevertheless it is also important to keep in mind the centrality of the subjectivity of the researcher to the production of ethnographic knowledge. Anthony Cohen and Nigel Rapport's point that our understandings of what informants say or do is solely 'an expression of our own consciousness' (Cohen and Rapport 1995), problematises Walsh's proposition. If the researcher is the channel through which all ethnographic knowledge is produced and represented, then the only way reality and representation can interpenetrate in ethnographic work is through the ethnographer's textual constructions of 'ethnographic fictions'. Rather than existing objectively and being accessible and recordable through scientific research methods, reality is subjective and is known only as it is experienced by individuals. A reflexive approach is thus important in that focusing on how ethnographic knowledge about how individuals experience reality is produced, through the intersubjectivity between researchers and their research contexts, we may arrive at a closer understanding of the worlds that other people live in. It is not solely the subjectivity of the researcher that may shade his or her understanding of reality, but the relationship between the subjectivities of researcher and research participants that produces a negotiated version of reality (see, for example, Fortier 1998).

One way to account for this as a researcher is to maintain an awareness of how different elements of our biographies, existing experiences, and elements of our identities become significant during research. On the one hand it is only through our own existing experiences and knowledge that we can begin to come to empathise with and understand the experiences of others – or indeed distinguish their experiences from our own and attempt to imagine what these might have been like. On the other hand elements of our identities such as gender, age, ethnicity, class and race are important to how researchers are situated and situate themselves in ethnographic contexts. Therefore as ethnographers we need to be self-conscious about how we represent ourselves to research participants and to consider how our identities are constructed and understood by the people with whom we work. These subjective understandings will have implications for the knowledge that is produced from the ethnographic encounter between researcher and participants. Such situating of the researcher also needs to be considered in relation to other themes, such as social and economic class. In some fieldwork situations the types of digital and visual media used by an ethnographer might be prohibitively costly for most local people, in others research participants themselves may have far more sophisticated equipment. Thus their use in research needs to be situated in terms of the wider economic context as well as questions of how the ethnographer's own identity as a researcher is constructed by participants in research.

Therefore being a reflexive visual ethnographer, involves interrogating how we are situated within the ethnographic research context. There are a number of ways in which this can be approached, and in part the analytical emphasis taken may depend on the research question. For instance, in my own experience of doing research about gender in Spain I was concerned with the question of how my identity as a woman and photographer shaped the ways that I could produce knowledge. This focus on gender was indeed coherent with the kinds of interrogations that were at the time happening in the reflexive methodology literature, where the gendered nature of fieldwork itself was a key theme (see especially Bell et al. 1993; Kulick and Willson 1995) and also developed in discussions of visual research (e.g. Barndt 1997). In other contexts researchers might be more concerned with exploring these questions through, for instance, regional, class, ethnicity or generational identity. For instance, when doing research about Slow Cities in the UK, I had a sense of 'closeness' and common reference points when I did research in towns close to the place where I had grown up, and I was interested in reflecting on how this shaped the way I understood these contexts. Other researchers have similarly reflected on how different elements of their identities have shaped their fieldwork experiences. For instance Daniel Sage, in the context of his ethnographic research in the construction industry, shows how his educational qualifications and status contributed to the way he was situated during his fieldwork (Sage 2013). These various forms of situatedness that might emerge in different projects are also important in determining the types of power relations, collaboration and image that tend to be produced in research projects.

Reflexivity was also a key theme of the visual methods literature that emerged since the beginning of the twenty-first century, and continues to be important in contemporary works in this field. It was advocated strongly (although in slightly differing ways) in single author books (e.g. Ruby 2000a; Banks 2001; Rose 2001; and see Pink 2006 Chapter 2 for a full review of this) and a number of good edited volumes containing case studies that demonstrate how contemporary researchers are reflecting on their visual methods in *practice* in visual anthropology (Pink, Kürti and Afonso 2004; Edgar 2004; Grimshaw and Ravetz 2004; Schneider and Wright 2005) and visual sociology (Knowles and Sweetman 2004; Pole 2004). This period of methodological reflection, clearly informed by the postmodern turn of the 1980s and 1990s, played an important role in characterising not only the visual methods literature, but also qualitative research literature more generally. As we move on further into the twenty-first century and visual methods become more consolidated as a field of practice (see Pink 2012a) the process of not only doing visual research but reflecting on the processes and practices through which it is produced has become further embedded (e.g. Martens 2012; Ardévol 2012; Hindmarsh and Tutt 2012).

Unobservable ethnography, invisibility and the problem of reality

Visual ethnography does not necessarily involve simply recording what we can see, but also offers ethnographers routes through which to come to understand those very things that we cannot see. This point can be applied very broadly. It invites us to consider how video ethnography methods might enable us to research how invisible and intangible resources such as electricity and gas are consumed in domestic homes (e.g. Pink and Leder Mackley 2012) as discussed in Chapter 5, or how hand-over-the-camera methods might provide routes into comprehending other people's embodied workplace knowledge or ways of knowing (e.g. Tutt et al. 2013) that would otherwise remain unseen by the ethnographer.

Simultaneously, such an approach enables us to recognise how images are also part of our imaginations and interior worlds (Edgar 2004; Irving 2010), as well as inviting us to imagine (Ingold 2010a). Researchers are increasingly attending to the human imagination, dreams and interior thoughts as a site of ethnographic fieldwork and visual ethnography methods are playing an interesting role in this field. Iain Edgar's 'imagework' and 'dreamwork' approaches involve accessing and analysing the images that are produced through our imaginations and dreams – 'both refer to the mind's spontaneous production of imagery that people may consider "good to think with"' (2004: 10). As Edgar points out, imagework is largely non-verbal, it tends to produce verbal narratives about intangible images, which form the materials that the researcher then analyses. Other approaches that also seek to understand interior thoughts make images and visual practices more central throughout the research process. For instance Andrew Irving also uses visual practices as a route to understanding other people's thoughts, but in this case Irving invites participants to photograph and narrate their feelings as they follow familiar paths through urban environments. In his publications Irving uses both photographs and transcribed recordings to represent these affective and interior experiences (e.g. Irving 2007, 2010); I return to his innovative practice in later chapters of this book. Inspired by Irving's discussions of the question of interiority and the use of photography in his work, in my own work with Susan Hogan we have explored questions around the relationship between visual ethnography and interior feelings. Drawing on Hogan's scholarship in art therapy we have identified correspondences between visual ethnography and art therapy approaches and suggested that the image making methods of feminist art therapy as engaged by Hogan, can offer ways of doing a visual ethnography of interiority (Hogan and Pink 2012). The relationship between seeing and knowing in visual ethnography research is therefore by no means straightforward. Photographs, videos and other images produced in material or imagined form as part of the research process do not necessarily take on the status of being knowledge about the research question or findings in themselves, but rather can be understood as routes to knowledge and tools through which we can encounter and imagine other people's worlds.

As these examples demonstrate, visual ethnography cannot be defined as a simply observational method. Moreover, while visual ethnographers might video record or photograph things that other people do, perform, point out or otherwise engage with, such recordings tend to be made from the embodied perspective of the participating ethnographer. Whether or not holding a camera, it is through our personal and embodied engagements in activities and environments that ethnographers learn about other people's lives. Anthropological critiques have been particularly important in problematising an observational approach (e.g. Fabian 1983) leading us to understand that simply using video or photography as an observational tool might be seen as objectifying. Ingold has suggested that anthropology's objective is to understand 'human being and knowing in the one world we all inhabit'. He has distinguished this from ethnography's objective, which he writes 'is to describe the lives of people other than ourselves, with an accuracy and sensitivity honed by detailed observation and prolonged first-hand experience' (Ingold 2008b: 69). He sees anthropology thus as 'an inquisitive mode of inhabiting the world, of being *with*' (Ingold 2008b: 88). Re-defining ethnography, and as such visual ethnography as a collaborative and reflexive exercise (as we have seen has happened across the 'ethnographic' disciplines discussed in Chapter 1), acknowledges its roots in anthropology, yet simultaneously connects with the participatory and collaborative trends in other disciplines and interdisciplinary fields.

These discussions moreover show that not only is the idea that we might produce objective knowledge as detached observers problematic, but that similarly we cannot record it with the camera. This has long since been a question for scholars across disciplines. As Chris Jenks argued in the 1990s, while material objects inevitably have a visual presence, the notion of 'visual culture' should not refer only to the material and observable, the 'visible' aspects of culture (Jenks 1995: 16). From anthropology we have also learnt that the visual forms part of human imaginations and conversations (Edgar 2004; Orobitg 2004). The material and visual cultures that we encounter when we do ethnographic fieldwork may therefore be understood from this perspective: material objects are unavoidably visual, but visual images are not, by definition, material or permanently inscribed on the screens or surfaces through or on which we view them. Nevertheless, the intangibility of an image that is described verbally or is imagined makes it no less real. This approach to images presents a direct challenge to definitions of 'the real in terms of the material, which can be accessed through the visible' (Slater 1995: 221). This rupture between visibility and reality is significant for an ethnographic approach to the visual because like the arguments outlined in the above paragraph it implies that reality cannot necessarily be observed visually, recorded and then analysed. It thus demands that we consider exactly what it is that we do record when we participate in a particular social, sensory and material environment with a camera. I discuss these questions further with regard to the examples of photography and video practice in visual ethnography in Chapters 4 and 5 respectively, focusing on the ways that ethnographic photographs and videos are made and move. The principle for both photography and video is the same, however. Both are produced as we move with our cameras through the environments that we are part of. In this sense they are composed through not simply the capturing of what is in front of the camera lens. Rather they are made in relation to what is behind and around the camera and photographer. This means that they are, on the one hand, as the anthropological filmmaker David MacDougall puts it, 'corporeal images' which stand for the positioning in the world of the body of the person who was holding the camera (MacDougall 2005). Yet simultaneously they are framed by the totality of the environmental configurations that also encompassed the person who took the photograph. Ingold's provocation around the question of the status of drawings and paintings also helps us to think about this question. He asks:

> Should the drawing or painting be understood as a final image to be inspected and interpreted, as is conventional in studies of visual culture, or should we rather think of it as a node in a matrix of trails to be followed by observant eyes? Are drawings or paintings *of* things in the world, or are they *like* things in the world, in the sense that we have to find our ways through and among them, inhabiting them as we do the world itself? (Ingold 2010a: 16)

Following Ingold's points we might propose that photographs and video are taken in the world and not simply of it or of persons and things in it.

The above understanding of images as emergent from particular configurations explains how we might potentially treat images as part of a research process. Yet the ways images are interpreted and given meaning is also situated and is culturally and biographically specific: different people use their own subjective knowledge and biographical experiences to interpret them. At this level a discussion of the relationship of photographic and video images to reality becomes relevant in a different way. As Terence Wright pointed out, this may be because '[a]s products of a particular culture, they [in this case photographs] are only perceived as real by cultural convention: they only *appear* realistic because we have been taught to see them as such' (Wright 1999: 6, original italics). As ethnographers, we may suspend a belief in reality as an objective and observable experience, but we should also keep in mind that we too in everyday life as well as in research situations might use images to refer to certain versions of reality and treat images as referents of visible and observable phenomena. Wright noted that 'As Alan Sekula (1982: 86) has pointed out, it is the most natural thing in the world for someone to open their *[sic]* wallet and produce a photograph saying "this is my dog"' (Wright 1999: 2). While Sekula was writing around forty years ago, most of us will have turned on our camera phones to show images of people, things and localities in similar ways. In this sense, often the ways in which we live in the world and the ways we theorise it might not coincide. These ambiguities are part of any research project. They can be resolved to some extent through a commitment to the reflexivity I have called for earlier in this chapter. Thus, realist uses of photographic and video images, such as their treatment as visual records of environments, arrangements of persons and things may in some situations be appropriate in ethnographic research and representation. However, realist uses of the visual in ethnography should be qualified by a reflexive awareness of the intentions behind such uses, the cultural conventions that frame them, their limits as regards the representation of truth, and the theoretical approaches that render them ambiguous.

Images, technologies, people

Photography and video have been appropriated in varying forms and degrees by many individuals in almost all cultures and societies. However, visual and digital images and technologies are not only elements of the cultures that academics study, they also pertain to the academic cultures and personal lifestyles and subject positions from which contemporary ethnographers approach their projects. As Chaplin argued for sociology, ethnographic disciplines should not distance themselves from the topics they study (1994: 16). For Chaplin, this meant thinking not simply of 'the sociology *of* visual representation' but of sociology *and* visual representations as elements of the same cultural context. The same point stands in a contemporary context in that ethnographers should treat visual and digital images and technologies as an aspect of the material culture and practice *of* social scientists as well as a practice and material culture that is researched *by* social scientists.

Most ethnographers, and an increasing number of research participants, own or have some access to digital and visual media. As I discuss further in Chapter 4, Smart phones and other mobile media have made what would in analogue and early digital times be a heavy combination of equipment easily portable within the same technology, thus creating a context where new and emergent digital and visual practices are part of the lives of both researchers and participants. Yet, we should also be cautious about claiming that we now live in a context of constant digital connectedness, or seeing this as a complete departure from analogue practices. Indeed, my own ethnographic research in slow cities has demonstrated that in some ordinary everyday contexts digital and analogue practices are used in relation to each other in the production, archiving and presentation of images (Pink 2011e).

During the reflexive turn of the 1990s, anthropologists (e.g. Okely and Callaway 1992; Kulick and Willson 1995; Okely 1996) stressed the inseparability of personal from professional identities and the importance of autobiography and personal experience in the production of ethnographic knowledge. The same point applies to the ways that ethnographers use visual and digital images and technologies, in ways that interweave the personal and the professional. This is demonstrated especially well in autobiographical ethnographic work that emerged in the 1990s, where the ethnographer's own existing personal images are appropriated or drawn into academic work. For example, Okely has analysed her past experiences of attending a girls' boarding school anthropologically, using photographs and memories from this period of her life in what she called 'retrospective fieldwork' (1996: 147–74). Working with film, Rosie and Ivo Strecker's ethnographic documentary, *Sweet Sorghum* (1995), is about Rosie's childhood experiences of living with the Hamar people in Ethiopia while her parents (anthropologists and filmmakers) were doing anthropological fieldwork. In making the film they cut their own old 'home movie' footage with a more recently shot interview with Rosie.

In my own fieldwork I have also been just as much a consumer of images and technologies as those who participated in these projects (although maybe in different ways). Conventionally when we study consumption, the focus is on how other people consume. Yet we might also turn the lens onto ethnographers, to develop a reflexive awareness of how we too are consumers of digital and visual technologies and images. Ethnographers' photography, video and online practices and skills may interweave their professional fieldwork narratives or personal biographies. Moreover, photographs and video can represent an explicit meeting point, or continuity, between personal and professional identities. They are given new meanings as they move through different situations. Photographs of research participants who are also friends will be found in research archives and vice versa. As I discuss in Chapter 7, digital archiving makes it possible for a photograph to simultaneously be involved in multiple localities in new ways. Yet the example of analogue photography is instructive: when I returned to England from fieldwork in Southern Spain in 1994 I had two sets of analogue photographs: one of friends and one of 'research'. As time passed these photographic prints shifted between categories as I reflected on what I learned from them and what they meant to me. They moved out of albums and eventually into a series of envelopes and folders. The personal/professional visual narratives into which I had initially divided them gradually became dissolved into other categories as I worked through the experience of fieldwork as life in an attempt to translate it into ethnographic knowledge. Some of the photographs had been copied for research participants and therefore they developed simultaneous biographies in these contexts gaining other situated meanings in other people's photography collections. As the work of Edgar Gómez Cruz shows, the boundaries between life and fieldwork can become equally blurred in digital visual ethnography. In his ethnographic research about contemporary digital photography practices in face-to-face photography clubs and online platforms, Gómez Cruz became as much a participant as a researcher (Gómez Cruz 2012). Writing of the people who participated in his research he describes how: 'I took photographs with them, ate with them, we were in constant contact through the Internet and mobile phones, I interviewed them, they guided me and taught me a lot about photography and about life' (2012: 25, my translation from Spanish). The work of the visual ethnographer can thus become part of life, while at the same time life becomes part of research.

Image-makers as practitioners

Photographers, video makers, digital artists, or web designers, whether or not they are ethnographers, are individuals with their own intentions working in specific social, technological and cultural contexts. In order to understand the practices of both ethnographers and research participants as image-makers it is important to consider how relationships develop between individuals, visual and digital technologies, practices, society and culture. Visual practices are also framed by institutional and corporate contexts. As Evans and Hall suggested for analogue photography (1999: 3) visual practices would intersect with camera and film manufacturing industries and developing and processing companies. In a digital context the literature is already demonstrating how the ways in which we experience and engage with the internet and social networking platforms (see Miller 2011) and digital mapping (see Farman 2010; Lapenta 2011) are framed likewise by corporations and software (as discussed in Pink 2012d). While these framings do not singularly determine the ways we enact digital photography and video practices, we need to comprehend the ways that they intersect with other elements.

The quest to understand visual production and images has long since been part of academic scholarship and a review of selected key existing contributions shows the complexities of this task and some of the debates and issues it raises. To understand visual ethnography as a practice we therefore need to turn our attention to the ways that scholars who already work on questions relating to visual media have approached these questions. Such approaches offer us ways to analyse the media and digital practices of research participants, and to comprehend our own uses of visual media and digital technologies in the ethnographic process within the same theoretical frame. The sociologist Pierre Bourdieu (1990) made an early attempt to theorise photographic practices and meanings to explain why individuals tend to perpetuate existing visual forms and styles in their visual work. Bourdieu proposed that while everything is potentially photographable, the photographic practice of individuals is governed by objective limitations. He argued that 'photography cannot be delivered over to the randomness of the individual imagination' but instead 'via the mediation of the *ethos,* the internalization of objective and common regularities, the group places this practice under its collective rule' (Bourdieu 1990: 6, [1965]). According to this interpretation, images produced by individual photographers and video makers would inevitably express the shared norms of that individual's society. Thus, Bourdieu argued 'that the most trivial photograph expresses, apart from the explicit intentions of the photographer, the system of schemes of perception, thought and appreciation common to a whole group' (1990: 6, [1965]). Individuals undoubtedly produce images that respond and refer to established conventions that have developed in and between existing visual cultures. However, the implication of this is not necessarily that individual visual practices are dictated by an unconsciously held common set of beliefs. Bourdieu's explanation represents a problematic reduction of agency, subjectivity and individual creativity to external objective factors. It is difficult to reconcile with both theories of agency and selfhood that emerged during the 1990s as well as with more recent understandings of the contingencies of practice (see Pink 2012d). For example, in terms of the 1990s debates, the anthropologist Anthony Cohen's proposition that individuals are 'self-driven' (1992: 226) 'thinking selves' and the creators of culture (1994: 167), viewed 'society as composed of and by self-conscious individuals' (1994: 192), and Nigel Rapport argued in favour of a recognition of the individual 'as a seat of consciousness, as well-spring of creativity, as guarantor of meaning' (Rapport 1997a: 7). Whether or not we wholly take up the views of these thinkers, their arguments caution us against the reduction of individual creativity to collective norms. While it is likely that individuals will to some extent reference known visual forms, styles, discourses and meanings through the content and form of their own visual images, as recent studies of the ways skills are learned and practiced shows, it is just as likely that they will modify and appropriate these skills as they learn and practice them (e.g. Marchand 2010). We need to account for the reality that research participants and visual ethnographers are creative and innovative individuals, with unique biographies and skills, and moreover seek to identify these differences alongside similarities. Recently a focus on practice and practice theory has become popular amongst sociologists and anthropologists and applied to the study of photographic and media practices.

Sociological approaches have focused on digital photography as a practice. For instance, Elizabeth Shove and Mika Pantzar discuss how 'people who use these [digital] devices continue to draw upon traditions established by film', but point out that nevertheless '*digital* photography—whether reproduced by casual "snappers" or devoted enthusiasts—is defined and constituted by distinctive forms of equipment, competence and know how, and by changing understandings of what amateur image making involves'. They argue that therefore 'it represents a substantially new practice, the details of which continue to unfold' (Shove and Pantzar 2007: 157). Gómez Cruz, on the basis of his in-depth ethnography, has argued that digital photography practices seem different from analogue practices and they 'acquire meaning through the constitution of assemblages and socio-technical networks which in turn give meaning to this digital culture' (2012: 231, my translation from Spanish). For these scholars, digital photography, which is still an emergent practice, is itself a field of research, reinforcing the importance for digital visual ethnographers of not only studying others but also reflecting on the meaning and meaning-making of their own practice.

Media anthropologists have also explored practice theory as a route to understanding how people use media (e.g. Bräuchler and Postill 2010; Postill 2010). This work can likewise inform the ways we understand our own media practices as we use audiovisual and locative media and methods in the making of visual ethnography. For example John Postill has argued for the importance of an engagement with practice theory for understanding 'what people do with media' (2010: 6). His point applies equally to the question of what ethnographers do with media when they use it in their research. Therefore Postill suggests that a practice approach can help us to understand media in everyday life (2010: 12), 'the relationship between media and the body' (2010: 14) and media production (2010: 15). As we have seen in the preceding discussions, each of these themes is similarly relevant to the practices of the visual ethnographer whose everyday life and research often become blurred, whose uses of photography, video and locative media are embodied, skilled and adaptive/innovative, and who is a (co)producer of media texts (see Ardévol 2012; Martens 2012, for practice-oriented discussions of visual research). Yet media anthropologists have also advanced criticisms of the use of a practice approach (e.g. Hobart 2010; Peterson 2010; Pink 2012d), which point to its limitations in enabling us to understand human agency, and the deeper and more general limitation of using a single theoretical prism through which to comprehend the 'messiness' (Law 2004) of reality.

Some of these limitations, I have argued elsewhere, can be resolved to some extent through a theory of place. Such an approach acknowledges that practices are analytical constructs designed to appreciate and analyse the otherwise unstoppable ongoingness of practical activity, and how this activity is contingent on the changing configuration of things with which it is co-implicated (Pink 2012d). Existing media theory also offers useful ways of understanding how media is part of a wider context, for instance, the concept of 'mediaspace' as developed by Nick Couldry and Anna McCarthy (2004) invites us to start thinking about how digital media and everyday life form part of the same spatial realities. These shifts towards spatial theory and towards approaches from human geography (see Chapter 1) therefore enable us to bring together two different analytical prisms of practice and place (as developed in Pink 2012d) which offer us a way of understanding how both ethnographers' and participants' uses of digital and visual media are contingent on a number of elements, including these individual differences, collective understandings and the contingencies of the environments of which they are a part (see Pink 2012d). It is not my agenda here to make an argument for one or another theoretical approach to understanding the practices and ecologies of digital and visual media use in ethnography (although I do advance such arguments elsewhere). The point that I hope to have demonstrated above is that there is a need for ethnographers to attend to such questions in ways that suit their own projects, practices and disciplinary orientations, and to theorise their own practice as much as they do that of the subjects of their research. This is all the more important, given the potential mutuality of the relations between researcher and research participants discussed above.

When we do visual ethnography, especially when it involves making images with, in ways parallel to and/or for participants, we can become implicated in some way in their visual and digital practices. This might involve learning to make the same types of images as participants, and publishing them, exhibiting them or simply collecting them in the same ways or participating in the same web platforms as research participants. When we start to contribute to these activities through our own images or sharing images we begin to also participate in the making of the places and visual cultures we are researching. The images we produce and the practices we engage in thus belong simultaneously to the different but connected material and digital cultures of visual scholarship and of the culture being 'studied'. This invites a series of questions, the consideration of which can create interesting reflections on the ways we make ethnographic knowledge. For instance: what happens when ethnographers start to produce the very material, visual or digital culture they are studying; what happens when ethnographers participate in and contribute to the visual and digital practices and innovations they are analysing; and, what happens to ethnographers' images when research participants appropriate them for their own purposes? Some of these scenarios arise in the examples discussed in the following chapters.

Visual ethnography and the sensory turn

In Chapter 1, I discussed how recent interest in the senses has impacted on the ways that the visual is now understood and studied across the social science and humanities disciplines. The sensory turn in scholarship (see e.g. Howes 2005), accompanied by developments in nonrepresentational approaches (Thrift 2008; Ingold 2011), has pushed forward new agendas for research and scholarship. These moves have contributed to scholarship in visual ethnography, particularly (see Chapter 1) in questioning how the visual and vision are understood in ethnographic practice. Indeed the turn to the senses by no means renders visual ethnography irrelevant (see also Pink 2006) and it has moreover been led in several ways by visual anthropologists themselves: for example, attention to the senses was already integral to the visual anthropology of MacDougall in his earlier writing (e.g. MacDougall 1998) and central to my own work on *The Future of Visual Anthropology* (Pink 2006). Some of these debates are also followed up in *Doing Sensory Ethnography*

(Pink 2009). I understand visual ethnography as a practice that attends to the visual elements of the worlds that we inhabit in terms of their inseparability from other elements of sensory experience, and to visual and digital media in relation to how we might use them to produce ways of knowing that acknowledges this interrelatedness of the senses. As the examples discussed in the following chapters reveal, doing visual ethnography offers a route to comprehending those aspects of experience that are very often sensory, unspoken, tacit and invisible. The twenty-first century turn to the senses and the nonrepresentational is, for visual ethnography practice and scholarship, an equally welcome move as was the reflexive turn of the late twentieth century.

Summary

Ethnographers themselves are part of the contexts in which photography, video and other digital and analogue media practices are already experienced and understood in particular ways. How individual ethnographers approach the visual in their research and representation is inevitably influenced by a range of factors, including theoretical commitments, disciplinary agendas, personal experience, gendered identities and their visual and digital skills and cultures. Fundamental to understanding the significance of visual and digital media and the practices associated with them in ethnographic work is a reflexive appreciation of how such elements combine to produce visual meanings and ethnographic knowledge.

Further reading

Edgar, I. (2004) *Guide to Imagework: Imagination-based Research Methods*. London: Routledge (an introduction to Edgar's image work methodology, which could usefully be used as a complementary method to the visual ethnographic methods described in this volume).

Howes, D. (2005) *Empire of the Senses: the Sensory Culture Reader*. Oxford: Berg (a volume of key readings about sensory aspects of culture, which usefully contextualises the place of vision).

Pink, S. (2006) *The Future of Visual Anthropology*. Oxford: Routledge.

Pink, S. (ed.) (2012a) *Advances in Visual Methodology*. London: SAGE.

Ingold, T. (2010) 'Ways of mind-walking: reading, writing, painting', *Visual Studies*, 25(1), 15–23.

Additional material is available on the book's companion website: www.uk.sagepub.com/pink3e

3

Planning and Practising Visual Ethnography

We cannot predict, and should not prescribe in advance, the precise methods that we will need to use in any one ethnographic research project. Equally, following Morphy and Banks, visual methods do not need to be used 'in all contexts', rather 'they should be used where appropriate, with the rider that appropriateness will not always be obvious in advance' (1997: 14). In practice, decisions about if visual methods should be used, which ones should be selected and precisely how they should be engaged are often best made once researchers are in a position to assess which specific methods will be appropriate or ethical in a particular research context. This kind of familiarisation with the context allows us to account for their relationships with participants and their experience and knowledge of local visual cultures as a basis upon which to decide and develop the methods to be used. Such opportunities are, however, often not the reality: more often than not certain decisions and indicators about the use of visual images and technologies in research need to be made before the fieldwork starts. Often research proposals, ethical review procedures, preparations and plans must be produced or completed before a project can be started. In other situations the fieldwork may be in an area where technologies are difficult to purchase or hire. Moreover if we are applying for research funding, we need to be able to anticipate and identify the methods that we will use, the technologies we need, and their costs, so these can be budgeted for at proposal stage. Indeed such pre-planning is not only needed for grant applications. Many researchers who plan or develop visual ethnography projects are employed by, may collaborate with or study in universities and other organisations. Usually such institutions require that their committees should formally scrutinise and approve the ethical procedures that are in place for research projects before the fieldwork stage can begin.

The appropriateness of visual methods

In an earlier work, Banks has divided visual research methods into three broad activities: 'making visual representations (studying society by producing images)';

'examining pre-existing visual representations' (studying images for information about society); and 'collaborating with social actors in the production of visual representations' (Banks n.d.). In a contemporary context where applied visual methods are increasingly developed we might add to this the practice of creating (or co-creating with participants) visual interventions (see Pink 2006, 2007a), and we should account for ways digital technologies and the Internet are implicated in these processes. As a general range of ways in which ethnographers would anticipate using images in their research, these activities are not necessarily chronologically ordered, and might overlap or interweave in practice. Of course, in reality our specific uses of visual images and technologies tend to develop as part of the social and technological relationships and activities that ethnographers engage in during fieldwork. Yet, the activities outlined above can be used as a guide to planning, mapping out and conceptualising the methods that will be involved.

While it is useful to think of visual methods as always being in progress, this is not to say that visual ethnographers do not pre-plan and apply existing methods that have already been developed in new projects. Doing this provides us with an important starting point in any project. In Chapters 4, 5 and 6, I discuss a range of already established visual ethnography research methods – including photo-elicitation, the video tour and participant-produced images. However, as I show in those chapters, the specific applications of these general models of visual research methods vary in practice, and moreover, in the case of the video tour method, which I have applied across several different research contexts (home, garden and town), the method and our understanding of it can also grow through its application across different projects (see Chapter 5). In other cases, unanticipated uses of the visual may be discovered by accident and retrospectively defined as visual methods. Ethnographers might repeat such activities (sometimes in collaboration with participants), thus developing and refining the method throughout a research project. This was my experience in my PhD research about Spanish bullfighting culture. I began photographing people at the many public receptions held to present trophies, exhibitions and book launches. After my first reception I showed my photographs to the organisers and participants and they asked me for copies of certain photos, some of which they gave to their colleagues. By keeping note of their requests and asking them questions about the images I gained a sense of how individuals situated themselves in relation to other individuals in 'bullfighting culture'. As I attended more receptions I consciously repeated this method and developed my use of the camera and the photographs in response to the relationship that developed between local people participating in events, the technology, the images and myself as photographer (Pink 1999b). This method of researching with images was appropriate in bullfighting culture partly because the ways I took and shared photographs imitated and was incorporated into local people's existing cultural and individual uses of photography. Yet in other fieldwork contexts it will not work in the same way; we should not simply assume that methods developed within one research context will be directly transferable to, or appropriate in, others. The use of photography in the bullfighting context was directly linked to local visual practices, therefore to replicate the method would involve not doing the same thing, but following the same principles. Achieving this would involve learning how to photograph in ways that corresponded with the photographic culture and practices of the research context, working with local photographic conventions and their personal meanings, and attending to the economic and exchange values that photographs might have in any given research context. In some contexts this might mean that the ethnographer does not become the photographer her or himself, but instead participates in the ways other people use photographs. For instance, an increasing number of social scientists do research with people who are more technology literate and wealthier than them. A good example is John Postill's research about uses of the internet in suburban Malaysia. Postill found that many of the people who participated in his research, who were mainly middle class Chinese suburban residents, had more sophisticated cameras and mobile phones than he did. At public events he was often surrounded by local people photographing the proceedings with camera phones, while key local actors, who were also participants in his research, used digital cameras to produce images for their own web sites. One local politician had a portable printer that he used to print out a photograph taken of himself with Postill at a community basketball match (an enviable technology for most visual researchers at the time in the early 2000s) (Postill 2011: 74).

In other research contexts photography might not be an obvious element of the everyday cultures being researched. Radley, Hodgetts and Cullen's photographic study of how homeless people both survive and make their home in the city is a good example of how in a context where photographic practice was not part of the everyday lives of the people who participated in their research, photography was nevertheless an appropriate research method. In this study they asked twelve homeless people, using disposable cameras, to take photographs of their lives at 'key times in their day, of typical activities and spaces, or anything else that portrayed their situation' (Radley et al. 2005: 277). These photographing activities were both preceded and followed by an interview. The researchers argued that their emphasis on the visual 'as a way of engaging the participants' (2005: 292) meant that for this research, with a particular focus on appearance, materiality and the use of space (2005: 293), the data provided more information than from simply interviewing. Importantly, they also report that 'the participants said that they enjoyed making the pictures, enjoyed having the opportunity to show as well as to tell about their lives, their constraints and their possibilities' (2005: 292).

Therefore we can see that while there are sets of 'established' visual methods, the ways they are applied can vary across projects. The method of interviewing with photographs used by Radley et al. (2005) is often called 'photo-elicitation' and is discussed further in Chapter 4. As we will see, it is in fact performed and practiced differently in different research contexts. Methods, thus, can be seen to have their own trajectories, biographies and transformations. As discussed elsewhere (Pink and Leder Mackley 2012) it is useful to think, in this sense, of the notion of the 'biographies of methods'. By this I mean that a method, such as a video tour, photo-elicitation or other, is not a static or fixed model. Instead, if we see methods as having biographies we can trace and understand how they change temporally and contextually, how they evolve in each application, and how they are redeveloped in the light of new findings, theories and experiences. In doing so we are thus able to simultaneously ask how these developments impact on the types of knowledge we are able to produce through methods as they are re-developed in different projects.

Therefore, a first task before planning visual ethnography research is to begin by reading up on how other ethnographers have used visual methods in similar research contexts and/or to answer similar research questions. The same methods may not be directly appropriate for the project in mind, yet their previous applications in similar fields will offer relevant insights into the ways they have been and might be used and the status of the types of knowledge they have the potential to produce. This includes considering how visual methods, images and technologies will be interpreted by research participants in specific fieldwork contexts and scenarios, in addition to assessing how well visual methods suit the aims of specific projects. In some situations visual methods will just not be appropriate, and moreover it is important not to have fixed, preconceived expectations of what it will be possible to achieve by using visual research methods in a given situation. Sometimes visual methods simply do not support the aims of a research project. For example, Hastrup's (1992) description of her attempt as a woman anthropologist to photograph an exclusively male Icelandic sheep market demonstrates this well. Although this is a relatively early example it continues to be relevant. Hastrup described the difficulty and discomfort she experienced while photographing this event but notes that having accomplished the task she felt a sense of satisfaction 'to have been there and to have been able to document this remarkable event' (1992: 9). She had left with the sensation that she 'even had photos from the sacred grove of a male secret society' (1992: 9). However, her photographic method was not appropriate for recording the type of information she had anticipated and she wrote of the disappointment she experienced on later seeing the printed photographs: '... they were hopeless. Ill-focused, badly lit, lopsided and showing nothing but the completely uninteresting backs of men and rams' (1992: 9). She emphasised the difference between her experience of photographing and the end results: 'While I was taking them I had the impression that I was making an almost pornographic record of a secret ritual. They showed me nothing of the sort but bore the marks of my own inhibition, resulting from my transgression of the boundary between gender categories' (1992: 9). Hastrup's expectations of what she may obtain by using this visual research method were not met. She anticipated that her photographs would represent ethnographic evidence of her experience of the event, 'a record of a secret ritual'. To assess why this was not achieved she generalised that 'pictures have a limited value as ethnographic "evidence"', and the 'secret' of informants' experiences can only be told in words (1992: 9). As I have emphasised in Chapter 1, the idea that the images we produce as visual ethnographers will necessarily serve as objective recordings or visual evidence of what was there and what was felt, is likely to lead to disappointment. Therefore, as ethnographic 'evidence', photographs have limited value and Hastrup's interpretation would hold. Yet I would caution against taking this to mean that one may only invoke ethnographic and participants' experiences with words. In other contexts and uses photography and video can be used to invoke these more experiential elements. In Chapters 4, 5 and 6, I examine a series of examples in which ethnographers have sought to bring out empathetic elements of the experience of research contexts through the use of photography and video.

Planning visual research

As the discussion above has shown, even when we already know the research context in which we are working well it is not always easy to predict exactly how and to what extent visual images and technologies may be used. Likewise, judgements about how appropriate, ethical and viable visual methods might be in any given ethnographic context are often best understood as contingent on that context itself, rather than simply determined by external guidelines and measurements. Sometimes the best formulated plans, based on in-depth training in using video or photography in ethnography, need to be revised once we become more familiar with the local or cultural context of fieldwork. For example, when I originally proposed to do research about bullfighting culture in Southern Spain, and having trained in ethnographic documentary making, I anticipated that I would use video quite extensively. However, once I began my work as an ethnographer in Spain in the early 1990s I found that local bullfighting fans only occasionally used video cameras. Instead photography was a dominant source of knowledge and representation about bullfighting and it was usually more appropriate for me to participate in local events as a photographer than as a video maker. Since some bullfight fans also participated in their bullfighting culture as amateur photographers, I was able to share an activity with them as well as producing images, which interested them. At the time photography fitted the demands of the project and offered me a role to play as a visual ethnographer in that context. Retrospectively, I was able to identify ways in which video could have supported the research, fitted into the local bullfighting culture and also served my informants' interests. Yet, my point is that these insights were based on my in-depth ethnography of that context, and would not have been knowable before. Such insights could have been used as the basis of future research plans, but would need to be reviewed on the basis of any changes in contemporary local practices in relation to new developments in visual and digital technologies. In Chapter 6, I outline how this research would be developed and planned differently if commenced now, 20 years later in a digital visual context.

Usually ethnographers with some experience of working in a particular culture and society already have a sense of the visual and technological cultures of the people with whom they plan to work. This kind of knowledge can help us to

The woman bullfighter Cristina Sanchez performing. © Sarah Pink 1993

Figure 3.1 When researching gender and bullfighting in Spain, one of the roles I played was as amateur bullfight photographer. My photographic prints, taken mainly in black and white, using a traditional stills camera, provided me with a way to fit in with and share one of the activities that local bullfight *aficionados* were involved in at that historical moment. Since doing that research both technologies and local practices have shifted. Were I to begin similar fieldwork now in 2013 I would not be able to take for granted that exactly the same method would be appropriate. I would need to review the extent to which amateur bullfight *aficionados* now use digital photography and the implications of this for their practice.

consider how their photographic/video research practices will develop in relation to local practices and provide a sense of how we may learn through the interface between our own and local visual practices. Such background knowledge makes it easier to present a research proposal that defines quite specifically how and to what ends visual technologies and images are to be employed. This may entail developing insights from prior research in the same culture, doing a short pilot study, or researching aspects of visual cultures from library and museum sources, ethnographic film and the internet. Online research would be an initial starting point for locating both digital and material resources in this process. Thus, to begin a visual ethnography the first step need not be solely a traditional literature review about visual culture. The first stage of the research process may be an exploration of web sites, blogs, online discussions, and video and photography sharing platforms, where elements of the visual culture of a research area are represented. It might involve discussing issues related to the research through social networking or email, and contacting the owners of web sites, online archives, bloggers, photographers and video makers. The internet is part of many contemporary ethnographic field sites, and visual ethnographers will often find themselves moving between or being simultaneously part of online and offline socialities and materialities as part of the process of doing visual ethnography. In this sense, engaging with the online constituents of ethnographic localities offers an opportune starting point for research projects, in particular those that are located in physical localities that researchers are not permanently based in or near to.

Pre-fieldwork surveys of literature, digital and other visual texts and examples of how other ethnographers have successfully worked with visual and digital images and technologies in specific research contexts can indicate the potential for using visual methods in particular social, cultural, technological and practical situations. Combined with some considered guesswork about people's visual and digital practices and discourses, this can form a basis from which to develop a research proposal. However, neither a researcher's own preparation, nor other ethnographers' accounts can predict how a visual method will develop in a new project. Just as ethnography can only really be learnt in practice, ethnographic uses of visual and digital images and technologies develop from practice-based knowledge. Moreover, as projects evolve, novel uses of photography or video may develop to explore and represent unexpected issues. Indeed some of the most thought provoking and exciting instances of visual research have emerged unexpectedly during fieldwork. A good example is Gemma Orobitg's research amongst the Pumé Indians of Venezuela. Orobitg writes that 'During the initial design of my fieldwork ... I did not consider using a camera. Rather it was a fortunate coincidence that led me to first experiment and then reflect methodologically on the value of visual technologies in anthropological research and for anthropological analysis' (2004: 31). Orobitg was asked to take photographs for some documentary filmmakers who wanted to develop a film project in the area and needed some images to support their application. However, from the moment she showed these photographs to the Pumé people she was working with, the images began to inform her research in some key ways: as a visual notebook; as a way of communicating with the Pumé; and as a medium through which to reconstruct the imaginary sphere of Pumé life (Orobitg 2004: 32). In Chapters 4, 5 and 6, I discuss a series of examples that are intended to offer ideas and inspirations through which ethnographers may develop their own styles. Yet as Orobitg's example shows it is important to remain open to new possibilities throughout the research process.

Choosing the technology for the project

As I have discussed above for images, technologies do not have single meanings or uses but are appropriated for new purposes, given meanings and become part of everyday life in different ways in different contexts and by different individuals. Likewise, usually we cannot know in advance how our own cameras, computers or locative media technologies will be given meanings in research contexts, and how these meanings will extend to the way research participants define us. Moreover our choices of technology (which could range for example between a digital or analogue camera, a semi-professional video camera, the cheapest hand-held domestic model or a smart phone) can be contingent on a range of factors, which might be related to skill, funding, energy supplies and personal taste.

Nevertheless, the equipment we use will become part of our identities during fieldwork and in academic circles. The brands and models of camera, laptop, tablet and phone that we use to undertake and present ethnographic research are all attributed meanings across both cultures. They are also significant for the types of conversations we can strike up with research participants about technology, and for the ways in which we might be able to share images with them and collaborate in visual projects. Our technologies help us to situate ourselves in fieldwork contexts, both in terms of our identities, but also in terms of the practical activities of sharing, collaborating or co-creating that their software and hardware permits us to engage in. Some research participants may have a shared interest in digital media, photography or video, and might have better computing and visual skills than the ethnographer. For example, in Spain my amateur interest in bullfight photography was shared with several local people. This led us to discuss technical as well as aesthetic aspects of bullfighting photography. Then in the early 1990s this included themes such as the best analogue film speeds, zoom lenses and the best seating in the arena for photographing during the performance. Later in 1999 and 2000 in video interviewing projects in the United Kingdom and Spain, interviewees appeared relaxed with my domestic digital video camera simply seeing it as one of the latest pieces of new video technology. In comparison to solitary field diary writing, photography and video making can appear more visible, comprehensible activities to informants, and may link more closely with their own experience. Photographic prints, videotapes, DVDs or digital files themselves become commodities for sharing, exchange and the sites of negotiation, for example, among participants, among researchers, between researchers and participants and between researchers and their families and friends at home. Participants might want to use our cameras or computers to create, find, or work on images of things they want to show us. In contemporary contexts it is most likely that ethnographers will work with digital images. Yet, as I have already stressed, it is important to recognise that we live in a world where digital photography exists alongside photocopying, printing and other techniques that are continuous with the practices and materialities of analogue contexts. In my own experience of research in slow cities, research participants combined the use of a digital archive, digital image projection, photocopies, and a display of printed analogue historical photographs within the same event (Pink 2011e). This is however not surprising, if we stop to consider how, as scholars, we often work online, using digital cameras and archives, while it is likely that many of us will have at least one printed and framed photograph on her or his desk, print out our writing and photographs and distribute photocopied information as well as email attachments. These mixes of the new and the old are part of everyday life. However, their combinations and the way they are engaged in different contexts has meaning that we as ethnographers need to be aware of since the technologies we use will also enable participants in our research to construct our identities and thus impact on our social relationships and experiences.

Therefore, when selecting and applying for funding for technology it is important to remember that a camera and the computing hardware and software that is to be used with it will be part of the research context and an element of the ethnographer's identity. It becomes part of the social relationships we are involved in and part of the way participants engage with us. It might become the topic for conversation, collaboration and shared interests. In Chapter 6, I discuss in more depth Edgar Gómez Cruz's ethnography of what he calls 'flickr culture'. This is an excellent example of how an ethnographer's own technologies, and visual practices can become part of the context in which she or he is working. As Gómez Cruz shows through his own experience and his research into those of other members of the photography club where he did his fieldwork, photographic technologies can be important in social and technological relations (see Gómez Cruz 2011: 204–7). In other contexts the technologies we use to do visual ethnography impact on identities and relationships in different ways. In Gómez Cruz's work the camera mattered particularly because he was doing research with fellow photographers (see Gómez Cruz 2011, 2012). In other situations the portability of the technology might be most important, or using a camera or other equipment that is inconspicuous in its size, design or branding might be more suitable. In some cases image quality may have to be forsaken to produce images that represent the type of ethnographic knowledge sought. For example, the ways that a relationship develops between an ethnographer and participant will be different, if framed by the use of professional lighting and sound equipment, to that which emerges when an ethnographer is working in the same environment with just a small hand-held camcorder or stills camera. The images may be darker and grainier, the sound less sharp, but the ethnographic knowledge they invoke may be more useful to the project.

The use of digital video for research in the home is a good example. Homes are generally not already lit in ways that are designed for video ethnography, images of participants are often back-lit by the sunlight streaming in through large windows, and some corners of the home are darker than others. Some of these issues can be resolved by asking participants to collaborate by switching on lights. However, bringing additional lighting for such a task would seem inappropriate when seeking to understand the home as it is actually made by participants, rather than how it looks when lit for a video documentary.

In tandem with the social and cultural implications of the use of visual technologies, practical and technical issues also arise. How will a camera and other equipment be powered and transported? (Will there even be electricity? And what kind of energy sources could be available?) What post-production resources will be available? Finally, what resources will be available for showing the images to research participants? Will a big screen, monitor or projector be available in case the images need to be shared with groups? Will research participants have their own computers, so that video and photographs can be shared with them online or delivered on DVD or a memory stick? Does the researcher need a small laptop that is easily transportable for taking images to show participants? Might tablet computers be used for these tasks? Or could much of the project be done using just a smart phone? When purchasing equipment it is important to keep track of technological developments and also of post-fieldwork equipment requirements. How and where will editing be carried out? Will any extra computing hardware, software or expertise be needed? The precise technology available and skills needed can change within a year or so. For example, for my 1999 video ethnography research I needed to ask skilled computing staff to support me by digitalising my video footage and saving it on CD. In contrast by 2006 I could do this myself using the software that was supplied with my domestic digital video camera and laptop computer. However, additional equipment, advanced video editing software and additional production facilities, if they are used, can be costly. It is important to seek up to date expert advice and budget realistically for the use of facilities, equipment and, if needed, training.

Ethics and ethnographic research

A consideration of the ethical implications of ethnographic research and representation should underpin any research project. Most guides and courses on research methods dedicate a section to ethics. Such texts in the past usually covered a standard set of issues such as informed consent, covert research, confidentiality, harm to informants, exploitation and 'giving something back', ownership of data, and protection of informants. These indisputably relevant issues are critically reviewed later in this chapter. However, the issue of ethics in ethnographic work refers to more than simply the ethical conduct of the researcher. Rather, it demands that ethnographers develop an understanding of the ethical context(s) in which they work, a reflexive approach to their own ethical beliefs, and a critical approach to the idea that *one* ethical code of conduct could be hierarchically superior to all others. Because ethics are so embedded in the specific research contexts in which ethnographers work, like decisions about which visual research methods to employ in a project, ethical decisions cannot be concluded until the researcher is actually doing ethnography.

In practice, ethics are bound up with power relations between ethnographers, informants/research participants, other professionals, sponsors, gatekeepers, governments, the media and other institutions (see Ellen 1984: 134). Project specific ethical codes might also include researchers from across different disciplines, each of whom needs to engage with different other groups in the development of these. Ethical decisions, within the context of ethnographic practice, are ultimately made by individual ethnographers in relation to the specificity of different situations. Yet even so such decisions need to be made with reference to personal and professional codes of ethical conduct, the intentionalities of other parties and possibly other factors. Ethics are therefore complexly situated (see Clark 2012). Here I do not intend to offer a guide to ethical conduct, as this would be too complex a task given the wide disciplinary and interdisciplinary applications of visual ethnography practice. Instead to design the ethics for any specific projects, ethnographers would need to refer to a range of appropriate sources, including ethical guidelines of the professional association that they feel most closely aligned with, and at times to those of other related disciplines when their work crosses disciplinary boundaries. Most professional associations now keep their ethical codes and other guidelines and discussions relating to this online. In Britain, the Association of Social Anthropologists (ASA) and the British Sociological Association (BSA) provide important documents. Ethics are also bound up with the epistemological concerns of academic disciplines – they both inform and are informed by theory and methodology and indeed in such contexts ethics can become an area of philosophical debate in itself (see for example Rapport 1997a). In addition, the ethical practices of academic researchers are now often scrutinised by the Research Ethics Committees that have been set up in the institutions in which they work. They are also a concern for research funding councils and other funding organisations. The personal dimension of ethnographic research, the moral and philosophical beliefs of the researcher and his or her view of reality also impinge greatly on the ethical practices that he or she applies in research and representation. Therefore while these organisations and institutions offer frameworks, guidelines and indeed processes though which ways of dealing with ethical issues are approved, ethnographers still bear responsibility for ensuring that research is undertaken ethically and appropriately.

As ethnographers we have to evaluate the ethical implications and possible issues raised by the research practices and representations we plan, before these are held up to the scrutiny of others. Similarly, we may find ourselves in situations where we are required to address questions relating to the ethics of participants in our research, and the ethics of studying and/or making moral judgements about them. Indeed this might include having to anticipate how others will judge their actions in our subsequent representations. In other cases the ethics that guide ethnographers may be a critical discourse on the ethics of the people they study, or of an individual or institution who has power over them. As Peter Pels has pointed out for anthropology, in the contemporary world:

> Globalising movements have resulted in a situation in which the ethics of anthropology can no longer be thought of simply in terms of the dyad between researcher and researched: anthropology is placed squarely within a more complex field of governmentality, cross-cultural conflict and global mobility. (Pels 1996: 8)

It is not solely ethnographers and participants in their research who are implicated in the ethical issues researchers confront during fieldwork. Therefore, in a sense, part of our research necessarily entails an ethnography of the ethical landscape of any given fieldwork context. In the context of visual ethnography, this would include developing an understanding of the ethical considerations that are important or used as guidelines when the people who participate in our research themselves make, show and share images. A range of other parties and agendas may shape the ethical conduct of ethnographers and research participants either by enforcing their own guidelines, or by posing a threat to the safety of those represented in ethnographic work. This means that depending on the research contexts, ethnographers may need to develop an understanding of how plural moralities are at play in any ethnographic situation, and how the different ethical codes associated with them are constructed and interpreted in relation to one another. We might need to ask ourselves where research ethics intersect with these other ethical codes and practices.

Visual research methods and ethical ethnography

In recent years much debate and research has been generated around the question of ethics in visual research, and much of the discussion that this relates to is relevant to the question of ethics in visual ethnography. In this section I discuss a series of issues relating to ethical practice and the use of visual images in ethnographic research. However, I start with a disclaimer, in that my words are not intended as either recommendations or endorsements of what individual ethnographers 'should' do in any given situation. Rather, such decisions, I stress, should be made in the context of specific projects, in relation to the guidelines of professional associations, and with recourse to the ethical committees of the institutions through which researchers are developing their projects. Researchers also need to account for legal issues relating to the production and use of images in online and offline contexts, and neither do I offer advice on this. Rather this should be sought and established nationally and locally and also in relation to the use of internet images. There is however a growing interest in visual ethics, making it a field of methodological discussion and debate in itself. Here, the work of Jon Prosser, Andrew Clark and Rose Wiles and others who have written with them (e.g. Prosser et al. 2008; Wiles et al. 2011, 2012) stands out as offering a series of insightful reviews and arguments about the ways that visual ethics may be interpreted and implemented. Of particular interest in this debate is the notion of situated ethics, discussed by Clark (2012) and the comprehensive discussion of ethics relating to participatory visual research offered by Claudia Mitchell in her book *Doing Visual Research* (Mitchell 2011), and Jeremy Rowe's (2011) discussion of legal issues in visual research. The discussion below takes a different focus. I consider a series of ethical issues that specifically arise through the use of visual methods in ethnographic practice. My aim is to alert readers to these issues and where appropriate offer examples of how they have been addressed in specific contexts.

In developing this I add to the existing literature a discussion underpinned by the understanding of the relationship between vision and reality established in Chapter 1. This emphasises the specificity of the visual meanings that operate in the different contexts in which ethnographers work and in the different ways 'ethnographic' images can be interpreted by other bodies such as academics, research participants, professionals, sponsors, gatekeepers, governments, the media and other institutions. However conscious we are of the arbitrary nature of photographic meanings, ethnographic images may still be treated as 'truthful recordings' or 'evidence' by other viewers. This means we need to attend to how different approaches to the visual and different meanings given to the same images may coincide or collide in the domains in which we research and represent our work.

Below I critically review existing conventional issues in and approaches to ethics in ethnographic research methodology, to consider their implications for the use of visual images.

Covert research and the question of informed consent

As a scientific-realist strategy, covert research was assumed to enable ethnographers to better observe an objective reality. Therefore following this rationale would be that covert use of video recording and photography through a hidden camera, or in contexts where people were unaware images were being made of them, could allow researchers to produce images of an objective reality, less 'distorted' by their own subjectivity and by the self-consciousness of their informants (see Banks 2001: 120–1). As I argued in Chapter 2, such objectivity can never actually be achieved, therefore making this type of justification for covert photographing or video recording redundant. This is, of course, not to say that covert recording would not produce a unique form of visual record, yet in the case of visual ethnography there is a further question, in that if we regard visual ethnography as a practice that involves a collaborative encounter between researcher and participant, it is hard to see of what potential interest such materials would be for a visual ethnographer. Although some would argue that not all covert research is necessarily unethical (see, for example, Hammersley and Atkinson 1995: 263–8) any type of covert research requires a careful consideration of ethics and any decisions made should be contingent on the specific research context. In my view, however, it would be extremely difficult to justify undertaking covert research as part of a visual ethnographic project.

The approach to photography, video and web media in ethnographic research that I propose in Chapters 4, 5 and 6 emphasises the idea of collaboration between researcher and participant (which is also fundamental to Banks' approach to visual research (see Banks 2001)). Covert research implies the researcher videoing and photographing the activities of people in a secretive rather than collaborative way, for example, using a hidden camera or using the camera under the guise of a role other than that of researcher. A collaborative method, in contrast, assumes that researcher and participant are consciously working together to produce visual images and specific types of knowledge through technological procedures, discussions and embodied types of empathy. However, this does not mean we should simply ignore the issue of covert image making. For example, there may be occasions where covert image making unintentionally becomes part of a collaboration, for instance, if a participant in the research photographs an event for an ethnographer as a way of expressing her or his 'visual perspective' but photographs others who are not aware they are being photographed, or at least not aware that photographs of them will become part of a research project.

The distinction between overt and covert research is further complicated when we consider its relationship to the notion of informed consent. The idea of informed consent itself is not necessarily straightforward. This is, first, because cross-culturally or in different circumstances within the same cultural or national context, consent may take different forms, involve different individuals and relationships and have different meanings. Second, people may be keen to participate in research without sharing the ethnographer's own understanding of the research aims and the reasons why certain activities are photographed or video recorded. Indeed even when the research is shared by ethnographers and participants there are likely to be some variations between their understandings or at least their intentions relating to the project and the images produced through it. In such cases, the extent to which consent can be fully informed might vary. Consent to participate in visual ethnography therefore often involves going beyond the simple process of having a consent form signed off, and may require further, and careful explanation and negotiation, that may be revisited later in the project or on an ongoing basis.

Harm, representation and permission to publish

While ethnographic research is unlikely to cause harm as, for example, drugs trials may, it can lead to emotional distress or anxiety (Hammersley and Atkinson

1995: 268). Sensitivity to how individuals in different contexts or cultures may experience anxiety or stress through their involvement in research is important in any ethnographic project. However, rather than prescribing actual methods of preventing harm to participants in visual research, my intention is to suggest a way of thinking about how research, anxiety and harm are understood and experienced in different ethnographic contexts. General methods of preventing harm to participants may not be locally applicable. First, there are culturally different ways of understanding harm and of causing it with images. Therefore, in order to prevent harm being caused, a researcher needs a good understanding of local notions of harm and anxiety, how these may be experienced by different people, and how they relate to images in that specific context. Secondly, the idea that people may find the research process distressing is usually based on the assumption that they are having the research *done to them*. In this scenario the researcher is supposed to be in control of the research situation and therefore also assumes responsibility for the potential harm that may be done to the participants. This approach requires that in taking responsibility to protect their participants, researchers should be sensitive to the visual culture and experience of the individuals with whom they are working. For instance, ethnographers need to judge, or ask (if appropriate), if there are personal or cultural reasons why some people may find particular photographs shown to them in interviews or discussions offensive, disturbing or distressing, or if being photographed or videoed themselves would be stressful.

However, anxiety and harm to participants might also be limited and at best avoided by taking a collaborative approach to visual research. This might involve degrees of and joint ownership, or at least joint control of the uses that can be made of visual materials, ongoing consultations and re-negotiation of consent, along with participant input into the question of what images might be used and produced and how. In this scenario researchers and participants would together discuss and agree questions relating to the production and content of visual materials and their subsequent uses.

The publication of the research raises new issues. Sometimes this is already a concern when the images are produced, especially if the ethnographer's project is to produce a documentary or photographic exhibition. In such scenarios it is possible to make these intentions clear to the subjects of the images from the outset. Some ethnographic filmmakers ask the subjects of their films to sign consent forms (see Barbash and Taylor 1997; Banks 2001: 131–2; Marvin 2005), and if this is not done, moral and legal issues of ownership of the images and of consent may arise. Yet, even when people have consented to being photographed or video recorded, it cannot be assumed that they have, in anticipation of the images being produced, been able to even imagine what these images will be like, let alone contemplate how they would feel if the images were in a publicly screened documentary video, posted on the internet or exhibited in a gallery. This raises a series of questions relating to the process of staged consent that I have referred to above, whereby consent is re-negotiated at different stages of the project to ensure that participants are fully informed. Often ethnographic research involves making private aspects of people's lives public and it seems only appropriate to involve those same people in questions of how this is done, if they wish to be involved.

Questions relating to consent are however only one element of this. The issue of harm to individuals, or institutions is equally important to consider. For photography and video this is particularly important since it is usually impossible to preserve the anonymity of people and places. Ethnographers have to make choices regarding if and how photographs or video footage will be incorporated into the final publication of the research. This requires a serious consideration of both ethical issues relating to participant approval and consent, but also in relation to the potential harm that the materials might cause to other persons and organisations. The publication of certain photographic and video images may damage individuals' reputations; they may not want certain aspects of their identities revealed or their personal opinions to be made public. People express certain things in one context that they would not say in another, and in the apparent intimacy of a video interview a participant may make comments that he or she would not make elsewhere. When a participant has already agreed for the materials to be used in publications, sometimes the ethnographer may be left with the task of deciding whether or not to publish.

These issues outlined above require the personal, cultural and ethical sensitivity of the ethnographer, which should be rooted in her or his in-depth engagements with the people she or he has worked with, the target audience for her or his work, and the wider context where it might have implications. Yet, once visual and other representations of ethnographic work have been produced and disseminated publicly neither author nor subjects of the work can control the ways in which these representations are interpreted and given meanings by their readers, viewers or audiences. In Chapters 8 and 9, these issues are raised again in the context of a discussion of the visual representation of ethnographic work.

From 'giving something back' to empowerment and collaboration

Usually ethnographers stand to gain personally from their interactions with research participants, through an undergraduate or masters degree project, PhD thesis, consultancy project or a publication that will enhance their career. In contrast, participants may not accrue similar benefits from their participation in research projects. Conventional responses to this ethical problem focus on how ethnographers may 'give something back'; how the participants in the research may be empowered through their involvement in the project; or that research should be directed at the powerful rather than the weak (Hammersley and Atkinson 1995: 274–5). None of these responses, however, provide satisfactory solutions to the exploitative nature of research (see Hammersley and Atkinson 1995).

The idea of 'giving something back' implies that the ethnographer extracts something (usually the data) and then makes a gift of something else to the people from whom he or she has got the information. Rather than making research any less exploitative, this approach merely tries to compensate for it by 'giving something back'. Ironically, this may benefit the ethnographer, who will feel ethically virtuous, while the participants may be left wondering why they have been given whatever it was they 'got back', and what precisely they got it in return for. In some cases where payments are made to participants because they are giving up their time to be part of a research project that is commercially sponsored or that has funding for this purpose, this seems an appropriate transaction, and indeed it is made clear what it is that participants are getting and what it is compensating them for. However, in much ethnographic research our involvement with participants is less clearly defined in terms of time commitments, it relies on good will, their interest in the project and on the development of mutual trust.

Yet the relationship between researcher and participants is often characterised as one of inequalities, whereby it is the researcher who stands to gain. Rather than try to redress the inequalities after the event, it would seem better advice to attempt to undertake ethnography that is less exploitative from the outset. If ethnography is seen as a process of negotiation and collaboration with participants, through which they too stand to achieve their own objectives, rather than as an act of taking information away from them, the ethical agenda also shifts. By focusing on collaboration and the idea of creating something together, agency becomes shared between the researcher and participant. Rather than the researcher being the active party who both extracts data and gives something else back, in this model both researcher and participant invest in, and are rewarded by, the project. Both historically and more recent projects with video and photography show how these media can be used to develop very successful collaborative projects. In some cases this has empowered participants and can serve to challenge existing power structures that impinge on the lives of participants and ethnographers. For example still in the twentieth century Barnes, Taylor-Brown and Weiner (1997) developed a project in which a group of HIV-positive women collaborated with the researchers to produce a set of videotapes containing messages for their children. This use of video allowed the women to represent themselves on videotapes to be screened in the future. Simultaneously, the agreement allowed the researchers to use the tapes as research materials. A number of other collaborative projects are discussed in my book *Visual Interventions* (Pink 2007a).

Thus, the concept of 'giving something back' often depends on the idea of ethnography as a 'hit and run' act: the ethnographer spends a number of months in the field gathering data before leaving for home where this data will be written up. Very little remains once ethnographers leave their field sites, apart from (in the case of overseas fieldwork) those domestic and other things that did not fit into a suitcase. Field notes and papers are of little use or interest to most participants, and at any rate researchers may feel these are personal documents. However, videos and photographs are usually of interest to the people featured in them and the people who were involved in their production. If an ethnographer

© Sarah Pink 2005

Figure 3.2 As part of my research in Aylsham, Norfolk, I provide copies of my own photographs of the Slow Food and Cittàslow events to the people who are developing local projects. In 2005 the town was a finalist in the international LivCom Awards (see www.livcomawards.com/), where it won a silver award. As part of the preparation for the event, I sent a set of photographs and video clips of the town and from its carnival and regional agricultural show which, combined with images produced by other peoples, provided a range of materials used to develop the presentation given at the awards event in Spain.

is working on the 'giving something back' principle, copies of video and photography of individuals and activities that research participants value could be an appropriate return for the favours they have performed during fieldwork. However, a collaborative approach to ethnographic image production may do more to redress the inequalities that inevitably exist between participants and researchers. For example, writing in the 1990s, Beate Engelbrecht discusses her collaborative work with ethnographic film. This shows how visual work can become a product in which both informants and ethnographer invest. Engelbrecht (1996) describes a number of filmmaking projects that involved the collaboration of local people in both filmmaking and editing. In some cases people wanted their traditional festivities or rituals to be documented, and were pleased to

Image first published in Pink and Leder Mackley (2012) in *Sociological Research On-line* **@ http://www.socresonline.org.uk/17/1/3.html**

Figure 3.3 Rhodes revisiting her video tour with Kerstin in July 2011. © LEEDR, Loughborough University, 2011

As part of the LEEDR project we supply our participants with copies of the video tours we have made with them then discuss these in a follow-up session. At this time we check that they are happy with us keeping copies of these recordings, and ask for their informed consent for the showing of all or part of the recording in presentations, at conferences or in publications. However, in other cases we also ask for consent to show images on an ongoing basis, giving participants the chance to opt out if they wish to during the course of the project.

work with the filmmakers to achieve these ends. Others realised the commercial potential of their participation in film projects. For example, Engelbrecht notes how the artisans who were represented in her film *Copper Working* (1993) participated actively in the film and 'were also thinking of the potential of film as a marketing instrument [for their copper artifacts]' (1996: 167). In this case, the subjects of the film had their own agenda and were able to exploit the project of the filmmakers for their own purposes: 'it was agreed upon that one copy of the film should be given to the local museum exhibiting the best of the recent copper work of the village so as to use it for tourist information' (1996: 167).

A further problem with the notion of 'giving something back' is that it does not account for the ways in which, when we do ethnography, often our personal autobiographical narratives become intertwined with the research narrative. Often in ethnographic research fieldwork, everyday life and writing-up may not necessarily be separated either spatially or temporally in the ethnographer's life and experience. Ethnographic research may not entail the researcher going somewhere, taking something away and being morally obliged to 'give something back' as a conclusion of both the research and her or his encounter with the participants. Instead, often the ethnographic research process may be, or may become, part of a researcher's everyday interactions. There may be a continuous flow of information, objects or online communications between the ethnographer and participants. This might include the exchange of images, ideas, electronic files, emoticons, and both emotional and practical exchanges and support, each of which are valued in different ways.

Ownership of research materials

In some cases visual research materials are jointly owned by a set of different parties such as the ethnographer, other researchers who are involved if it is a larger project, participants, funding bodies, persons or organisations involved in post-production, and other institutions and universities or organisations. In such contexts it is important to ensure that approaches to ethics, use of materials, issues relating to ongoing consent as outlined above, and any other ethical questions and issues relating to the project are made explicit and agreed in advance. While on the one hand this issue is concerned with managing the ways that researchers share materials amongst themselves, it is also concerned with the question of how participants may wish to use shared materials, and the implications this may have if one or more participants is shown in a video recording or photograph. To attempt to avoid such problems it is advisable to clarify rights of use and ownership of video and photographic images before their production. Such an agreement might also need to incorporate the possibility of ongoing negotiations around consent as discussed above. This will inevitably bear on the ethical decisions taken during the research and may influence the types of images that are produced. Other contingencies may also arise in contexts relating to digital image sharing.

Summary

Preparing to do visual ethnography involves a range of academic, practical and ethical considerations that should ideally come together in ways that support each other to create a viable framework through which to plan and start the research. Yet there are also many unknowns and uncertainties, things that we cannot predict and questions that are as yet unanswered. In reality, many decisions about how to use visual technologies and web-based media and the ethical questions they raise will need to be confronted during the ethnographic research process. Sometimes it is hard to make evaluations in advance as they are ideally informed by an ethnographic appreciation of the ways visual and digital technologies are already part of the context of the ethnography. Yet this impossibility of knowing exactly what will happen is part of doing visual ethnography, and brings with it the possibility of learning about the otherwise invisible and the unexpected.

Sometimes taking photographs and video recording research participants or using web technologies in the research process is inappropriate for ethical reasons, because such methods do not suit the context, or because they will not create a route to the types of knowledge that are being sought. Yet we should also be open in the latter case to knowledge that we did not expect to produce. Indeed, the challenges of doing visual ethnography that is ethical and appropriate should not be seen as obstacles to the application of pre-determined methods, but rather as opportunities to work with participants and others to create ways of working ethically and appropriately.

Further reading

Pink, S., Kürti, L. and Afonso, A. I. (eds) (2004) *Working Images*. London: Routledge. (An edited volume of case studies about the use of visual research methods. The first set of chapters in particular tell the stories of how different types of visual research projects developed.)

Wiles, R., Coffey, A., Robison, J. and Prosser, J. (2012) 'Ethical regulation and visual methods: making visual research impossible or developing good practice?', *Sociological Research Online*, 7(1)8, <http://www.socresonline.org.uk/17/1/8.html>.

Wiles, R., Clark, A. and Prosser, J. (2011) 'Visual research ethics at the crossroads', in E. Margolis and L. Pauwels (eds), *The SAGE Handbook of Visual Research Methods*. London: SAGE.

Rowe, J. (2011) 'Legal issues of using images in research', in E. Margolis and L. Pauwels (eds), *The SAGE Handbook of Visual Research Methods*. London: SAGE.

Additional material is available on the book's companion website: www.uk.sagepub.com/pink3e

PART 2

Producing Knowledge

Doing ethnographic fieldwork is a unique and personal experience. Although on the surface it might seem that different ethnographers use the same methods, the way we develop these uses in different circumstances tends to mean that in practice they emerge in different ways, perhaps through subtle innovations or through more radical changes. Indeed the process of doing ethnography itself can be seen as a process of making methods as well as that of producing knowledge. In Chapters 4, 5 and 6, I draw from some of my own and other ethnographers' experiences of doing research with photography, video and the internet to offer some ideas and possibilities for reflexive visual ethnography practice.

The discussions in Chapters 4 and 5 respectively acknowledge the role played by digital and web-based media in contemporary ethnographic photography and video practices. However, in these chapters I draw on good examples of visual ethnography practice that have been developed using analogue as well as digital cameras. My aim in these chapters is to employ the best examples available to demonstrate how the methods discussed can work and the implications they have for ethnographic knowledge/knowing. As we will see there are usually continuities between the ways that visual ethnography methods have been used through digital and pre-digital technologies, and that often we will find ourselves as researchers dealing with digital and print media in the same contexts. It is in Chapter 6 that I move to a more dedicated consideration of digital media through a focus on web-based digital visual ethnography. This emergent context is contextualised through understandings developed in media anthropology and internet studies, again with an emphasis on the relationship between online and offline, and digital and material.

In ethnographic processes analysis is not necessarily a stage in the research process that is completely separable from other elements of knowledge production. It might take place ongoingly during and as part of different moments of our involvement with fieldwork and with research participants. Analysis might be combined with

and/or feed into the development of and innovation in the methods described in Chapters 4, 5 and 6. Therefore in Chapter 7, I continue the discussion of analysis through a focus on the organisation, and interpretation of research materials, focusing on the relationships between visual and other materials and on situating them, rather than offering a guide to the analysis of visual materials in isolation.

4

Photography in Ethnographic Research

Photography has a long and varied history in ethnography. Supported by different methodological paradigms, over the years a camera has been an almost mandatory element of the 'tool kit' for research for several generations of ethnographers. In the late nineteenth and early twentieth centuries, photography, seen as an objective recording device, flourished as a method for the 'scientific' documentation of cultural and physical difference (see Edwards 1992, 1997b) and early anthropological uses of photography in research were developed by the British Alfred Cort Haddon, Franz Boas in the US, and Baldwin Spencer and Frank Gillen in Australia (Jacknis 1984; Morphy 1996). From 1915–1918 Bronislaw Malinowski used photography as part of his long-term fieldwork method (Young 1998) and later, in the mid-twentieth century, Bateson and Mead (1942) used photography to record and represent Balinese culture (see Chaplin 1994: 207ff; Banks 2001). Between the 1970s and the end of the twentieth century, photography was initially employed to fit the needs of scientific-realist approaches to ethnography, which were then critiqued by the reflexive and critical stance (e.g. Edwards 1992) that has endured and now informs most ethnographic practice (see also Edwards 2011 for a critical discussion of the history of photography in anthropology).

In this chapter, I take this reflexive reassessment of the place of photography in ethnography as my point of departure. I draw from examples both from this recent past in the 1980s and 1990s, which produced rich interrogations of photography in ethnographic practice, as well as contemporary examples from the digital era.

Ethnographic photographs and ethnographers as photographers

As I pointed out in Chapter 1, no visual image or practice is essentially ethnographic by nature. This applies to photographs in a way parallel to Edwards's point that 'an anthropological photograph is any photograph from which an anthropologist could gain useful, meaningful visual information' (Edwards 1992: 13). She emphasised how viewers subjectively determine when or if a photograph is anthropological, pointing out that '[t]he defining essence of an anthropological photograph is not the subject-matter as such, but the consumer's classification of that knowledge or "reality" which the photograph appears to convey' (1992: 13). Similarly, using as his example the categories of visual sociology, documentary photography and photo-journalism, Becker noted that the definition of the genre of a photograph depends more on the context in which it is viewed than it pertaining to any one (socially constructed) category (Becker 1995: 5).

Therefore the same photograph may serve a range of different personal and ethnographic uses; it may even be invested with seemingly contradictory meanings. As Edwards noted, '[m]aterial can move in and out of the anthropological sphere and photographs that were not created with anthropological intent or specifically informed by ethnographic understanding may nevertheless be appropriated to anthropological ends' (1992: 13). Similarly, a photograph created by a researcher with a particular ethnographic agenda in mind may travel out of 'the research' and into the personal collections of informants or other individuals, therefore being appropriated for *their* own ends (see Pink 1996). For example, one photographic slide that I took of Encarni, a friend and participant in my research in Southern Spain, was duplicated as a print and used in a variety of ways, in her personal collection and family album, in my discussions with other local people, in my PhD thesis (Pink 1996), my book (Pink 1997a), in a conference paper (Pink 1996), as well as being part of my own personal collection of photographs of friends. Similarly, my photograph of the woman bullfighter Cristina Sanchez entitled 'The Bullfighter's Braid' was in one context an 'ethnographic photograph' that appeared on the front cover of my book *Women and Bullfighting* (1997a). This photograph also won a prize for artistic journalistic photography, was used to publicise the visit of a female bullfighter to Córdoba and became part of the personal collections and wall displays of research participants. Therefore, during the fieldwork this photograph had no single meaning, but it was re-appropriated and given new significance and uses in each context. In Chapter 7, I discuss how the diversity of meanings invested in these two images was fundamental to my subsequent analysis of them and informed the academic meanings I gave to them. While these examples are taken from an analogue research project the same principles can be applied to the ways that we understand the meanings invested in digital photographs. Research participants are often interested in photographs of activities related to their own interests, and when this coincides with the research project then photographs might be shared. Take, for example, the following extract from a transcription of a meeting I attended during my research about slow cities in the UK in 2006:

Sue: If there are any photographs, especially digital photographs of any of these barbecues and events that are going on they would be really good because we are going to be putting together a presentation for the LivCom awards and it would be very good. What I want to do is to build on the application we put in and so it mentions the community garden, so it would be nice to treat the presentation as almost an update on when we submitted the application and say 'here are the community garden people' doing their garden or enjoying their space or whatever, and so moving it on. So I'd be really grateful for, especially digital but I can get photographs scanned so I would be grateful.

Sarah: I'm going to take some photos when I interview the chairman, it won't be of activities.

Sue: Yes that's fine.

Jenny: That's useful.

Sue: Anything at the moment, I'll just kind of mop it up.

As this particular extract, which has also been cited in a slightly longer version in an article on this topic (Pink 2011e: 92) shows, digital and analogue photography are not necessarily separated out in terms of the priorities of research participants. Therefore we might think in terms of the exchanges and sharing of images between research archives and research contexts as material and digital.

In my research about slow cities, exchanges of photographs do not only flow from researcher to participants, but also, because my relationship with some slow city projects has meant that I have become 'their researcher' as much as them being 'my participants', I have had 'project' photographs sent to me, varying between photographic prints, paper prints of digital photographs, and emailed digital images. Sometimes this was to show me activities I could not attend, or to keep me up to date at distance. For example, during my research about Slow Cities I found that participants often kept detailed photographic records of their project activities and events. Several times they sent these to me, often including images in which I had been photographed myself. Again the status of these images changes, as they move from participants' memory or project archives to my ethnographic archive.

Therefore any photograph may have ethnographic interest, significance or meanings at a particular time or for a specific reason. The meanings of photographs are contingent and subjective; they depend on who is looking, and when they are looking. The same photograph may have different or changing meanings invested in it at different stages of the ethnographic process, as different audiences view it in diverse temporal, spatial and cultural contexts. Edwards's work on historical photography (1992, 1997b) demonstrates well how this can happen. The contributors to her volumes critically deconstructed the theories, philosophies and political agendas that informed the intentions of those who produced and used these images. By revealing the historical meanings that these photographs were given, the authors thus gave them new meanings by embedding them in new discourses. Re-situated, the images were made to represent a critique of the intellectual and scientific environment and framework of beliefs in which they were produced. However, it is not only historically that the meanings given to photographs may be renegotiated. For example the meanings that anti-bullfight or animal rights activists might invest in the series of bullfighting photographs shown in Figure 4.1 would be quite different from the meanings the bullfight *aficionados*, who participated in my research would use to interpret them. The latter group, when viewing performance photographs of women performers would focus on the details of the bullfighter's technique and her female body. Readers might examine these photographs to elicit their personal responses, to ask what other stories could be told with these photographs, and how these stories might be compared with the two rather opposed and dominant interpretations of the images I have suggested that animal rights activist and bullfight fans might invest in them. In a contemporary context there is a wealth of online visual materials that promote and celebrate the bullfight as well as those that condemn it and campaign against it, where it becomes clear how such images might be situated within the arguments of either side. Yet there is another dimension to this to keep in mind when we produce images as ethnographers, because our task goes beyond the comparative study *of* visual culture, to our participation in it. For me, however, the slides are also ethnographic photographs. They were shot as part of ethnographic fieldwork in which I was seeking to document the performance of a woman bullfighter in such a way that I could discuss it with participants later, while also being part of my project to learn the art of bullfight photography.

Therefore the ethnographicness of photographs is in this sense contextually defined. Photographs are also framed by the photographers' subjectivity, an awareness of which is also relevant to the ways we comprehend their meanings in ethnographic research. When ethnographers take photographs, like any professional or lay photographer, they do so with reference to specific understandings of photography and in the context of particular social and technological relationships. Moreover as Terence Wright pointed out, 'anyone who uses a camera or views a photograph, will most probably be subscribing, albeit unwittingly, to some or other theory of representation' (1999: 9). A reflexive approach to ethnographic photography means researchers being aware of the theories that inform their own photographic practice, of their relationships with their photographic subjects, and of the theories that inform their subjects' approaches to photography.

In projects where ethnographers collaborate with photographers rather than taking the images themselves, the same question applies to reflecting on the photographers' own subjectivity. The sociologist Dawn Lyon discusses how this process played out in her visual ethnography of a renovation project undertaken in a building in Chatham in the UK. Lyon describes how she and the visual artist Peter Hatton developed what she calls 'strategies of looking' (2013: 25). She reflects on how her own strategy involved 'incidental attention' which

Figure 4.1 These photographs were taken at a performance of the woman bullfighter Cristina Sanchez during my research in Spain. Here in this sequence Cristina gets into some difficulty with the bull. She is tossed into the air, falls to the ground, and then gets up to kill the bull.

Yet, this sequence of images and the events in the performance that it represents can be invested with different meanings by different viewers.

Based on my own research I could identify at least three different interpretations that would be made by bullfighting fans who were in favour of women performers, bullfighting fans who did not feel that women were able to participate as 'real' bullfighters, and people who were against bullfighting.

Each different standpoint would enable viewers to invest different meanings into the story of Cristina being tossed into the air. One group might see them as showing how Cristina was able to recover her position and successfully complete her performance as well as a man could; another might argue that this demonstrates that women cannot perform as well as men; and another might interpret this as showing a triumph for the bull.

How do we explain this?

Fans of women bullfighters would assess Cristina's ability to 'prove' that she is able to conclude the performance with the bull well; those against women performers would see her being tossed as a sign of her lack of physical strength and skill; and those against bullfighting might interpret the performance as a 'fight' between the bullfighter and the bull, with the option of either of them 'winning'. These are based on very different interpretations of the performance, because bullfight fans do not see it as a 'fight', but as a performance, therefore the idea that the bull could 'win' would not make sense in a bullfighting narrative about the sequence of images.

was 'casual, not trying too hard to see everything but to absorb the sensory feel and activity of the space, and taking photographs as part of that process' and focusing on photographing work as it was done (2013: 26). In contrast, the second strategy followed by Hatton, was one of 'steady concentration' which Lyon writes was 'a more structured approach' and 'a deliberate act of looking ahead and noticing what was going on in a bounded and specific space, and the result is several sets of images from multiple but fixed perspectives' showing how the work impacted on the building (2013: 26). These two techniques therefore produced different types of image and different ways of knowing about the building work. As this example shows, a reflexive awareness is key to understanding how photographic ways of seeing are bound up with intentionalities and subjectivities.

Developing a reflexive awareness also involves considering how ethnographers play their roles as photographers in particular cultural settings, how they frame particular images, what is behind, above and below these frames, and how these choices are related to the expectations of both academic disciplines and institutions as well as those of local visual cultures and relationships. As we will see in Chapter 6, these contexts and considerations also include the ways that software is used, and the power relations associated with the web platforms and other digital technologies that are integral to the ways we do digital visual ethnography. Below, I discuss existing uses of photography in ethnography. While I distinguish between different methods, each method is not usually used in isolation but often interlinks and overlaps with others.

Getting started: taking the first picture

The question of when to take the first photograph varies from project to project. In some contexts photographing can help to initiate the research process and to establish relationships with participants, while in others it may be more appropriate to wait several months before beginning to photograph, or to hand the camera over to participants so they can photograph instead. These decisions can be informed by the kinds of knowledge about the meanings of photography in the research context discussed above, as well as by discussing and negotiating with participants and in relation to ethical issues.

Several examples demonstrate how photography may initiate and support research. In one of the earliest texts on photographic research methods, Collier and Collier (1986) described the idea of the camera as a 'can-opener' in two ways that can help establish rapport with research participants. First, they noted how playing a photographer role can put researchers in an ideal position to observe the culture or groups they are researching. Secondly, showing photographs to their subjects can provide feedback on the images and their content while also forging connections with members of the 'community'. This can provide excuses or reasons for further meetings, which might include visiting people in their homes and building up connections with them. In this way ethnographers may also use such photographic practices as ways of communicating about themselves and what they are interested in, to participants. Taking the first images with a digital camera with a good enough view finder to be able to show images to participants, or even using a portable printer, may speed up the process, allowing participants to be able to see the ways they, or things and persons that matter to them, are being photographed almost instantly, and if they are comfortable with these to engender their trust and interest.

Sometimes, to be able to photograph the activities they are interested in, ethnographers first have to establish themselves locally as someone who is trusted to take those photographs. Again, earlier accounts still provide good examples: Shanklin (1979) has described her role as ethnographer/photographer during research in rural Ireland. She had intended to take photographs of people working, that she could subsequently discuss with her informants, but initially she found this was inappropriate. However, she learnt, by observing people's domestic displays of family photography, that photographing children was an appropriate activity and would provide parents with valued images: 'Just as I had to learn something about patterns of social interaction in order to become more a member of the culture I studied, so too I had to learn something about their use of photographs in order to integrate my own picture taking into the roles to which I had been assigned' (Shanklin 1979: 143). Once she had established herself as someone who took photographs within the local community, she found she could proceed by photographing agricultural workers at work and interviewing as she had originally intended.

In some projects photographing may come first and can be a means of making contact with local people. For example, Schwartz (1992) began her research by photographing the physical environment of Waucoma, the town she was studying. On arrival, she began photographing buildings to both inform the residents of her presence and to observe the goings-on of everyday life. This provided her with an entry point into local interaction – seeing a stranger photographing the town made many people curious enough to approach her and ask what she was doing. The local people became interested in and supportive of Schwartz's work and the photographic aspect of the project became a key point of communication between her and her informants.

In my own research in Spain I began to photograph as soon as I made contact with the groups I was interested in working with. Photography provided me with an appropriate activity to engage in at the beginning of my research into bullfighting culture. As an unaccompanied woman at bullfighting receptions and public occasions and, at the time, still learning the language and unable to engage in any detailed conversation, I was grateful to have a role as 'photographer'. My photography was endorsed by the organisers and was not problematic for participants since at any such public event a number of press photographers were expected to be present. Once my photographs of the receptions were printed, I showed them to the organisers and other participants with whom I was in contact. We discussed the event and the people who were present, and people often asked for copies of particular images, usually of themselves with particular people, so that they could pass them on to their friends, colleagues or contacts within the bullfighting world. In this way I could not only gain feedback about the events I participated in as a photographer, but also a sense of how social relationships and alliances were mapped out and constructed amongst bullfighting experts, fans and enthusiasts. I did this by studying who wanted to be photographed with whom during the events, and by tracking the collection and distribution of the copies of the images that people asked for.

In other contexts photography might begin in a more formalised way, in conjunction with the use of other methods. For example, in my Slow City research I began my encounters with most key participants in the research with an audio-recorded interview (which would later be transcribed and sent to them for their approval and corrections), after which I usually took a portrait photograph of each participant in the location of the interview, in a way that they chose themselves (see Figure 7.1).

As these examples show, the camera can lead us into fieldwork situations in unanticipated ways. Our photographic practices themselves and the research methods we engage develop alongside and are interwoven with relationships we build as our research evolves in any one situation.

Photographing (in) the environment: from the survey to the tour

Photographing the material physical environment in/about which we do research has been a common visual research practice, since Collier's photographic surveys of the mid-twentieth century to contemporary collaborative touring methods.

In earlier work the creation of photographic records has often been based on the assumption that the artefacts photographed have finite, fixed symbolic meanings. For example, Collier and Collier proposed a 'cultural inventory', where, for example, by producing a systematic photographic survey of visual aspects of the material content and organisation of a home, one may answer questions relating to the economic level of the household, its style, decor, activities, the character of its order and its signs of hospitality and relaxation (Collier and Collier 1986: 47–50). Collier and Collier's approach provided a way of visually comparing specific material aspects of different households or even cultures. However, such photographic records are limited because they do not indicate how these objects are experienced or made meaningful by those individuals in whose lives they figure. Since then this photographic survey approach has been employed mainly by visual sociologists – for example, Secondulfo's (1997) study of the symbolism of material items within the home and Pauwels's (1996) study of the material environment of the Brussels office of a Norwegian chemical multinational. Pauwels has sought to contextualise his visual survey through interviews and an analysis of other aspects of office life. These types of realist surveys present useful materials that can be used to provide statistical data and background knowledge, and in some cases this will be sufficient, when related to other data, to justify their use.

However, combining photographic surveys with a subjective collaborative approach can bring further benefits. For instance Schwartz's (1992) collaborative approach to photographic survey work in the North American Waucoma farming community led her to define her survey photographs as neither 'objective visual documents' nor 'photographic truth'. Rather, they 'represent a point of view' – in this case her 'initial inferences about life in Waucoma' (1992: 14). She used her survey images of the Waucoma physical environment, together with old photographs of the same places, in interviews with local people. Rather than basing her analysis of the images on their content, her interpretation 'is informed by insights gained through ethnographic fieldwork and informant's responses to them'. Schwartz assumed that her photographs 'would prompt multiple responses'. She 'sought to study the range of meaning they held for different members of the community' (1992: 14). Therefore, she made the understanding of the arbitrariness of visual meanings a key element of her research method.

Thus the photographic survey as conventionally developed in this work brings elements of the material environment together with personal narratives and meanings. More recent developments in the use of photography in relation to the environments we inhabit or move through enables us to take this further. In Chapter 2, I introduced the idea of understanding image making as something that happens in movement. We can understand photography as a mobile ethnographic method, a process of making images as we go through the world, often accompanied by others, who, as participants in the research may share some of our aims. One of the most obvious ways in which the status of photography as happening in movement is recognised is methods that involve and combine walking and photographing. These methods advance the idea of the photographic survey by offering us alternative ways of understanding the process and meanings of photographing (in) an environment as we move through it. For example walking, touring and photographing with people has been important in my own work about slow cities, as described in Figures 4.2 and 4.3. Walking and photographing enables us to attend to elements of the ways that people experience and give meanings to their environments, and in this sense also enables a focus on the sensoriality of place (see Pink 2009). Here I depart from the survey method of photographing the environment, to focus on the idea of photographing and viewing as we move *through* and *in* and *as part of* environments, keeping in mind Ingold's point that 'knowledge is grown along the myriad paths we take as we make our ways through the world in the course

© *Sarah Pink 2006*

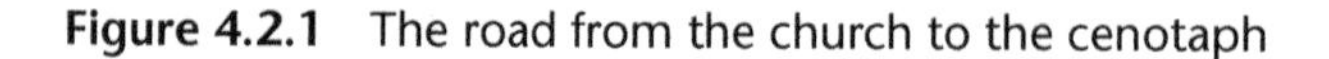

Figure 4.2.1 The road from the church to the cenotaph

of everyday activities, rather than assembled from information obtained from numerous fixed locations. Thus, it is by *walking along* from place to place, and not by building up from local particulars, that we come to know what we do' (Ingold 2010b: S122–123).

A good example is developed in the work of the anthropologist Andrew Irving who develops walks around urban areas (in Kampala, New York and London) in which audio-recorded verbal narratives are combined with photographing meaningful locations or things during the walk. Much of Irving's work has involved asking people who have been diagnosed as being HIV positive to re-walk the route that they took to and returned from the clinic on the day of their diagnosis. He has worked with different research combinations in that in some of his published work he discusses narratives that have been made by two research participants walking together and recording and photographing one another's experiences (Irving 2007) and another where he walked with, recorded and photographed while the participant narrated (Irving 2010). He has also used different publication strategies, in some cases including the photographs in his publications, and in one (Irving 2007) leaving blank pages to very powerfully stand for photographs that could not be included.

© *Sarah Pink 2006*

Figure 4.2.2 A view from the Hill

During my research in the Welsh Cittaslow town of Mold in the UK, I was invited to tour the town with a series of different town leaders, each of whom took me to experience a particular Cittaslow element of the town. For this trip I carried with me a rucksack with a digital stills camera, a video camera, an audio recorder and my notebook and pens, not to mention my mobile phone and a printed map I had been sent. During this tour, as I describe in an article that reflects on this research process, I used all of these technologies at different moments depending on the appropriateness of the technology to the moment. The following extract from the article explains the context in which each of these photographs was taken, and as such invites us to imagine their meanings as part of an ethnographic tour, not in terms of their objective content or aesthetic value:

> 'At the church we were met by Bryan Grew the current Mayor of Mold. Bryan was to take me to the cenotaph and to meet Ray Dodd with whom I would have lunch. It was now raining gently. Walking up to the cenotaph we followed another local route (Figure 4.2.1). There is a remembrance service and event every year which involves a walk along the same, although then crowded, road to the cenotaph. The material symbols remained, now plastic poppies replacing the real flowers used historically. We walked further up the hill, imagining the past where there was once a bowling green and where a children's playground remains. We appreciated the view out to the hills, the modern buildings of the theatre and district council offices, and a local cement factory which Bryan told me is a significant local employer. Visual experience became increasingly important and I felt compelled to continue our search for a suitable view to photograph through the trees (Figure 4.2.2), despite feeling increasingly cold and wet.
>
> The photograph achieved, we walked back down to meet Ray ...' (Pink 2008: 187)

(Continued)

(Continued)

Figure 4.3 When I toured the Spanish Cittaslow town of Lekeitio in 2011, with Lisa Servon with whom I was researching the town and our hosts Nekane and Xavi (see Pink and Servon 2013), I used different technology to that discussed in Figure 4.2 (above). The iPhone I was using could take images, video record and audio record. iPhone photos can moreover be digitally tagged onto a map, leaving a record not only of what is in front of the camera, but a geo-location of where it was taken. The four photographs shown here were taken in the harbour area during our walking tour. Each stands for the materialities of the town that we encountered and for the ways that they reminded me of themes that were emerging in our research, including the relative isolation of the town, the routes that crossed in it and its relationship to the sea. These images were made as part of the process of moving through the town, and in this sense I have come to understand them as representing what was in front, behind and around them as much as what is 'in' them. Indeed digital media enable this type of understanding (see also Chapter 5) because these images have been geo-tagged to google maps which allows me to view them as moments in a route, and as part of an environment rather than as flat pictures of it.

In his (2010) essay 'Dangerous Substances' that focuses on a walk that he undertook with Alberto, in New York, Irving puts it:

> By placing the lived experience of the walking body directly into the field, the ... photo essay, 'Dangerous Substances', combines *image*, *voice* and *walking* to try to uncover how a city's streets, buildings and neighbourhoods are mediated by ongoing interior dialogues and imaginative lifeworlds that are based in a person's current existential concerns. (Irving 2010: 24–5)

Irving uses walking, narration and photography as ways of exploring and communicating to readers about the specificity of one person's interior experiences of traversing a route across a particular urban landscape. In the essay, each of the seven pages of written narration is shared with a set of four photographs that head the page. These photographs were taken by Irving as they walked. Therefore, just as Ingold writes with reference to painting and drawing, 'we have to find our ways through and among them, inhabiting them as we do the world itself' (2010: 16), the same practices of engagement are integral to how we might understand the experience of Irving's text. Irving's written and visual narrative takes us on a walk in a very literal sense, as it invites us to follow the narrative of the route that he and Alberto took that day. Yet at the same time the reader/viewer has to take a journey through the text that is experiential and imaginative. Here, photographs are not static objects, waiting for use to interpret their content. Rather they are images that were created in movement, as part of the process of *walking through* the city and exploring the interior feelings associated with it and not simply *looking at* it. They are, as such, also part of a journey that the reader takes through the essay, and in doing so she or he is invited to imagine these feelings. As such we can think of this as an empathetic and experiential text as well as being a piece of theoretical and scholarly work.

The method of walking and photographing is becoming increasingly popular in research that seeks to both represent the experience of, and issues related to, particular environments. In doing so researchers are able to use the environment itself as a prompt or probe in the research process. Recent works in this area include the work of Maggie O'Neill and Phil Hubbard (2010) and Susan Hogan (2011) all of whom use walking and photographing together in articles that discuss experiences of urban environments in contexts related to policy and to local politics. Another example of how walking and photographing can be effective in the research process is developed by Nick Emmel and Andrew Clark (2011) as they discuss how the practice of photographing enabled them to think reflexively during the research process. Here they are writing of photographs taken during walkabouts in the fieldwork locality by the researcher, in contrast to the collaborative exercises described above. They comment that such practices and images 'allow us to map our reflexive engagement with the research field. They are a kind of visual research diary, offering clues to how we respond to the field over the course of research. They sharpen our gaze through framing the field in the viewfinder' (2011: 39). In the next section I discuss participatory and collaborative photography. These methods overlap with those discussed in the latter part of this section, which have likewise involved participants in directing the content of the photographs.

Participatory and collaborative photography

Ethnographers have collaborated with research participants to produce photographs in a variety of ways. Existing examples involve working alone with a single informant (e.g. Collier and Collier 1986), with groups engaged in creative (e.g. Chaplin 1994) or ceremonial (e.g. Larson 1988) activities, in eclectic ways within wider ethnographic projects (e.g. Banks n.d.; Lammer 2012), and in ways more systematically built into a research design (e.g. Radley et al. 2005; Clark 2012). When photographs are produced collaboratively, they combine the intentions of both ethnographer/photographer and participant and represent the outcome of their negotiations.

Collaborative photography usually involves ethnographers engaging in some way with the photographic culture and/or practices of research participants. For instance an ethnographer might try to produce the kinds of images that are popular in participants' photographic cultures, or that refer to local photographic conventions but simultaneously conform to the demands of an academic discipline. The intentions and objectives of researchers and participants combine in their negotiations to determine the content of the photographs in ways that vary in different projects. For instance, participants might be interested in collaboratively producing family photographs, images that will provide legal evidence, documentation of local traditions or of work processes, artistic exhibits, souvenirs or publicity photographs. Yet within such collaborations, as ethnographers we may wish to please our participants in such ways but at the same time ensure that this leads to us producing images we can publish in articles, a blog, as part of an interactive web project or in an exhibition. Furthermore, we may wish to learn local photographic styles, conform to the conventions of their academic discipline, or produce images that follow a particular photographic tradition, such as realist documentary, expressive or art photography.

Existing ethnographic examples indicate that people are usually quick to teach a potential photographer what kinds of images they would like to have taken. Sometimes the photographs participants request challenge the assumptions behind ethnographers' original intentions and thus change the meaning of the method used. For example Pinney described how, during fieldwork in India in 1982, he learnt how local people wanted to be represented through his attempts to photograph his informants in terms of his own aesthetic designs. He took a photograph of his neighbour that fitted the type of image he wanted to produce: 'candid, revealing, expressive of the people I was living among' (Pinney 1997: 8). This photograph was a half-length image taken around 5pm in the fields: 'a good time to catch the mellowing sun' (1997: 8). But his informant was not satisfied with the image. He 'complained about the shadow and darkness it cast over his face and the absence of the lower half of his body. The image was of no use to him' (1997: 9). Pinney's informants wanted a different type of photograph, one that was taken according to another procedure. These photographs 'could not be taken quickly since there were more lengthy preparations to be made: clothes to be changed, hair to be brushed and oiled (and, in the case of upper-caste women, the application of talcum powder to lighten the skin)' (1997: 9). Moreover, their content and symbolism conformed to different expectations: 'These photos had to be full-length and symmetrical, and the passive, expressionless faces and body poses symbolised for me, at that time, the extinguishing of precisely that quality I wished to capture on film' (1997: 9). Here the portraits indicated informants' existing expectations of photography and their personal and cultural uses of images. Often we learn through experience, as described above. Therefore we can see the benefits of paying attention to the personal photograph collections people show us, to interpret how they would like to be photographed and to understand what they are referring to when they describe the sorts of images they would like to have; when following the process, our visual methods are usefully shaped through our interactions with the people and institutions we encounter during the research process, rather than being preconceived.

Anthropological ethnographers have a long history of photographing at ritual or other collective activities. In urban India, Banks found much of his photography was at communal ritual events. Sometimes his informants actively 'directed' his photography: at one event his informants insisted that he 'took a pre-posed photograph of the woman who had paid for the feast, ladling a dollop of a rich yoghurt-based dessert on to the tray of one of the feasters' (Banks n.d.). Banks interprets this photographic event to show how this collaborative photography was informed by his own and his informants' knowledge:

> It was composed and framed according to my own (largely unconscious) visual aesthetic and is part of my own corpus of documentary images of that feast. But it is also a legitimization and concretization of social facts as my friends saw them: the fact that the feast had a social origin in the agency of one person (the feast donor) as well as by virtue of the religiously and calendrically prescribed fasting period that preceded it; the fact that this was a good feast during which we ate the expensive and highly-valued yoghurt dessert. (Banks n.d.)

For Banks, this 'directed' photography became a way of visualising and reinforcing his existing ethnographic knowledge because, he writes 'I "knew" these social facts, because I had been told them on other occasions, but by being directed to capture them on film I was made aware not only of their strength and value but of the power of photography to legitimize them' (Banks n.d.). I had similar experiences during my research about women and bullfighting in the 1990s. For example, during an evening reception given after a talk by the woman bullfighter, Cristina Sanchez, at which I had been photographing, people who had already been involved in my research directed my photography. They asked me to photograph them posing in groups with Cristina, making me a collaborator in creating photographs that followed local conventions in bullfighting culture. On another occasion I was attending a performance with some women members of a bullfight club. One of the younger women began to tell me what and when to photograph – this included both the conventional stages covered in bullfight photography and the important moments in her personalised narrative of the event such as when her favourite bullfighter waved to the part of the ring where we sat with other members of his supporter's club. When it came to the moment that he was about to kill one of his bulls she asked for my camera to photograph this herself. In a way parallel to the experience Banks described, I already knew that for most bullfight fans the kill is a pivotal moment of the performance, and thus also the key photographic moment. Through her actions she both demonstrated this in practice, and used the camera to express her own in-depth embodied knowledge of the bullfight, which enabled her to follow and predict the movements of the performance, to know when to ask for the camera and the right moment to actually photograph. In both these contexts the photographs I later had developed were images that had already been imagined by the people in them or who had wanted to take them: they followed the existing conventions of social and performance related bullfight photography as seen in magazines and displays, and they connected the participants personally to bullfighters through these images.

A similar pattern emerged in a more recent project, this time with a digital camera. As part of our ethnographic research into migrant workers' safety and health on UK construction sites, Dylan Tutt was photographing as he researched communication processes on one construction site. We have described how 'On the twelfth floor [of a building in construction] Dylan asked if he could photograph what Viktor could see and who he could communicate with when he worked'. In this situation the participant took charge to show Dylan what he would see – 'Noticing Dylan's awkwardness and reluctance to lean over the edge – with no head for heights – Viktor offered to take some photographs himself'. It was these photographs that enabled us to gain a sense of Viktor's perspective, and 'made us question our own assumptions about the scene' (Tutt et al. 2013: 45).

If we now return to the discussion of photography and movement in the last section we can also see how in the taking of such photographs, a configuration of different things came together to inform the moments and movements through which they are taken and the ways they are composed and negotiated. By attending to these we can learn about social relationships, the actions, things and persons that matter and how photography is engaged in the processes of establishing, reinforcing and standing for these connections and feelings.

Returning the gaze: ethnographer as photographee

In this section I discuss situations where the ethnographer has become the photographic subject of research participants and reflect on what we might learn from these sometimes spontaneous or unexpected moments. In many contemporary contexts where most people have cameras or camera phones, being photographed by the people we are researching with is not necessarily surprising, and it has happened to me through several research encounters in Spain and England. These serendipitous moments when the people who we are learning from take control of the camera are infrequently discussed in the literature, yet they can provide striking insights and are worth attending to.

My first experience of such a moment was during my PhD research when in 1993 Cristina Sanchez, who was then a famous woman bullfighter, visited Córdoba in Spain where I was doing my research. The Director of Museums, who was hosting her day in the city, invited me to accompany them and a local bullfighting journalist during their tour of the town. My role was to photograph their day in Córdoba and the Director frequently told me what to photograph. When we were all sitting in a bar during the visit he asked for my camera, and photographed me sitting at the table with Cristina. Essentially he had taken the photograph that, according to the standards of the visual culture of bullfighting photography, I should have wanted to have (see Pink 1997a: 102). I connected this photograph to my existing knowledge. I had already studied bullfighting fans' personal photographic collections and historical images of bullfighters and their associates and knew that this was a recurring image composition. In fact it was similar to the photographs I had already taken, guided perhaps subconsciously by my knowledge of these conventions, of Cristina being interviewed by a local bullfighting journalist. The important point about the Director's photograph was that by situating me within the conventional composition it confirmed for me visually the knowledge that I was already developing from other sources.

Local photographic practices and images that incorporate the ethnographer can teach us other unexpected things. During his ethnographic research in Malaysia in 2003–4, John Postill was photographed with a group of people with whom he was doing research, standing behind a banner. Postill writes:

> It all started when a web forum user opened up a thread on the trouble he was having getting the municipal council to fix a drain that had collapsed outside his backyard. The forum thread grew longer and longer and eventually a group of residents, led by the person who started the thread, decided to take action and organise a demonstration to draw media attention to this issue. Being a dutiful fieldworker, I joined the demo but tried to keep a low profile. Yet this was a poorly attended demo, and when I was asked to stand behind the only banner to make up the numbers I foolishly obliged. As a result, the following day my portrait appeared in the Chinese-language press, alongside that of the demonstrators. This photograph was the cause of much strife and conflict, both online and offline, as the web portal founder accused the demonstrators of misusing the portal's domain. He felt that the banner in question was not only rude about the municipal council; its author had also tarnished the portal's domain name (USJ.com.my) by displaying it on the banner. He demanded a public apology on the web forum, as well as to the municipal council. (Postill 2005)

Having appeared in the photograph, even though he was not intending to be part of the demonstration, Postill also had to apologise and explain his mistake to the town council. The incident nicely shows how photographic meanings are generated on several different levels. First, the photograph was needed to transform a small demonstration into a reportable reality for the news media. Once digitalised and distributed online, the photograph took on another meaning as it was used as a form of evidence that the web portal's name had been misused, and by whom.

© Sarah Pink 2005

Figure 4.4 Through the very act of researching the community garden I myself became subject to David's own process of documenting the project, as he likewise photographed me sitting at the same table for his own records. When we proceeded outside so that I could video David as he showed me the plot of land and explained the plans for it, again my own visual production was balanced by his: the video still above, shows David photographing me.

Through this Postill learnt how, identified photographically, he had inadvertently become implicated in this. To explain his appearance in the photograph he needed to refer back to the intentionalities and motives that had informed its moment of production (Postill, personal communication).

I later found myself photographed as part of my work about the UK network of the Slow City movement. Here I followed several projects in the movement's member towns, one of which involved the transformation of a piece of disused land in a residential area of the town into a community garden that local people could comfortably walk through on their way to town, take their young children to play in, and sit and relax in. Supported by a local charitable organisation, the Aylsham Care Trust (ACT), the project is managed by a committee of neighbours from the streets that surround the plot of land, chaired by David Gibson. To follow this project as it developed I first interviewed David. I arrived at his and his wife Anne's house one very rainy morning and was welcomed into their living room. We sat around the table with coffee and biscuits and discussed many things relating to the town and the community garden and David talked me though his file on the project. As part of my research process I am creating portraits of the people I work with, and I photographed David and Anne holding a photograph of the type of path they were proposing to have put down across the garden (Figure Intro. 2.). I was interested in how memories of slow cities and their projects are created in the present and for the future and as we talked I learnt how in his file David was meticulously documenting the development process of the community garden project, visually through photographs and garden plans, in written documents and by taking notes on the stages and activities. As the researcher studying the project I was also a subject of the documentation process. As David put it, it was 'tit-for-tat'. He photographed me for his records. First, sitting at the table during the interview, and later, standing outside in the garden itself, with a jacket and umbrella kindly lent to me by Anne, as I videoed him showing me around the plot in the pouring rain (Figure 4.4).

A further example of putting the ethnographer in the frame is shown in the work of Christina Lammer who, in her work about facial reconstruction and plastic surgery, often turns the camera onto her own body as she seeks to comprehend the experiences of others. These exercises can be seen as processes of learning and also sometimes become part of the arts practice through which Lammer represents some of her work. One photographic example of this can be seen in Figure 1.2.

Collectively these examples of the ethnographer being put in the frame remind us that as visual ethnographers we are not the only people who actively use photography to explore, construct and understand other people's experiences and worlds. Indeed we can learn much by attending to how other people use photography to insert us into their categories, projects and agendas, or by seeking to expand our own experiential knowledge, placing ourselves in similar embodied and photographic frames.

Viewing ethnographers' photographs: interviewing with images

In this section I explore the roles photographs may play in interviews or conversations. In Chapters 1 and 2, I emphasised the situatedness of visual meanings and how viewers create meanings with photographs through biographical experiences and knowledge as well as contextually and culturally specific understandings. Meanings do not exist in photographs, and when we talk with research participants about photographs we need to attend to how meaning and significance are constituted through the image. It is not simply a matter of asking how participants provide information in response to images but rather as ethnographers we should seek to understand how people use images to produce and represent experiential and affective ways of knowing that might not so easily be expressed in words.

The term commonly used to refer to photographic interviewing is 'photo elicitation' which Harper writes: 'is based on the simple idea of inserting a photograph into a research interview' but also goes beyond that in the interview in that 'the photo elicitation interview seems like not simply an interview process that elicits more information but rather one that evokes a different kind of information' (Harper 2002: 13). There is a growing literature on this method and the different forms it takes in research (e.g. Lapenta 2011). In the context of visual ethnography the connotations of the term elicitation itself however might be problematised. Taken literally it seems focused on the idea that information might be extracted from a participant, and my own preference is to think of photographic interviewing as informed by the ideas of inviting, co-creating and making knowledge with photographs rather than the notion of eliciting knowledge from respondents through them.

The photo-elicitation method was established in the work of John Collier Jnr. (1986 [1967]), which still offers useful examples and can now be followed up by viewing the online archive of Collier's photography at http://americanimage.unm.edu. For instance, researching farming families who were also employed in urban factories, Collier used his photographs of work locations as reference points in photographic interviews to examine his informants' attitudes to city life, factory work and migration to the city. His work provides a useful example of how his informants talked about the images and of how a photographic research project may evolve over time. Yet, when it is situated historically we can see that Collier's analysis was based on the assumption that 'the facts are in the pictures' (Collier and Collier 1986: 106; Collier 1986 [1967]) and the idea that the ethnographer may elicit knowledge about this visual content from informants. Later, the visual sociologist Douglas Harper developed an approach that related photo-elicitation to the 'new ethnography' of the reflexive and postmodern turn of the 1990s, redefining it as 'a model of collaboration in research' (1998a: 35). For Harper, photographs are not simply visual records of reality, but representations interpreted in terms of different understandings of reality. When informants view photographs taken by an ethnographer they will actually be engaged in interpreting the ethnographer/photographer's visualisation of reality. In a photographic interview, therefore, ethnographer and informant would discuss their different understandings of images, thus collaborating to determine each other's views.

Taking a similar approach Donna Schwartz shows how interviewing with photographs led her to new knowledge. She identifies her photographs of a Waucoma community as representations of her own vision of the physical and social environment. Basing her analysis on the principle that 'the photograph prompts personal narratives generated by the content of the image', she describes how her use of photographs in interviews 'was informed by the unique and contradictory nature of the medium ... photographs elicit multiple perceptions and interpretations' (Schwartz 1992: 13).

In these earlier examples, therefore, we see how participants responded to specific series of survey type images produced by the researcher prior to the interview.

In my own work I followed a similar pattern when seeking to learn about the bullfight. However, here the layers of knowledge produced and referred to were further complicated in relation to the genre of bullfight performance photography. For example, when learning to photograph the bullfight myself I first studied existing bullfighting photography and then photographed the performance myself from my position in the audience – as did many keen amateur photographers. I showed my photographs to local people who were knowledgeable about the bullfight and had well informed opinions about how it should be photographed. In commenting on my prints, they were actually commenting on my intellectual and embodied knowledge of the bullfight as expressed through my formal knowledge of the right stages to photograph and the extent to which I was developing an ability to

Figure 4.5 These photographs of Cristina Sanchez (above) and Finito de Córdoba (below) became part of the way I discussed bullfighting during my fieldwork in Spain. Informants used these photographs to comment on the bullfighters' performance skills and on the development of my own skills in learning to take the photograph at the 'right' moments of the bullfight. In doing so, they were able to represent their own expert knowledge of the bullfight. From these discussions I was able to learn about the knowledge that was meant to inform appropriate bullfight photography as well as the values and knowledge that my informants used to inform their commentaries on the images.

be able to predict the moves, and take the photograph at the right instant. At the same time they invested their own knowledge in developing evaluations of the performances of the bullfighters whom I had photographed, to judge how their postures and skills were manifested in that moment (Figure 4.5).

Photographic interviews can thus provide a context where ethnographers and research participants discuss images in ways that connect or compare their experiences of realities. In doing so they can bring to the fore normally unspoken dimensions of experience, meaning and knowing and enable ethnographers the routes into understanding participants' perspectives in new ways.

Viewing other people's photographic collections: interviewing with images

We often show images, in our homes, our wallets, or stored on our camera phones as ways of expressing those things we might be talking about that are hard to put into words. Sometimes people speak about photographs or paintings, either of personal relevance or well-known images when seeking to describe or refer to something else that is difficult to express verbally. During video interviews these forms of expression are also quite common, especially when participants have the images they are referring to at hand and know that they are 'showing' an image to the researcher and for the video. During my video ethnographies of the home, participants have often discussed people and things with reference to photographs they have on display or kept somewhere. The showing of photo albums or collections can often both help participants to describe, and researchers to understand, the changing biographies, relationships and materialities of people's lives. This is also demonstrated well in some ethnographic films. Good examples are found in David and Judith MacDougall's *Photo Wallahs* (1991) where the photographers or owners of photo albums shown in the film discuss the qualities, histories and meanings of the photographs with the filmmakers. In Paul Henley's *Faces in the Crowd* (1994), scenes where the film's protagonist discusses his photographs of the Royal Family both with the filmmaker and likewise when he presents them to members of the Royal Family at public events, show us how these photographs are part of experiences that cannot be expressed just in words and enable him to communicate about them across different contexts.

The biographical nature of photographic collections means that they are often used to talk about personal histories and memories. Judith Okely describes how her informants' own photograph collections became important in her research about the 'changing conditions and experience of the aged in rural France' (Okely 1994: 45). When an elderly woman in a nursing home led her to her room and took out a box of old photographs Okely 'found a route to her past through images' that stood for 'profound recreations of her past' (1994: 50). For Okely, these images were not merely illustrations of her informant's oral narrative, but were evocative descriptions and comments. She argues that the introduction of the photographs into their conversation enhanced the sensory dimension of the interview: 'A mere tape recording of her speaking in a formalised interview could not have conjured up the greater sense of her past which we mutually created with the aid of visual images' (1994: 50–1). Okely notes that a history related through a series of 'selective images of the past', and captioned by a verbal narrative, is inevitably subjective, selective and fragmented. Nevertheless, she also shows how this enabled them to collaboratively create a version of the past that extended beyond the limitations set by the linearity of a verbal or textual narrative:

> Both of us pieced together the memories from whatever was picked up from the box, and created a synthesized whole. In reacting to the visual images, randomly stored, the woman was freed of linear chronology, any set piece for a life history and a purely verbalised description. The images did some of the work for both of us in ways which adjectives and other vocabulary could not supply. (1994: 51)

Okely emphasises the need for reflection on how researchers experience people's photographs. She notes how in her own experience she was 'watching, listening and resonating with the emotions and energy of her living through the photographs' (1994: 50).

When people use photographs to tell stories about their experiences, identities and practices these images become embedded in personally and culturally specific narratives. They might, actually purposefully, and unprompted by the researcher, seek out photographs to employ as part of the narratives that they are also developing verbally. In other contexts we might engage with people and their photograph collections or displays more purposefully. In this section I have focused on how analogue and printed images have been used in earlier work. We should remember that in a contemporary digital context many biographical photographs remain in this material form (see Pink 2011e), yet web-based social media and archiving shift the context and possibilities for this, as is shown for example in the work of Gómez Cruz (2012), Forrest (2012) and Fors et al. (2013) discussed in Chapter 6.

Participant-produced images

It is increasingly common for ethnographers to ask research participants to photograph for or with them in participatory research. In the past researchers have given participants disposable cameras to use and then return to them for processing although affordable digital cameras would also be appropriate. Participants' photographs often allow the researcher access to and knowledge about contexts they cannot participate in themselves. For instance, such methods have been used to create routes to understanding children's worlds (e.g. Mizen 2005). Working with older people, Suzanne Goopy and David Lloyd (2006) have used participant photography in a project about quality of life amongst ageing Italian Australians. Participants were asked to photograph 'those places, people, objects and/or situations that lend them identity and express or add to their quality of life' to produce series of snapshots that represent 'a spatial discourse of place and self'. They interviewed the participants

Red Roses. © Alan Radley and Diane Taylor 2001

Radley and Taylor's writing (cited above) and images from this research can be found online on the Visualising Ethnography website at www.lboro.ac.uk/departments/ss/visualising_ethnography/

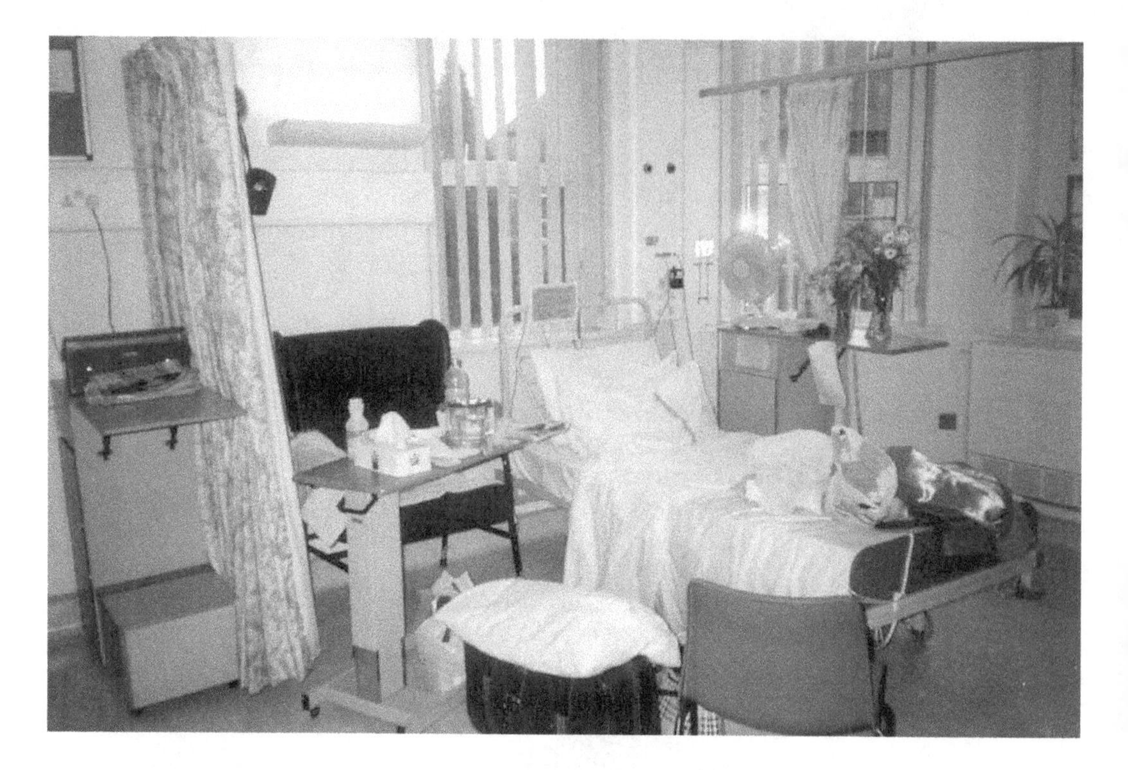

4-bedded Ward. © *Alan Radley and Diane Taylor 2001*

Figure 4.6 In their research into experiences of hospitalisation and recovery, Alan Radley and Diane Taylor asked patients to take their own photographs of the hospital ward. They suggest that to learn about the hospital ward – a space in which patients spend extended periods of time – 'it seems sensible to use a form of record that allows patients to show what matters to them while in hospital'. By asking patients to photograph twelve of 'the objects, spaces and places that they found most significant', Radley and Taylor 'aimed to capture some of the most important features of recovery after surgery'. Although they had not originally planned to be there, the researchers were required to be present when their informants took the photos and in several instances assisted them with this. They later interviewed each patient about the images both during their time on the ward and later once they had returned to their homes. Radley and Taylor argue that, although these photographs could not depict respondents' actual experiences of being in hospital, they did have significant meaning for the patients involved. This meaning was made (was narrated) when participants spoke about *why* and *how* they took the pictures, as well as about what was depicted *in* the pictures. To get closer both to patients' experiences of being on the ward and to understanding the meaning the *act of photographing* had for them, Radley and Taylor explain why it is important for the researcher to be present when participants take photographs. As for informant-directed photography, as I have noted above, when it is possible to access and participate in the context of photographic production this can add significantly to our understandings of the ways they can become meaningful.

about these photo-diaries and then asked then to produce a second photo-diary. The second stage was crucial because Goopy and Lloyd report 'the participants became more intimately involved in creating an amateur auto-ethnography'. The final stage of the research built on these diaries and interviews: the researchers and participants collaborated to produce a composite photographic image from photographs taken by the researchers. This aimed to reflect 'their [the participants'] overall sense of identity and quality of life'. These composite images contribute to the research process by giving 'the participants the opportunity to select and emphasise aspects of their domestic environment' and are part of the final published representations of their understandings of quality of life (see Figure 8.3).

In these contexts participants' photographs allowed researchers to access and gain understandings of situations that would be difficult for them to enter themselves. However it might be that the researcher can be present, and as Alan Radley and Dianne Taylor's (2003) research with people in hospital wards represented in Figure 4.6 shows, this can create a different type of research encounter which, reflexively considered, can be equally beneficial.

When participants take photographs for us the images they produce do not hold intrinsic meanings that we as researchers can extract from them. Rather they create routes through which we can explore in interview how people experience and act in the material, social and embodied elements of their environments. If we understand such photographs as emerging from photographic moments that were meaningful to the people who took them within a particular experiential narrative of events and of movement in a specific environment, one task is to engage with the image to explore these meanings. Yet photographic meanings will be renegotiated and remade in the interview context and this remaking is part of the process of creating ethnographic knowledge.

Displays, exhibitions and archives: viewing semi-public and public photographs with participants

Viewing photographic displays or exhibitions with participants offers further ways to explore the relationship between visual and spoken ways of knowing. This may involve visiting public exhibitions, viewing photographs displayed publicly (e.g. in schools, clubs, bars, town halls), or simply talking around photographs displayed on the wall or mantelpiece of someone's home. By attending to how people interweave such images with verbal narratives, researchers may learn about how these individuals construct their lives and histories.

When we enter people's homes, work stations, or other areas they have appropriated for themselves, we usually encounter photographic displays. Anthropological studies of the home demonstrate the importance of attending to the domestic material culture (e.g. Miller 1998, 2001; Pink 2004b). This includes photography which is part of the visual, material and sensory composition of the home *and* a medium through which people represent and communicate their identities to themselves and others in the semi-public areas of the home. Rose Gilroy and Peter Kellett's work in the North of England demonstrates the importance of photographic display for older people in their own homes, and as they move into sheltered housing and nursing homes where private space becomes increasingly limited (2005). Likewise in France, Okely found that elderly people drew the photographs they had on display into their conversations with her: 'The selected icons of photos which the aged displayed at institutional bedside or on familiar sideboard in their own home were both cultural and individual presentations' (Okely 1994: 51).

In Spain I discussed individual collections and public displays of images to explore people's visual representation of their 'bullfighting world' and its history, and to see how individuals used these visual representations to situate themselves within that bullfighting world. In photographic displays individuals and groups often used photographs to establish identities and to imply relationships. Most bullfighting bars and clubs owned permanent exhibitions that mapped out a local version of the history of bullfighting. People tended to take me to see their own bullfighting bars or clubs and gave me guided tours of the bar's photographic display. As I was led through these photographic wall displays, narratives of history, place and kinship were developed as people emphasised the family relationships between different bullfighters, their historical authenticity and their local links. The histories I was told when viewing the images were, as in the case of the box of images that Okely's informant drew her faded prints from, multilinear. The chronological history of bullfighting that participants outlined for me was intersected with family histories as links between fathers, sons, nephews and great uncles and formed particular routes across the various different photographic maps of the bullfighting world that I was shown. For a bullfighter, it was especially important to be situated in this world by having his photograph included in the exhibition, since inclusion in a display and the social relations involved in achieving this are crucial for a bullfighter's career. The cultural construction of history and the contemporary configuration of the bullfighting world depend on the strategic inclusion and exclusion of photographs of certain people (Pink 1997b: 56). Bullfight *aficionados* used similar strategies in their semi-public displays at home. These included photographs of themselves in amateur performances, or photographed with famous bullfighters, and thus mapped personal versions of the 'bullfighting world' that placed the owner of the exhibition at their centre. I was also invited to the openings of many exhibitions of bullfight photography during my research in Spain. At these events I discussed photographs with informants as we milled around the exhibition spaces. Their comments about the content and style of photographs gave me a better understanding of how different photographic representations fitted with each person's vision of the contemporary and historical world of bullfighting and of how they constructed their own place and identity in that world (see Pink 1997b).

In Spanish bullfighting culture photographic exhibitions pertain to the visual culture of a group. Public photography archives and displays are also often produced with a locality focus, and can contribute to processes through which the identities and histories of towns or other settlements are produced. Làszlò Kürti discusses a community archive project he was involved in setting up in the town of his birth, Lajomizse in Hungary. He found that although the town had been labelled a place without 'serious history', in fact what this 'masked was the fact that there was no written history'. The first project was the creation of a Digital Photo Archive (DPA) that aimed to 'collect, analyse and archive family photographs'. Kürti writes: 'As more and more photographs were offered and scanned into our DPA, the more the town's past began to emerge as unique and colourful'. Analytically, this produced two areas of knowledge about the past focusing on 'the moment the picture was taken, and the post-photographic event that the pictures clandestinely suggested' (Kürti 2004: 51). Kürti's detailed analysis of the images that composed the DPA provides an insight into the sorts of academic knowledge that can be derived by studying community archives. As he points out, 'These postcards of a single settlement chronicle the diverse practices, cultural and political commitments that have generalised the past century. They reveal that the visual representation of a community is always suspect to being a momentary snap-shot-like description manipulated both by the makers and users' (2004: 65).

In my research about the Cittaslow movement in Aylsham Norfolk I have also witnessed the role of photography in the constitution of local history, through the production of a digital community archive that is exhibited at public events. As part of a carnival in Aylsham in the summer of 2005, an exhibition of historical photographs sourced from the town's community archive and local people's own collections was presented in the town hall. In one section of the exhibition local people were invited to identify people featured in old photographs by writing their names on photocopied sheets, thus participating in the process of the production of this archive of local history. In the main room of the town hall a series of tables upon which photographs were laid out, covered past carnivals and more generally local history. Here as I talked with people from the town they pointed out how their own families, memories and histories were interwoven with this exhibition (see also Pink 2012d). The use of photographic displays at community events, or digital projections is a significant way in which local people create identities, histories and memories. Increasingly such practices are extending to Facebook and other social media platforms, and I comment on this further in Chapter 6.

Summary

This chapter has emphasised two dimensions of ethnographic research with photographic images and technologies: an appreciation of both the local and academic visual cultures in which ethnographers work; and how researchers may employ photography and photographs in the production of knowledge. Ethnographic image production and discussions of images both respond and refer to local and academic visual cultures. Ethnographers should recognise that neither local nor academic visual and written cultures are superior to the other. As the individual through whom the experience of each of these verbal and photographic cultures is mediated, photographers/ethnographers should attempt to maintain a reflexive awareness of how the demands of each inform their work.

Usually the processes of learning about local visual cultures and the production of one's own images go together. However, in different projects photographing, collecting, and interviewing with/talking about images will inevitably develop in different ways. The photographic research methods described above are not intended to be comprehensive, but to present a series of ideas and examples of existing work and of the potential for photography in ethnographic research. Variations in the methods developed in different projects are not just contingent on the cultures in which researchers work, but also on the personal styles of ethnographers and the social relationships in which they are involved. The key to successful photographic research is in understanding the social relations and subjective agendas through which they are produced and the discourses through which they are made meaningful.

Further reading

Harper, D. (2002) 'Talking about pictures: a case for photo-elicitation', *Visual Studies*, 17(1): 13–26.

Radley, A., Hodgetts, D. and Cullen, A. (2005) 'Visualizing homelessness: a study in photography and estrangement', *Journal of Community and Applied Social Psychology*, 15: 273–295.

Pink, S. (2011e) 'Amateur documents? amateur photographic practice, collective representation and the constitution of place in UK slow cities', *Visual Studies*, 26(2): 92–101.

Irving, A. (2010) 'Dangerous substances and visible evidence: tears, blood, alcohol, pills', *Visual Studies*, 25(1): 24–35.

Additional material is available on the book's companion website: www.uk.sagepub.com/pink3e

5

Video in Ethnographic Research

Film and subsequently video have long since been used in ethnographic practice, being defined broadly into uses for filmmaking and uses for research. In this chapter, I focus on how video recording practices have developed as routes to knowledge in ethnographic practice. First, to set the ground for understanding the debates that inform these contemporary uses, and to account for their key points of departure, I outline the academic and technological history of the use of video in ethnography.

Visual anthropologists became interested in video in the 1980s, applauding new developments in video technology for the convenience, economy, durability and utility they offered. In comparison with film, which was used extensively in anthropological research in the 1970s (see Morphy and Banks 1997: 5), video was relatively cheap and could record for considerably longer periods of time. During this period the potential of video was often harnessed to serve a scientific-realist approach. For example, Collier and Collier saw the idea that a video camera may be left running continuously for several hours as an advantage compared to the relative selectivity imposed by both the cost of film and the need to reload a camera more frequently (1986: 146). During the 1990s, video cameras became increasingly affordable, smaller and more portable and easier to operate. By the late 1990s researchers from different social science disciplines were engaging with video anew and as distinct from ethnographic film, and increasingly so with the digital video cameras and editing. In this context also reflexive approaches to using video in research became increasingly appreciated. Over the last 10 or so years, the increasing accessibility of digital video technologies, easier uploading of files to personal computing equipment and editing has made it possible for ethnographic researchers to use video at relatively little cost. Ethnographic video-making is still a specialised genre and a skilled practice, which has to be learned, and this is especially the case for the production of finished films. Yet the accessibility of digital cameras and smart phones has opened up new possibilities for reflexive uses of video recording in ethnography, as a medium through which ethnographic knowledge is created.

In Chapter 4, I discussed how researchers' choices of camera are significant to the ways in which they work and are categorised by others in ethnographic field sites. It is also worth reflecting on the design of video technology used and how this affects the video ethnographer. To put this in historical context a key shift in design was in the 1990s when Chris Wright described how the Sony PC7 digital video camera differed from the larger and heavier earlier video cameras. In place of a viewfinder, the PC7 had a fold-out mini-TV screen that created distance between the camera operator's eye and the camera, allowing the ethnographer thus to see both the camera screen and the scene recorded. The camera no longer followed the operator's eye but allowed him or her a split vision and to see and decide what was being recorded in relation to the scene in front of the camera (C. Wright 1998: 18–19). While we might now take this for granted as a common feature in digital video cameras, the shift was important as it helped to define not only the camera operator's view, but also what the video subjects saw. Using the open camera screen of the video, a researcher can maintain better eye contact with video subjects because the camera itself is not hiding his or her face. Video footage can also be viewed directly with participants on this screen and listened to through the external speaker. In comparison with viewing playback though the small camera viewfinder with headphones as one would have done with earlier cameras, this also allowed researcher and participants to discuss the images during viewing. As technology developed and digital downloading of video directly for viewing on a laptop became possible, then viewing video with participants directly after its production has become possible in further new ways. Video is of course not simply visual – it is an audiovisual medium and sound recording is part of video recording. In many instances the camera's internal microphone will be sufficient for the type of video methods discussed in this chapter. However, to achieve good sound quality, especially when not close up to the source of the sound, researchers might also consider using an external microphone and at times a radio microphone. A further contemporary option is to use camera phones and smart phones for ethnographic video recording. These have the advantage that they can also be used for other fieldwork methods including audio recording, note-taking and photography, as well as to share images produced with participants and co-researchers digitally.

As this short history of video in ethnography shows, it is not only our relationships with the participants that we need to be reflexive about, but we also need to consider how both relate to the camera, and to our different agendas regarding the video technology and recordings. In this chapter I draw on examples of video ethnography practice spanning the last 20 years or so. However, I write with the assumption that most contemporary video ethnographers will be using digital camcorders, smart phones or other new technologies to video record.

Defining ethnographic video

The review of existing historical and contemporary ethnographic films may form part of the visual reviews undertaken in preparation for visual ethnography research and therefore it is important to understand something of the history of ethnographic film and the debates around its relationship to research film (see also Durington and Ruby 2011 for a historical and critical review of the history of ethnographic film). In the 1990s, literature about ethnographic video and filmmaking often distinguished between 'objective' research film or video footage and 'creative' footage produced for ethnographic filmmaking. This distinction was informed by 1970s and 1980s debates about the relationship between cinematography and scientific ethnographic film (see Banks 1992). Some (e.g. Heider 1976) argued that ethnographic film should be objective, unedited, not 'manipulated', and it should be guided by scientific, ethnographic principles, rather than cinematographic intentions. Such footage was intended to be stored as a film archive and screened to anthropological audiences and was part of a project of recording an objective reality. During the same period others produced more creative, expressive films intended for public consumption. For instance, the filmmaker Robert Gardner 'distanced himself from realism' (see Loizos 1993: 140), producing films that used cinematographic and symbolic techniques that challenged the criteria set by Heider. Collier and Collier applied a similar distinction between 'research' film, which 'is made to contain relatively *undisturbed* process and behaviour from which to develop information and concepts' and 'ethnographic' film that 'is usually edited to create a narrative selected by the filmmaker-producer' (Collier and Collier 1986: 152). They dismissed the possibility of using 'ethnographic' film for research purposes, claiming that the selectivity involved in its production makes it invalid as an observational record. These categories persisted in publications of the 1990s (e.g. Barbash and Taylor 1997) where research footage was regarded as objective data, 'raw material' and a scientific document. In this view creativity is not part of research as the ethnographer's intentionality must be scientific to be 'ethnographic'.

The idea of video ethnography developed here is based on three main criticisms of this approach. First, it is usually impossible or inappropriate to video record people or culture 'undisturbed'; people in a video are always 'people in a video'. Moreover, like any ethnographic representation, research footage is inevitably constructed. Second, ethnographic knowledge does not necessarily exist as observable facts. As I argued in Chapter 2, ethnographic knowledge is better understood as originating from fieldwork experiences. Knowledge is produced in negotiation between research participants and researcher, rather than existing as an objective reality that may be recorded and taken home in a notebook, word processing file, audio recording, photograph or video. Third, and parallel to my discussion of defining ethnographic photography (Chapter 4), the question of the 'ethnographicness' of video footage does not depend entirely on its content or on the intentionality of the video maker, but its ethnographicness is contextual. In the broadest sense a video is 'ethnographic' when its viewer(s) judge that it represents information of ethnographic interest. Therefore video footage can never be purely 'ethnographic': a video recording that ethnographers see as representing ethnographic knowledge about an event and how it is experienced might, in their participants' eyes, simply be a video of a birthday party. Or, for instance when I have returned video recordings made of a garden tour (see Pink 2007b) to the participant who featured in them I have expected him to treat these as ways of remembering the past and as records of the progress made in his garden project. In contrast, as my written work shows, for me they are ethnographic records of my own experience, and process of learning and understanding about this project (Pink 2007b, 2011d). This broad and contextual definition of ethnographic video invites the possibility for a range of different genres of video to be 'ethnographic'. This includes not only ethnographers' video footage, but also (for example) home movies, events videoed by participants for ethnographers (see Morgan and Muir 2012), indigenous videos made for self-representation to external bodies and documentary videos made through collaborations between researchers and participants as part of applied research (see Pink 2004a, 2007a). Video can be used for ethnographic diary keeping (e.g. Holliday 2001; Chalfen and Rich 2004; Chalfen and Rich 2007), making recordings to show to and work on with participants (e.g. Capstick 2011) or for recording certain processes and activities (e.g. Dant 2004; Pink 2012d). None of these types of recordings are essentially ethnographic, but may become so when they are implicated in an ethnographic project.

There are different ways to record people as they engage in actual practices and different analytical techniques are attached to these. For example, the sociologist Tim Dant, reflecting on his video research about the work practice of car mechanics comments that 'Because of the capability of capturing the visible and hearable actions and interactions of people going about their ordinary life, it [video] would seem to provide a rich source of data for those social scientists interested in studying local social situations'. He goes on to suggest that 'The flow and pattern of life as it is lived is recorded and retained in the moving picture with sound to become available for close study and multiple replays' (2004: 41). Such recordings and work with them using methods such as conversation analysis (see for example Hindmarsh and Tutt 2012) offer one route to knowledge. However, to identify a difference between these approaches and visual ethnography practice as defined here, in video ethnography as I practise it the intervention of the researcher and the constructedness of the research encounter is made more explicit. Therefore while Dant writes that 'The flow and pattern of life as it is lived is recorded and retained in the moving picture' (2004: 41), in video ethnography it is the encounter between life as it is lived and performed and the event of doing research that come together to produce knowledge. Therefore, when I have asked people to perform their 'usual' everyday routines of washing up or doing the laundry this has created a reflective performance of practice 'in practice' (see Pink 2012d). The same principle applies to both participant produced video and researcher produced video, in that even if the researcher is not present the encounter with the technology is framed by the event of the research. Indeed, video ethnography practice can be seen as both a site of knowledge production, and as the process of making a reflexive video document that is itself a trace of that site.

My own interest is in conceptualising the processes of making and (re)viewing video as happening in and being part of movement. Elsewhere, drawing on the work of Ingold, I have argued that 'the process of walking with video is one of *going forward through* rather than mapping onto an environment, it offers a very particular way of creating a permanent trace of the routes we take through both the ground and the air. Moreover it provides a way of describing this trace and the experience of making it' (Pink 2011d: 146). Following on from this I have suggested that when we view video that we have recorded we should understand it not as being 'played back' which is how we would usually term it, at least in the English language, but instead we play video forward (Pink 2011d; Pink and Leder Mackley 2012). This point I believe is a crucial one to keep in mind when we are working with video as ethnographers – whether we are making video, viewing other people's video, re-viewing our own video, or asking other people to view videos with us. Video does not take us or anyone else 'back' either in time or to a place or locality. Rather, video invites us to move forward with it, and as such to make new knowledge as we engage with it.

Ethnographic video and local 'video cultures' and practices

People who participate in video ethnography usually already have their own uses for and understandings of video technologies and images. As Lomax and Casey noted from their experiences of videoing interactions between midwives and their clients, 'the camera ... is socially significant given both its ability to preserve interaction for re-presentation and participants' awareness of that ability' (1998: 6). However, reflexivity entails more than simply an awareness of how participants' interactions are affected by their 'camera-consciousness'. Rather, we need to firmly situate their self-awareness within the cultural and media contexts in which they live out their everyday lives, which also may be generational, gendered or informed by specialist interests and hobbies. Moreover, when it is the ethnographer her or himself who is recording, she or he becomes a person with a video camera, the camera becomes part of its user's identity and of how he or she communicates with others. It is not only the cultural and environmental difference that influences the way video becomes part of a project, but in each situation the camera will impact differently on the relationships researchers develop with other individuals and the social roles they play. An individual ethnographer does not have one single and fixed identity as a video maker, but this will be negotiated and redefined in different contexts. To be reflexive ethnographic video makers need to be aware of how cameras and video recordings (whoever is holding the camera) become elements of the relationships between themselves and participants, and how these are interwoven into discourses and practices in the research context.

In most contexts of contemporary ethnographic research television, film and video form part of participants' own consumption and production. An appreciation of local or multi-sited media and video cultures, people's interpretations of media narratives and how these inform their understandings of video images can also inform the ways we use video as a research method. In this sense existing literatures around media and internet ethnography offer a strong starting point for video ethnographers seeking ways to comprehend the contexts in which participants might make meaning of their ethnographic media practices (see, for example, Hughes-Freeland 1997; Ginsburg et al. 2002; Askew and Wilk 2002; Rothenbuhler and Coman 2005; Bräuchler and Postill 2010). Media ethnography was earlier formulated as a departure from 'audience studies' and 'reception studies' in media analysis to propose a reflexive ethnography of media reception that focuses on how 'audience creativity' intersects with 'media power' (see Morley 1996: 14). In its contemporary manifestations it offers an ethnographic approach to studying media forms and practices and their meanings within specific cultural contexts, individual narratives and social relations. This includes the possibility of going further than simply seeking to understand viewers'/users' individual and cultural understandings of media representations by doing participant observation with television, video or film audiences and internet users. Contemporary media ethnography extends to also cover media practices such as commercial, public and domestic media production. It can support ethnographic research with video by helping researchers to understand how research participants' interpretations of video cameras and 'ethnographic' video recordings are informed by the roles played by media practices and representations more widely in their lives. For example, the work of the visual anthropologists Manuel Cerezo, Ana Martinez and Penelope Ranera, demonstrated the importance of sensitivity to media narratives and the meanings that people invest in visual representations of themselves. The researchers were working with African immigrant workers in Spain. Since they had used photography quite extensively in the project, to the pleasure of their informants, they were surprised when video recordings they had made created moments of tension that were difficult to deal with (Cerezo et al. 1996: 142). The informants did not like the images of themselves in the video; while they admired its landscape scenes, they found themselves 'ugly' and 'poor' (1996: 143). The researchers situate these responses in relation to popular culture, pointing out that the immigrants, who work very long hours and have a low economic level, nevertheless return home every evening to watch television or videos. Thus for them the video images of themselves on a television screen were images of poverty (1996: 143). The researchers' self-reflexivity and discussions with their informants about the video representations revealed how each of them had gazed differently on the video footage. By exploring this they learned both why the video images were problematic and how their informants interpreted images of themselves with reference to contemporary popular media culture.

A second example of how culturally specific narratives inform participants' relationships with video emerged from my own video ethnography research in the home. From 1999–2000, I undertook two video ethnography projects that explored aspects of the relationship between self-identity and the home in Britain and Spain. The research involved an in-depth interview of about one hour with each participant, followed by a 'video tour' of their homes. The video tour entailed each participant showing me around her or his home while I video recorded her or him. Guided by prompts, each person led the tour discussing with me aspects of the visual and material home, their feelings about it and treatment of it (further reading about this method can be found in Pink 2004b, Pink 2004c). As the video tour method developed in the different sites and contexts of my fieldwork – that is, in the homes and personal narratives of different individuals – I realised that it was culturally embedded in specific ways. First, using a small domestic video camera (as described above), I was introducing a domesticated research technology that already fitted in the home. However, because this was also the 'latest' and smallest of the new domestic digital video cameras at the time, it aroused people's curiosity to hold and examine it. Second, all the participants in this research were conversant in video use. They had preconceived ideas about what to expect from and how to perform with a video camera. Although none of the participants had ever experienced a similar research exercise, each of our video recordings could be seen as a performance that had been informed by existing cultural and personal knowledge and experience about how one performs and communicates 'on camera'. Finally, the video tours are interesting because they show how each participant appropriated the video tour process her or himself by attaching it to a (usually subconsciously) chosen existing cultural narrative. For example, some people developed the tour by taking the stance used to show a prospective buyer around the home, others used what I have called a 'hello magazine' type narrative to communicate the idea of showing the home in a way that presents a lifestyle, and finally others linked the tour and the way that it encouraged them to reflect on their own personal trajectories to a counselling narrative. As such they were able to comment on both the material home, their embodied experiences of it and their self-identities as we toured it. These performances and uses of narratives can be seen as an element of the participants' negotiations with me – since they also used them as mechanisms through which to select what they would and would not show me within the private space of their homes. They did not ever ask me not to video but at the same time took control over what I could and could not access through video (see Pink 2004c for a more detailed discussion of the enactment of these narratives).

In contrast to working in domestic contexts, when researching the work of the slow city movement in the UK, I began to attend to public media narratives as a way of seeking to understand towns through their media cultures. I found that one town, Diss, already had an interesting video culture that was directly linked to my own interest in the experiencing of towns through touring them on foot. I have written about these experiences and video narratives elsewhere. First in an article (Pink 2008b) where I show how 'routes and mobilities are both invested in, and produce, local visual cultures. Thus examining how place is also constituted through the representation of routes and mobilities using (audio) visual media and techniques' (2008b: 1). I do this by examining how the town is 'made' in a series of local historical and contemporary filmic, video, photographic and drawn narratives, all of which involve partial walking tours of the town. Indeed, when I had asked Bas, a participant in my research, to take me on a walking tour of the town as a way of seeking to understand its Slow City identity, he had suggested that I view these films first. When we eventually walked around the town together with my camera, I was able to understand the route and the narratives that we followed as being in direct conversation with these existing contemporary and historical videos about the town. However, the story did not end there, and as I discuss in a later publication (Pink 2012c), the video research continued when I later found a YouTube video about the town which had been shown by town leaders at a Cittaslow conference. Again I was able to understand this digital video in relation to the historical videos of the town that I had already researched, as well as the video tour that Bas and I had walked. As this example also makes clear, it is of course not only ethnographers who make videos, in some cases it is at the intersections between these ethnographic and local and online visual cultures that knowledge is produced. In other projects, however, participants' and researchers' visual framings come together in different ways. I discuss some of these below with particular reference to participant-produced video (e.g. Chalfen and Rich 2007; Mason and Muir 2012).

Attention to the video practices and culture of research participants also entails learning about their technological practice and seeking to understand how these might both inform our understandings of how to work with video and simultaneously enable collaborative research practices. This could encompass using technology to share video recordings with participants, for their digital annotation or comments, or for co-editing.

Getting started

There is never any single 'right moment' to start using a video camera. In some cases video recording may become an element of a researcher's relationship with research participants right from the first meeting. For example, in my video ethnographies of the home in England and Spain, video recording was an unavoidable element of the fieldwork and was agreed with each participant from the outset. I introduced video as a matter of course as part of our interview process. In other projects, however, uses of video are negotiated on different terms. It may even be several months before the ethnographer considers it the 'right moment' to introduce video. Francisco Ferrándiz (whose work I discuss below) did not begin to use video in his research in Venezuela until he was already six months into the fieldwork, and then, as he notes, the 'most complex visual project had to wait a couple of months more' (1998: 26). Similarly, video work with different participants may start at different times in a project as relationships between ethnographers, technology, images and different individuals develop at different paces and in different ways.

Getting started is not solely a matter of finding the right moment but also involves a range of possible technological issues. This varies according to the equipment used and in the past was usually more complex than it might be now if one is using a camera phone or a small hand-held camera. However, in some contemporary video ethnography projects this might involve setting up a camera on a tripod, organising external sound recording, and perfecting the lighting. These processes do not only serve the video making processes but also frame the research encounter and become part of the research process. For example, even though they were using older technologies, Lomax and Casey's experiences during their research on midwife–client interaction demonstrate how this might work in practice. They found that even entering the home and setting up was of relevance since 'it is not possible to enter a person's home and set up camera without becoming interactionally involved' (Lomax and Casey 1998: 7). Similarly, when I toured their homes with people or videoed them as they performed and discussed domestic practices, I often collaborated with research participants to arrange that lights were strategically placed and switched on as we moved around video recording. Here the technical demands of video recording become a collaborative issue as both the interviewees and interviewer seek extra sources of indoor lighting, and indeed engage with the home in the embodied and material task of seeking to use its existing resources as a way of shaping the research encounter. This, again, should not be considered to mar the objectivity of the research but instead to serve as a collaborative route to knowing about the potentialities of the home and the participants' knowledge about these.

Learning to see with video

One of the opportunities afforded by doing long-term participant observation with a video camera is that one can learn not just about how other people do things but also become engaged in similar practices oneself. Where the practices one is learning about involve visual evaluation the camera can be an important tool. In Chapter 3, I discussed how I photographed the bullfight in ways that followed the conventions of existing bullfight photography and local people's instructions. Then by showing them these images, taking their criticisms of how I had *seen* (photographed) the performance and discussing what they *saw* in my photographs I came closer to understanding their visual knowledge about and criteria for evaluating a performance, the performer and the bull (see Pink 1997). Through a discussion of her video research about cattle breeding in Northern Italy, Cristina Grasseni has suggested that the visual ethnographer might, by apprenticing her or himself to their informants, develop what she has called 'skilled vision': the ability to see and thus understand local phenomena in the same way as the people with whom the researcher is working. Grasseni proposes that there is 'a parallel between the process of apprenticeship that a visual ethnographer has to undergo, and the process of education of attention that is required of anyone participating in a community of practice'. As such an ethnographer might learn to share 'an aesthetic code' (Grasseni 2004: 28) with her or his informants. In her own research working with a breed expert, Grasseni tried to 'develop an "eye" through an apprenticeship into looking at cattle'. As part of this process she used her video camera to keep a video diary, from which she showed footage to her hosts for them to comment on, allowing her to compare her own way of seeing with theirs (Grasseni 2004: 17). Grasseni describes how when she first began to tour farms with a breed inspector she 'did not know what to point the camera at, because I could not *see* what was going on'. She realised that in order for what she saw to become meaningful she would need to learn 'to share the breeder's vision' (2004: 20). Under the guidance of an expert, who explained to her how to evaluate a cow, Grasseni used her video camera as a research tool. She describes how: 'As a result of his instructions, I started to look at the udders from underneath, lowering the camera to knee-height. I concentrated on the volume of the udder, trying to shoot from under the cow's tail to line up her teats. I also began to frame the cows mainly from behind, keeping the camera high above their backs to show the line of the spine and the width of the shoulders'. The video camera was important in this exercise, since rather than simply looking at the cow as instructed, Grasseni video recorded this vision, as she puts it 'the camera functioned as the catalyst of my attention, tuning my eyes to the visual angles and the ways of framing the cow through the inspector's gaze' (2004: 21). As this example shows, video can be used as part of the process of learning to see as others do, in a directed way. Moreover, this produces audiovisual materials that informants can then comment on to produce a further layer of knowledge. Grasseni situates these uses of video in relation to a theoretical understanding of vision. She argues that the idea of participant observation should be reformulated as not simply imitating what other people do, but (drawing from ideas of ecology) as a way of learning about how people's shared visions (or understandings) 'co-evolve' (2004: 28–9).

Collaboratively exploring everyday experiences with video

In other projects long-term fieldwork may not be a possibility, either due to the timescale allowed for the research or the nature of the subject. My own 'Cleaning, Homes and Lifestyles' project (developed with Unilever in 1999) was an exploratory applied video ethnography. The project examined the relationship between people's self-identities, values, moralities, knowledge about housework, and the actual housework practices they engaged in, products they used and how they used them. We hoped to learn what domestic cleaning and the products used for it meant to people within the wider contexts of their lifestyles, homes and self-identities. I had six months to complete the research from the beginning to the final report and presentation. There was no time for the immersion in my research participants' lives that forms part of long-term participant observation. This was for two reasons. First, I needed to complete the fieldwork within three months.

Second, I was to study the relationships between forty individuals, their lifestyles, homes and cleaning and the fieldwork was to take place in their homes. Short of living with each of them for several months I would be unable to participate in their everyday lives for extended periods. For this study I developed the collaborative video tour method already mentioned above to achieve an in-depth understanding of the social and material worlds people live in (see Pink 2004b). Therefore I only had one meeting with each participant where we collaboratively set out to explore their homes using the video camera. Whereas Grasseni sought to learn the 'way of seeing' of cattle experts, and as such be able, using the camera, to imitate their practices herself, my approach was to ask my participants to show me their homes and to describe their practices to me on video both verbally and through embodied performance (see Pink 2004b). My meeting with each research participant lasted between two to four hours. The research meeting involved two tasks. First, a tape recorded interview covering areas including their self-identities, everyday lives, usual cleaning practices, moralities and values concerning dirt and cleanliness, knowledge about cleaning and definitions of clean and dirty etc. The interview was structured by my checklist, but was focused on allowing the research participant to talk and explain these areas her or himself. It was a collaborative interview in that we worked together to enable the research participant to define these areas of their life. Second, the video tour followed. This was a collaborative exercise that involved each research participant working with me to represent her or his experience of everyday life in the home and the routine practices this involved. Whereas in long-term fieldwork we would wait for events to unfold over a period of time, here we did not have that luxury. Instead we had one hour of videotape on which to represent the research participant's life in her or his home. Therefore we very consciously worked within a constrained time period to explore and represent the home and to discuss the human and material relationships, sensations, identities, emotions, memories, creativity and activity associated with the research participant's life there. This included participants giving demonstrations of how everyday domestic activities were performed. They used their whole bodies as well as words to show me what their lives and experiences were like in their homes as I probed and guided the 'tour' according to the objectives of the study. Through this research I aimed to produce, with each participant, shared understandings of their past experiences and current practices. To do so I had to depend on our collaborations and to work with them to help them draw out, reconstruct and represent the relevant experiences in a way that was meaningful to them, and to me. This produced a set of interview transcripts and recordings and videotapes. Their content which was at one level my audiovisual representation of the research experience, included descriptions and discussions of peoples' past experiences, demonstrations of how things are done, what has happened in a past situation, explanations of knowledge and meaning, values and moralities. The other layer of knowledge was based on my own first hand experience of the contexts in which the research participants lived and experienced their everyday lives, which I had gained through the video tour. While the participants used their bodies to perform and show the ways of knowing that were shown on the video, I also used my own body to seek to understand these ways of knowing. This type of video ethnography does not provide access to the level of experience and shared knowledge that might be produced through the type of involvement in people's lives permitted by long-term fieldwork. But it does allow us to explore collaboratively, and intensively, the visual and other sensory knowledge and experience that forms part of people's everyday lives.

This video ethnography touring method has been extended in the ethnographic strand of the LEEDR (Low Effort Energy Demand Reduction) project being undertaken at Loughborough University during 2010–2014. With Kerstin Leder Mackley I have written about and shown in online videos how we are using the method as a route to collaboratively exploring with participants the ways in which they make and maintain the sensory aesthetics of their homes. As we put it, 'The aim of the video tour is to move through the home ... following and discussing with the participant and, in doing so, to learn about the ways in which the sensory aesthetic of home is created. It involves particular attention to the textures, sounds, and the visual dimensions of home, how participants create atmosphere in their homes – as such, how they make their homes feel "right" and what they do about it when someone or something messes this up' (Pink and Leder Mackley 2012: 1.2). As in earlier video tour research, here our use of the video camera enabled participants to recall, perform and re-enact elements of their everyday experiences of home. We used the material and sensory home itself as a prompt, while also acknowledging that this was the very environment that we were seeking to understand. For example, reflecting on one of the video clips, recorded next to the front door of the house, we point out how 'The video context invited Rhodes [the participant who was leading the tour] to engage visually and through touch with the environment of the home, thus allowing us to appreciate the aesthetics of the front door and the thermal curtains, imagine the feel of the cold through her fingers, and comprehend the spatial proximity between entrance and thermostat' (Pink and Leder Mackley 2012: 5.10). The video tour method thus enables participants to represent their experiences to us as researchers, while simultaneously offering us ways to try to comprehend them.

Handing over the camera

Asking participants to film their own lives has a long history since Sol Worth and John Adair's (1966) 'Navajo Film Themselves' project which had as its main objective 'to ask the Navajo to show "us" (acknowledged researchers) how they saw themselves and their surroundings, or even better how they wanted to show themselves and their selves to outsiders' (Chalfen and Rich 2004: 19). Richard Chalfen (a visual anthropologist) and Michael Rich (a medical researcher) comment that the principle of handing the (now video) camera over to the research participants has been applied in a large number of studies across a wide range of disciplines (see Chalfen and Rich 2004: 19–20, and 2007). There is now a growing literature about this practice (e.g. Holliday 2001; Chalfen and Rich 2004, 2007; Mason and Muir 2012). Chalfen and Rich's own study was produced in the context of applied medical anthropology. They developed a method called Video Intervention/Prevention Assessment (VIA) by which 'Young patients were instructed to follow a specified protocol to "teach your clinician about your illness" by using consumer model videocams in their homes, neighbourhoods, schools, work, church and events of their own selection. They could also make a series of diaristic "personal monologues"' (2004: 17, and 2007). This means that 'VIA asks young people who share a medical diagnosis, such as asthma, obesity ... to create a visual illness narrative, documenting their experiences, perceptions, issues and needs on video'. Developed in the form of videotaped diaries these recordings represent the experience of illness from the patients' perspective. They provide a route through which clinicians, assisted by the analysis developed by the research team, might access patients' knowledge and understandings of their illnesses (2004: 18, and 2007). This is seen as a way of creating better understanding and communication between clinicians and patients in a context where each may understand the illness in different ways. As such, Chalfen and Rich refer to this method as offering a form of cultural brokerage (2004: 20–22, and 2007) (which is more generally characteristic of applied visual anthropology work). As is often the case in applied visual anthropological studies in this work it is not only the results of the research that impact on the lives of the participants, but also the process becomes empowering (see below). Chalfen and Rich note that (in the case of a study of Asthma) 'The process of self-examination had resulted in quantifiable improvements in patient's asthma status, possibly because of the cognitive dissonance between what they observed themselves to be doing and what they knew they should be doing' (2004: 23, and 2007). The work of VIA researchers is also shown and discussed online (see also Pink 2011b) providing an important introduction to and documentation of this work, including video clips (see http://www.viaproject.org/home/). I discuss this further in Chapter 10.

Another example of participant produced video, which includes the video clips in an online article, discusses Jennifer Mason and Stewart Muir's sociological research about family life. Mason and Muir developed their work though a genre which stands in relation to home movies and participant-produced videos as a way to gain a closer understanding of family Christmas celebrations. They describe how they 'invited several participants to record their Christmas using small handheld camcorders' in the hope (not dissimilar to the achievements of VIA discussed above) that 'participants could afford us a glimpse into a realm of their private life that would otherwise be difficult for us to access' (Mason and Muir 2012: 2.3). Mason and Muir reflect on how such materials enable researchers to 'get a feel for and insight into the multi-dimensional, multisensory, and embodied ways that personal lives are lived' and comment that video data 'can help us literally to see inside people's houses, into situated, sensory and physical aspects of their consumption and relational practices, and into interactions and occasions when a researcher cannot, for all kinds of reasons, join in and be present themselves'. This they suggest, in a context where social scientists are usually dealing with abstract categories like 'intergenerational relations, social class, gender relations, and sometimes even tradition itself' can bring the 'vitality' of such realities back into view (2012: 4.8). Comparing the videos with the interview – a dominant, but limited research method in sociology – their discussion shows how the use of participant produced video can take researchers into a sense of what is happening in the middle of everyday life or celebrations. They stress the capacity of video to show 'the situational dynamics of consensus or ambivalence and dissent', how 'what happens can be a jumble of practices, meanings, innuendos, misunderstandings and mishearings, mild subversion and ambivalence' (2012: 4.6). Video indeed, as I have argued elsewhere (Pink and Leder Mackley 2012), whether participant or researcher recorded, can take us to the centre of life as lived: it is a way of researching from the perspective of being part of an environment rather than from that of asking someone to tell you about it in spoken words.

Doing ethnography does not always involve creating and framing relatively controlled research encounters, but rather, we should expect the unexpected. An example of this is demonstrated in Francisco Ferrándiz's work with Venezuelan spirit cults (1996, 1998), which, although coming from the analogue age of video remains relevant today. In this case, also, we see how video can provide a route to visual and sensory knowledge and, interestingly, how the camera itself was appropriated within a culturally specific activity. Situating the role of video in his fieldwork in relation to the cult's existing relationship with, and experience of, media representation, Ferrándiz pays particular attention to the way the video recording developed through the intersubjectivity between himself and his informants. In some instances the video became a catalyst that helped create the context in which it was used, as in the case of a ceremony that was organised by his informants as part of the event of videoing it. However, of particular interest is that when Ferrándiz began shooting video, six months into his fieldwork, the informants with whom he was closely collaborating also took the camera to shoot footage themselves, each of them creating 'completely different visual itineraries of the same place' (Ferrándiz 1998: 27). Ferrándiz takes his analysis further than merely the question of how different people created different video narratives of the same context. He forms continuities between the video making and the ritual activities in which his informants were involved; the visual practices of video recording and the ritual practices coincided as people moved in and out of trance and in front of and behind the camera's viewfinder as the ceremony proceeded. In this research the video camera became part of the material culture of the ritual and its recording capacity an aspect of the ritual activity. Therefore Ferrándiz was able to learn about ritual practices both by observing the ritual uses of the camera itself and by analysing and discussing the video recordings that these uses produced.

Collaborative/participatory video and the empowerment of participants

As some of the examples discussed above have shown, ethnographic video production may become interwoven with local video cultures. Such work is by nature collaborative in the sense that it involves the active collaboration with research participants in the processes by which knowledge is produced. It is, as Banks (2001) has also pointed out, hard to imagine visual research that is not collaborative, however there are of course different ways that video ethnographers and participants work together and towards different ends. There is a growing literature about participatory video (e.g. White 2003) and participatory visual methods (Mitchell 2011) more broadly. These literatures overlap with visual ethnography in that they might share some types of video practice and/or inspire ideas in each other. Here my interest, however, is not in reviewing the development of participatory video methods, but rather to explore how video, participation and empowerment might overlap with theoretically informed video ethnography methodologies.

As I have argued in Chapters 1 and 2, visual ethnography is not just a set of methods, but rather the methods are engaged in ways that are theoretically informed, as part of academic disciplines and in the case of the examples discussed in this section also in relation to understandings of power and inequalities. Indeed it is not only these projects that play such a role, for instance the work of Chalfen and Rich discussed in the previous section could also be described as finding a route through which to empower patients. Of course video ethnography projects do not all fit into separate or neat categories. The field of applied visual ethnographic research is fast growing, along with a move towards a public visual anthropology (see also Pink 2006). Indeed often the two are combined in that, for example, as is demonstrated by the edited volume *Visual Interventions* (Pink 2007), visual ethnographers who are seeking to bring about change through their work tend to engage participants in video projects that enable them to reflect on their circumstances in useful ways, while at the same time seeking to bring critical or revealing arguments to general publics or to groups in authority or with the power to make change. Since the first years of the twenty-first century applied visual anthropology has developed further, especially in relation to attention to the sensory and digital elements of visual practice (see Pink 2011b). There is therefore a good range of examples through which we can now begin to learn about how video ethnography can be, and indeed is being, engaged in projects of empowerment and change. In fact while the institutional frames are rather different there are in methodological terms many correspondences between these projects and applied video ethnography as developed in organisational and corporate research contexts (e.g. Sunderland and Denny 2007). Below I discuss two examples: the work of the anthropologist Carlos Flores (Flores 2004, and see Flores 2007) which draws on the tradition of the work of the anthropological filmmaker Jean Rouch to develop a 'shared' anthropology; and the interdisciplinary projects of the sociologist Christina Lammer which are interesting because they show us how working with video explores and indeed constructs different contexts and dimensions of power relations in medical contexts.

Contemporary visual ethnographers are working in contexts where power relations are complex. They involve not only the relations between researcher and participant but also with other institutions and individuals. In some projects ethnographers have used video in collaborative work to create both academic knowledge and to empower people who have lived through political conflict. Drawing on Jean Rouch's notion of a 'shared anthropology', the visual anthropologist Carlos Flores discusses his collaborative video work with Maya Q'eqchi' filmmakers in post-war Guatemala. Flores shows how a community-based video project he developed collaboratively with local Q'eqchi' people simultaneously 'provided important ethnographic insights about an indigenous group and its transformations' and 'provided the communities with new mechanisms for sociocultural reconstruction and awareness after an intensely traumatic and violent period of civil war' (2004: 31). Attaching himself to, and initially adopting a participant-observer stance in, an existing NGO video project, Flores began to learn that existing practices clashed with his own expectations of indigenous video: they seemed to represent a development agenda rather than focusing on traditional indigenous practices or the recent history of conflict, and were made in Spanish rather than local languages (2004: 35). When, in the next stage of his involvement he began to contribute his own filmmaking skills and ideas he encouraged them to take up these other themes, focusing on planting rituals in one video and conflict in another. As Flores' work shows, such collaborative work both opens up possibilities and is constrained in what it can achieve (2004: 39). His work also reveals that (like other work in applied visual anthropology – see Pink 2004a, Pink 2006 Chapter 5, Pink 2007b) it is not simply the final film document that is important, but rather the collaborative processes by which it is produced, and it is through these processes that both new levels of engagement in thematic issues and of self awareness are achieved by participants and ethnographic knowledge is produced.

The work of Christina Lammer offers further interesting perspectives on how participants might be situated in a research process. Lammer works with a range of media including video. Her video work is interesting when we take it as a part of a body of work spanning over a series of projects and consider how she has used video differently and in ways that are adaptive to the collaborations she builds with different participants. I have followed Lammer's work through three projects, focusing on interventional radiology (e.g. Lammer 2007), breast cancer and cosmetic surgery (e.g. Lammer 2009, discussed in Pink 2011b) and facial reconstruction (e.g. Lammer 2012). Lammer often seeks to create new points of contact and understanding between patients and the clinical staff who treat them and uses a number of creative techniques. This has included developing video-based ethnographic techniques in relation to other visual, arts-based and ethnographic research methods in the contexts of medical consultations, treatments and interventions. In these contexts, her uses of video, rather than systematically repeating the same method, tend to be developed in ways that are appropriate to the particular circumstances. For example in her work in the operating theatres of interventional radiology, Lammer used the camera to research the 'non-verbal and sensual interactions during diagnostic procedures' (Lammer 2007: 97), following patients' stories with her camera, focusing through this (amongst other things) on the relationships between patients and clinicians. In her later work on facial reconstruction Lammer has developed a series of related body art projects, including, for example, the 'healing mirror' whereby she records patients who participate in her project while they go through a series of facial physiotherapy exercises, and recordings of her own endoscopic video (discussed in Lammer 2012). The different types of materials Lammer works with bring together different positions and ways of seeing and knowing clinical contexts and the lives with which they become interwoven. Yet it is these juxtapositionings that bring into relief the partiality of any one view through the lens.

Viewing video with participants

Another way to develop collaborative routes to producing knowledge with participants is by viewing video materials in which they feature together with them. Editing, distributing and viewing video footage with his informants was also an aspect of Ferrándiz's project in Venezuela (described above). Ferrándiz produced a tape when his informants asked to see copies of the video. He edited the footage to include expressive imagery by using slow motion to represent some trance sequences. The video was widely viewed and well received in the shanty town where Ferrándiz was working. The slow motion sections were to the satisfaction of his informants: 'it is important to stress the success of the use of slow motion, which seemed to embody with more accuracy the emotionality and fuzziness of the temporality experienced during the ceremonies, somewhere in the scales of trance, as opposed to the times where real time was used' (Ferrándiz 1998: 30). Viewing the video produced with informants can help researchers to work out what are and what are not appropriate representations of individuals, their culture and experiences. Indeed, it is possible to trace this type of practice through different types of research project. Another good example of involving participants in commenting on video representations of them is shown in Zemirah Moffat's reflexive ethnographic film *Mirror Mirror* (now online at http://queergiving.co.uk/). As part of the process of researching and making the film, Moffat involved the participants in a series of feedback sessions in different contexts: viewing footage of themselves individually on a laptop; viewing a rough-cut of parts of the film projected onto a stage that the participants usually use for performances in a bar; and then viewing and commenting on a rough-cut projected onto a screen in a university seminar room. In this case the participants, conversant about their own identities and active discussants of the process of representation and the extent to which the film was achieving its aims, continue to negotiate the way they are portrayed throughout the whole visual ethnographic and filmmaking process.

'Why ask Josephine?' © *Zemirah Moffat 2006*

'Do you like your penis?' © *Zemirah Moffat 2006*

Figure 5.1 Zemirah Moffat's film *Mirror Mirror* explores queer identities in London. Embedded in the research and film making process is her collaborative and reflexive approach that accounts for both her own identity and part in the film and how the subjects of the film wish to represent themselves. As part of this she screened her footage to them in various contexts and edited their responses into the film itself.

As I discuss in Chapter 3, through the example of the video footage follow-up meetings used in the LEEDR project (see Figure 3.3), such processes do not simply ensure that research has a strong reflexive awareness but might also be part of the ethical process through which research knowledge is produced. The follow-up meetings in this particular project also give opportunities to reflect on and discuss further elements of the video research encounter (Pink and Leder Mackley 2012).

Summary

In this chapter I have suggested a reflexive approach to video in ethnographic research that focuses on the question of how knowledge is produced through the relationship between the researcher and the subject of ethnographic video, the technologies used, and local and academic visual cultures. I suggest that we understand video as produced in movement and as the outcome of unique and changing configurations of persons and things, also in movement.

New uses of video in ethnographic research have developed in tandem with new technologies, innovations and theoretical perspectives. A growing interest in and range of collaborative approaches to ethnographic video have developed in academic research intervention projects and documentary. This field of practice continues to evolve with new technologies and practices that span the online and offline, and it is to this context I turn in the next chapter.

Further reading

Grasseni, C. (2004) 'Video and ethnographic knowledge: skilled vision in the practice of breeding', in S. Pink, L. Kürti, and A. Afonso (eds), *Working Images*. London: Routledge. (A useful methodological perspective on vision and seeing in ethnography and an example of using video in research.)

Pink, S. (2007a) *Visual Interventions*. Oxford: Berghahn. (An edited volume containing a series of case studies of video uses in applied anthropological research. The work of Chalfen, Flores and Lammer, discussed in this chapter are to be found in this text.)

Pink, S. (2011b) 'Images, senses and applications: engaging visual anthropology', *Visual Anthropology*, 24(5): 437–454.

Pink, S. (2011d) 'Drawing with our feet (and trampling the maps): walking with video as a graphic anthropology', in T. Ingold (ed.) *Redrawing Anthropology*. Farnham: Ashgate.

Pink, S. and Leder Mackley, K. (2012) 'Video as a route to sensing invisible energy', *Sociological Research Online*, February 2012, <http://www.socresonline.org.uk/17/1/3.html>.

Additional material is available on the book's companion website: www.uk.sagepub.com/pink3e

6

Doing Visual Ethnography with the Web

Some readers will find it hard to imagine a world when the internet was not part of everyday life; a time before digital videos and photos could be shared wirelessly as soon as they were taken and when social networking sites were not a common point of reference. Others will have witnessed the rapid changes that have occurred since I wrote the first edition of this book in the late 1990s. Likewise in just a few years' time some of our contemporary ways of engaging with the internet will probably appear absurd. In this chapter I cannot hope to document the place of the internet in visual ethnography for the simple reason that the chapter would be out of date before it was even published. Instead (using an approach I have also applied when writing of digital visual anthropology (Pink 2011f)) my intention is to draw on the ways that the potential of the internet has been engaged in existing work. My starting point for defining the internet as a contemporary site for visual ethnography is the web 2.0 context, which I elaborate on further below.

In this chapter, I focus on how visual ethnographers already have and might continue to work with this potential, by participating in new digital visual internet practices as they develop around emergent software and hardware. Therefore, while I might write of examples where researchers have used particular web platforms and media in their work, my point is not to simply show or prescribe how this or that particular platform or technology might be part of a digital visual ethnography. Rather my intention is to invite readers to engage similarly as new opportunities develop. I am concerned with how we might create entry points into learning through our engagement with other people's digital and visual web-based practices, how they are performed and how they are experienced, in a context where online/offline cannot be understood as separate from each other. In doing so I build on the basis for understanding visual ethnography practices developed for photography and video in Chapters 4 and 5: this chapter's focus is on how we bridge these techniques with a continually emergent digital environment.

How then might we imagine an ethnographic research project that engages with the visuality of the internet as part of a research process? Indeed although several of the examples I discuss below are visual ethnography projects that specifically explored the internet as part of their research question, as I have stressed in earlier chapters, I conceptualise visual ethnography as a way of doing research that attends to digital visual methods and media as appropriate, and as part of a research process – rather than simply using visual methods for the sake of it. The same applies to the use of the internet as part of an ethnography that uses visual methods and media. We should engage with the internet where it is part of the visual cultures, everyday lives and particular practices that our research focuses on as, in many cultural, social and regional research contexts the internet will already be part of the lives of people who participate in projects with us, and being connected to the technologies we use, in this sense inevitably already is a part of our work. Yet the extent to which, and ways in which, people are connected to the internet, and the visuality of these ways of being connected, vary enormously in relation to their access to different technologies, the specificity of practices of Internet use and economic and political systems. It is important to be aware of, rather than simply take for granted, the roles that contemporary and emergent technologies play in the research process. It is also important to realise that we should not take it for granted that simply because there is now available a range of web-based technologies for making, working with, storing and sharing images, that their use always constitutes the most culturally or ethically appropriate way to do visual ethnography. It is in this sense that I suggest that the principles for doing visual ethnography discussed in earlier chapters become a starting point for thinking through web-based practices. They demonstrate tried and tested ways of doing visual ethnography, which are being extended to web-based contexts. Therefore throughout this chapter, the same themes of appropriateness, reflexivity, and collaboration and participation will be explored in relation to the examples discussed.

As Nancy Baym shows, it is through the comparison of media that we can also gain understandings of their capabilities and consequences (2010: 6–7). She suggests that 'Seven concepts that can be productively used to compare different media to one another as well as to face to face communication are interactivity, temporal structure, social cues, storage, replicability, reach and mobility' (2010: 7). In earlier chapters I have discussed some of my experiences of using photography in my PhD research about women and bullfighting in Spain (Pink 1997a). Many of the principles of working with people and photography developed there still hold, but in other ways the context has vastly changed. While Baym's seven concepts do not map directly onto the narrative comparison of these two historical contexts, we can see that they are clearly relevant as structuring categories that can help us to reflexively consider how digital media are part of visual ethnography practice. One way to achieve this type of reflexivity is through historical comparison: when I went to Spain to do my fieldwork, twenty years ago, I did not have a computer, or a mobile phone. I bought a typewriter and went to the local telephone centre in the main Plaza to call home from one of the little cabins inside. To meet academics at the local university in Córdoba I presented myself in person at the beautiful old stone faculty building, followed the signs along its historic corridors and knocked on the door of the English Department. I researched and experienced the local visual culture of bullfighting by viewing films on video or at the cinema in the Filmoteca, I read books and magazines bought in local shops and kiosks, and viewed printed photographs displayed on walls in bars. I took photographs with an analogue camera, waited for them to be developed and then collected them from the shop. If I were to start a similar project now I would have access to very different routes to knowing and people and images. I would be able to identify, contact and interact with relevant people online before arriving and develop a study of the online visual culture of bullfighting before even going to Spain. Let us imagine one element of how I might go about this. It might include searching for and viewing videos on YouTube about bullfighting – videos made by bullfight fans, by those against bullfighting, by professional filmmakers, and by others. These different genres would offer me routes through which to interpret the different ways of seeing and filming the bullfight that I would be likely to encounter and to begin to imagine myself in those worlds. To make this online research ethically and ethnographically complete I would contact the people who had posted the videos to ask them to participate in my research by discussing their posts with me – again online, or later face-to-face once I had arrived in Spain. Likewise I might contact bullfight photographers using Flickr or through Facebook groups. This would enable me to learn further about the ways of seeing, making and creating understandings of the bullfight that intersect online and the material, technological and social contexts in which they are produced. However, all online research is related to a face-to-face material presence. If I wanted to know how the visual culture of bullfighting was produced then I should ask if these amateur or professional video makers would mind sharing with me the experience of making the videos they post in face-to-face contexts. This could mean researching, as the geographer Eric Laurier has, the processes of digital video production (e.g. Laurier et al. 2011 and see Laurier's web pages for this work at: http://www.ericlaurier.co.uk/assembling/). Following the example of Ardévol and San Cornelio (2007, discussed below) I might, once in Spain, begin to make, contribute and share my own videos, learning to participate as a practitioner in the very world that I was studying, indeed creating continuity between my 1990s research practice where, as I have discussed in Chapter 4, I participated as an amateur photographer of the bullfight, as a route to understanding how other people see and know.

Thus, as Baym and Markham rightly remind us 'The Internet changes the way we understand and conduct qualitative inquiry' (2009: viii), and this is equally the point for the way we do visual ethnography. Yet, as I have shown above, these changes might not be absolute departures, but may also have continuities with past methods. This is indeed an exciting time where some of the differences lay in that, as Elisenda Ardévol tells us:

> ... to enhance the field of visual methods to include Internet practices means reformulating the dimensions of visual research and expanding fieldwork

> from face-to-face encounters to virtual social contexts. Moreover, Internet technologies offer the opportunity to incorporate new methodologies and tools for visual data gathering and analysis, such as image searching tools, graph programs or geo-mapping. (Ardévol 2012: 86)

As the historical comparison above suggests, web 2.0 offers a new context for doing visual ethnography, yet there are also strong continuities in the ways that both research participants and ethnographers use video and photography in their everyday life and research practices. Our engagements with the internet also have implications for how we might theorise a world of which it is a part (see also Pink 2011a, 2012c). In what follows, I map out some of the theoretical and practical implications of doing visual ethnography with the internet and explore how the Internet is becoming part of visual ethnography practice.

Ethnography and the internet

There is already a vast and growing literature about internet ethnography. It is not my intention to review this literature here, but rather to focus on the question of how visual ethnographers might understand and develop the dimension of their work that goes online. This chapter is not, I would stress, intended as a contribution to the burgeoning literature on Internet Ethnography. Following the focus in Chapters 4 and 5 my interest is predominantly in the question of the implications of the internet and computing and web technologies for how uses of lens-based media are developed in visual ethnography. Readers who are interested in a comprehensive review and discussion of the relationship between visual ethnography and internet studies should refer to the recent work of Elisenda Ardévol (see Ardévol 2012). Ardévol's chapter demonstrates a number of correspondences between visual and virtual ethnography, showing how in both cases we need to go beyond the way the reflexivity in ethnography has focused on writing to what she refers to as 'the "mediation turn" [which] is a question of how we integrate other representational tools and digital technologies in our daily fieldwork practices and knowledge production' (Ardévol 2012: 75). This point is complicated further, as I elaborate in the following paragraphs, by continuous innovation in digital technologies, the fact that there is neither one single way in which digital media are incorporated into ethnographic practice, and nor one single definition of what a digital ethnography might entail as it moves across disciplines and priorities.

Because digital technologies are continually being developed, it would be unwise to order a discussion of media for digital visual ethnography in terms of the media that one might engage for this. It seems quite safe to speak of the mobile camera phone on the one hand and the internet on the other (see for example Baym 2010: 13) – although these are not necessarily separate entities either. Yet it is harder to separate out other digital media, especially in terms of their image producing, editing, storage and sharing capabilities, because often one technology will encompass more than one of these as either its primary or a secondary function.

For this reason, I discuss below digital visual ethnography not by technology, but rather I order the discussion into two sections that are continuous with Chapters 4 and 5 to discuss photography and video. While it is perhaps ironic that these two categories were historically created because they referred to two separate technologies, there is a strong case for continuing this distinction for the moment in that while in a digital era the technologies themselves are not so distinct, the practices, skills and genres of video making and photography remain culturally and practically separated in many ways in everyday, professional and ethnographic practice. However, within this claim to continuity we need to also recognise the breaks. Therefore while we may use specialised digital video and still image cameras, we might also do digital visual ethnography with a smart phone that can perform both of these functions and more.

As I outlined in Chapter 1, the ways that visual ethnography is actually practised will be framed by disciplinary agendas and theory. Likewise, each literature that focuses on internet ethnography is also often faithful to its disciplinary heritage, as regards ethnography. Therefore anthropologists tend to write about the ways that they have participated in the digital visual and web-based practices of other people as participant observers and practitioners of the same activities sometimes. For instance Michael Wesch's work on YouTube videos involves participating in this activity (2009, and discussed below) and Tom Boellstorf writes of his role as a participant observer on the platform Second Life (2008). In contrast, in an article published in the journal *Sociology* the research practices that the sociologist Dhiraj Murthy is concerned with include digital ethnography as an observational and often covert practice, the use of questionnaires and email interviews, and video diaries (Murthy 2008). These disciplinary differences are significant beyond the distinction between the main anthropological and sociological traditions: because ethnography is an increasingly popular methodology across a good number of disciplines and interdisciplines it is important to remain aware of how their agendas influence its practice. Contemporary literatures about digital research contexts are, moreover, being produced in a fast moving technological environment (as is this chapter) often the examples that they give of ways that we might do online research and the web platforms to which they apply tend to feel out of date in only a short time. This provides a broad context through which to discuss the implications and possibilities of the internet for digital visual ethnography.

In the context of this literature on digital ethnography there are also emerging new terminologies, including: Hine's earlier concept of 'virtual ethnography' (2000), Kozinets's 'netnography' (2010) and Murthy's definition of 'digital ethnography' (2008). In this chapter I depart to some extent from these labels. In Chapter 1, I pointed out that in reality the idea that ethnography can be simply 'visual' defies the way we actually practice ethnography. I also suggested that much of contemporary visual ethnography should be defined as 'digital' in that it usually involves the use of digital technologies, in the form of digital cameras and/or camera phones, web-based media, scanning, and more. My concern here is with where these ethnographic uses of digital and visual technologies intersect with the internet. In this sense I would stress that my definitions of digital, visual and internet ethnography may differ from those that readers will encounter in other literatures. This is because my approach to defining these practices is based on the premise that these cannot be pure, exclusive or clearly delimited categories. To take an example, Murthy defines digital ethnography by way of contrast with Hine's 'virtual ethnography'; he argues that in his definition, digital ethnography differs from virtual ethnography (something that does not involve face-to-face research). In contrast he sees digital ethnography as 'ethnography mediated by digital technologies'. He accounts for this as including 'digitally mediated field-notes, online participant observation, blogs/wikis with contributions by respondents, and online focus groups' and writes that 'it can also include accounts of off-line groups' (2011: 159). For Murthy thus digital ethnography is when 'its data-gathering methods are mediated by computer-mediated communication' (2011: 159). While I would concur that the role of computer-mediated communication is key to ethnographic engagements with the internet, here my aim is to push the definition further to consider digital video cameras and audio recorders, camera-phones, and other technologies as part of the assemblages that make up online web-based computing configurations. One might argue that there is a case for referring to all of these technologies as being 'computers' in some sense – a point that is particularly salient for smart phones. However, as Hine (2000) has also pointed out it is the performance of these technologies – how they are used in practice – that contributes to what they become. Therefore in the context of a digital visual ethnography, understanding computing and computers in a way that is defined through the relationality of technologies both to each other and with other people and things is a pertinent definition because it provides a clear way through which to incorporate audiovisual media as part of the research context, process and subject. Yet, this definition also has implications for the way we understand the interrelatedness of the technologies that we use for doing visual ethnography with digital and web technologies. We are indeed concerned not simply with an array of different technologies each of which is associated with a distinct medium such as video or photography, but our digital visual ethnography practice can be seen as an enactment of the potentialities of these technologies and of the ways that what was once a distinct medium (e.g. consider the technological distinction between analogue photography and video) now moves through and across different devices (e.g. from a camera to a laptop to a mobile phone) and across different web platforms.

Theorising the internet as a context for visual ethnography

As Ardévol has identified, visual and internet researchers generally tend to share sets of common concerns, this being related to the fact that they are both engaging with technologies as a route to knowledge in a number of ways (Ardévol 2012). Commonalities can be seen in the shared roots of visual ethnography as developed in the first edition of this book (2001) and Hine's virtual ethnography (2000). The two books were published in consecutive years and were informed by similar theoretical and methodological approaches emerging from the turns to reflexivity and multisitedness in ethnographic practices in the 1990s, and turning away from a holistic approach to ethnography (see also Pink 2009). As I have emphasised in the preceding chapters, the reflexive turn of the 1980s and 1990s had a profound influence on the ways visual ethnography could develop, and continues to inform its practice, the ways that contemporary visual ethics are played out, and our representational practices which are discussed in Chapters 8 and 9. Moreover, in common with visual ethnography, Hine's virtual ethnography led her to engage with both the theory and cultural understandings of the technologies involved. Her approach drew on both media sociology and the sociology of technology to understand the internet as both something that was performed and constructed through its use, and by its users (2000: 38), *and* as a technology (2000: 9). She stresses how meaning is produced in context, meaning 'the circumstances in which the Internet is used (offline) and the social spaces that emerge through its use (online)' (2000: 39) thus challenging the myth of holism in ethnography.

There is a fast expanding literature of social science and media approaches to the internet. As for other fields of scholarship each approach has its preferred disciplinary priorities and analytical scales and units. This, as has been pointed out in recent discussions (e.g. Baym 2010; Postill 2011) includes the dominant theories of the internet through theories of network (e.g. Castells 1996) or understandings of their being online communities (e.g. Kozinets 2010). Yet these concepts, which are already deeply debated contested in some social science literatures, have also inspired critical reactions in internet studies, not least from scholars whose work on the internet is rooted in anthropological ethnography (e.g. Miller 2011 Postill 2011) who have shown that the experienced and practiced realities of everyday internet use cannot be wholly explained by these grand theories, and indeed sometimes directly contradict their logics. This is not to say that sociological theories of network and community do not provide useful frameworks for understanding the internet and its relation to everyday media technologies (see Pink 2012d). Indeed, these concepts lead us to routes to knowledge that enable us to situate the way the internet is used, experienced, practiced, and co-created in everyday life in relation to wider societal, economic, corporate and other processes and on the terms of specific disciplinary trajectories and priorities. However, the task of the digital visual ethnographer is in part to focus on the detail that such theories cannot attend to and to do so in ways that await the unexpected, unanticipated and the invisible. In what follows I ask what theoretical framings might offer us both the freedom to do this and the opportunity to use digital media to build not only ethnographic knowledge but also theoretical contributions.

Another set of theoretical explorations that provide insights for visual ethnographers are those that explore the nature and relationships of the emerging digital environments in which we research. The media historian William Uricchio considers the invisible mathematical framing of the environment when he writes of what he calls the algorithmic turn, pointing out that 'although difficult to "see" (after all, we attend to the images before us and not to the underlying selection and organisation process), the algorithmic domain ultimately determines *what* we see, and even *how* we see it' (2011: 33). According to Uricchio, 'over the past decade or so we have had increased access to new ways of representing and seeing the world, ways dependent on algorithmic interventions between the viewing subject and the object viewed' (2011: 25). This is manifested, he tells us, in the ways we see participatory media such as Wikipedia and 'the dynamic and location-aware cartographic systems that we can find on our iPhones and TomToms' (2011: 26). Uricchio explores in depth what this means by looking at the example of Photo-synth software which synthesises multiple photographs to create a new perspective on the 'whole'. His argument is that: 'applications like Photosynth and augmented reality share a fundamental realignment of subject–object relations thanks to their algorithmic processing layer', they resituate 'human agency' and 'the stubborn fixities of the world viewed' (2011: 33). Thus, 'The algorithmically enabled interplay between the viewer's position in the physical world and this virtual information layer is transformative, creating sites of meaning and enabling action' (2011: 33). For web-based visual ethnography the implications are to invite us to add this to our reflexive awareness of what it is that we, and others, see when engaging with digital images, and to be aware of the invisible architectures that participate in the ways that we are situated as viewers.

In the context of methodological discussions Francesco Lapenta (2012), drawing on the work of Uricchio as well as Lev Manovich's work on information visualisation techniques (Manovich 2011), has focused on how digital mapping and its related technologies likewise create new invisible architectures that frame a context for the emergence of visual research methods. Focusing on the 'new forms of representation and visualization of communications and social interaction' (2012: 134) associated with these technologies, Lapenta argues that they have implications for sociological and ethnographic research that go beyond the approaches to online ethnography discussed above. Focusing on the visuality of the web 2.0 environment, he argues that web applications (such as 'Wikimapia, OpenStreetMap, Google Earth, Google Maps, Google Places, and Google Latitude, Foursquare, Gowalla, Flickr, Facebook Places, MyMaps etc') could be described as 'defining a new geospatial turn and new visual trajectory for the Web' in a context where 'the virtual aspects of individuals' Web 2.0 online interactions, identities and communications are localized and visually merged on a virtual map with the real spaces of users' existence' (2012: 134). In practical terms the implications for visual researchers are that 'These new technologies ... become meaningful elements to project, organize, make visible and study the social performances, personal identities, mediated interactions, and the "imagined" communities of the media users that created them' (Lapenta 2012: 147). While to date little attention has been paid to these invisible technological architectures of the internet in visual ethnography practice (an exception is Pink and Hjorth 2012) these investigations invite digital visual ethnographers to acknowledge the ways that their practice, and the types of knowledge that they may produce, are inevitably situated by their presence and framings of the web and its applications. Both Uricchio's and Lapenta's commentaries link nicely to the concept of the mobile web, in that they account for the way mobility and location-based technologies are implicated in how the visuality of digital environments is constituted and experienced. As I stress in earlier chapters, images are produced and experienced in movement; this point is equally applicable to those discussed in these paragraphs. Particularly (as discussed elsewhere), for instance, in the examples of how visual ethnographers might traverse web-based contexts such as Google Street View (Pink 2011a) and as Larissa Hjorth and I show elsewhere they can enable us to understand the digital environment within which camera-phone photography is practiced and experienced (Pink and Hjorth 2012).

These theoretical viewpoints offer us ways to conceptualise the internet as an environment or invisible architecture. Yet to understand the potential of visual internet ethnography we need to examine how the internet has been researched and understood ethnographically. This is not a straightforward task in that the Internet is not just one thing, and single web platforms tend to not have just one use or definition. Yet there is an increasingly rich series of ethnographic accounts and analyses which collectively demonstrate what the internet is like as an ethnographic site, how it is interwoven with non-digital realities and materialities and how we might engage with these using visual ethnography approaches. There is moreover an interesting visuality to internet or web-based ethnography that intertwines image production, manipulation, browsing and posting, which offers exciting practical opportunities for visual ethnography practice.

While definitions of web 2.0 (and its future transformations into web 3.0 and further) are debated, Nancy Baym's comments provide a solid starting point. Baym notes that although much of the content of web 1.0 was also generated by users, 'The hallmark of web 2.0 is often taken to be user-generated content' (2010: 16), characterised by wikis, and Social Network Sites (2010: 16–17). Yet web 2.0 has also coincided with the proliferation of digital visual technologies, meaning that, as we will see in the examples discussed below, the content that users generate includes photography, video and other visual forms. Moreover, web 2.0 is not a static form, it is a part of our lives, and neither is it just one technology, but rather because it is in part user-generated it comes into being in a continually emergent way through the use of a range of differentiated digital technologies. At the same time however, our understandings of the ways and extent that web 2.0 becomes part of everyday life, access to it, and more should necessarily avoid the elusive 'we' that characterises some accounts. This has implications for the ways we understand the roles of users to be in generating content. Larissa Hjorth points out that much of the discussion of web 2.0 has been characterised by an 'over-determined user-empowerment rhetoric' (2010: 74). We need to be critical of such tendencies and account for, as Hjorth puts it, the processes through which, as she describes it 'as the internet is transformed by the creative social networking potentialities of Web 2.0 localities, the fact of techno-social inequalities and the role of power collectively problematizes a "bottom-up" egalitarian model that participatory online popular culture claims' (2010: 74). The implication for digital visual ethnography practice is, perhaps unsurprisingly, that as ethnographers our role is, rather than to expect the theoretical and technologically focused possibilities of participation to be realities, to instead explore how and where user generated content and participatory online practices emerge. It implies that we should consider how these might be researched through participatory visual ethnography practices, and how forms of participation and user-creativity they involve enable digital visual ethnographers to learn through sharing these practices.

Photography, the web and visual ethnography practice

There is a growing literature about digital photography and its practice, which spans academic disciplines including anthropology, cultural studies, sociology and human computer interaction. This might involve a focus on the relationship between digital and analogue photography (e.g. Pink 2011e), digital cartographies and camera-phones (Pink and Hjorth 2012), how people become recruited to the practice of digital photography (Shove et al. 2007), or digital and personal photography (e.g. van House 2011).

Digital visual ethnography uses of photography as a research method have also produced studies that are at least in part about digital photography practices. For example Vaike Fors has researched Swedish teenagers' use of a photo-diary social media web platform called Bilddagboken (BDB) where users can microblog with photographs, connecting with friends whose photographs they can also comment on through links to their pages or to specific dates. To understand the meaning of this web platform and its uses, Fors focuses on the idea of 'websites as fleeting, temporary and ephemeral place-events', emphasising movement and the potentiality of the meanings that will be created as users move through this web environment (discussed in Fors et al. 2013). In this work the focus on the visual becomes one that enables Fors to create an analytical route to understanding the ways in which research participants create and practice a particular form of interactivity in relation to this web context that interweaves with their everyday lives, digital photography, and social relationships. She therefore uses her study of digital photography practices as part of a methodological approach since she has developed this in relation to another part of her project where she uses video ethnography methods to explore how the same teenagers engaged with and critically responded to interactive museum exhibits (Fors et al, 2013). When viewing this work the visual contrast between the teenagers' engagements with interactive museum exhibits and their uses of Bilddagboken is impressive. Using different media the research design creates different indirect routes to understanding how and why teenagers actively engaged with one form of interactive exhibition while another seemed

Image © Vaike Fors

Figure 6.1 Vaike Fors shows how a teenage participant in her research described and showed her photographs on the photo-diary web platform much less relevant to them (Fors et al, 2013). Such photo-diary web sites indeed provide rich contexts for understanding what is meaningful to the people who participate in youth cultures that are otherwise inaccessible to ethnographers of an older generation. For example, the anthropologist Francine Barone (2010) has also analysed the ways in which the Spanish photo micro-blogging site Fotolog is used by young people as a route to understanding elements of change.

These initial studies of digital photography practice start to reveal the range and nature of the everyday ways in which people are using digital photography in relation to the materialities of their homes and other environments alongside their use of web platforms and computing devices. This is not a static body of literature and I would predict that it will continue to grow in the coming years, as new studies, and new web platforms, new mobile visual technologies and new practices emerge, thus making it a key field to keep up to date with. What these studies show is that by engaging with people as they use visual and digital media in their everyday lives, we can create routes to understanding their worlds beyond these media. Given that mobile and visual computing technologies are increasingly ubiquitous and moreover central to everyday socialities amongst some groups of people, attention to these through visual ethnography methods and media offers important routes to understanding a contemporary technological and social world.

As we have seen through the discussion of Vaike Fors' work, the relationship between online and offline practices and environments is important to attend to, in ways that are both direct and indirect and visual ethnography methods offer us interesting ways to achieve this. Fors' work demonstrates how this can help us to see the breaks or incoherence between online practices and offline opportunities, as well as the continuities. Edgar Gómez Cruz's research about what he calls 'flickr culture' in contrast offers us an example of how online/offline relationships are co-constituted through digital photographic practices. Gómez Cruz's work, focused mainly in Barcelona, Spain (but with further research in Oxford, UK and Granada, Spain) is particularly interesting because he actually participated as a Flickr photographer as part of his long-term ethnographic research. His work is that of a reflexive digital visual ethnographer who was actively engaged in the same practices as the people who participated in his work and was involved in shared and common activities with them. Therefore we see through the example of his project not simply how participants' digital photography practices are part of contexts or places that span online and offline, but how the ethnographic research process involves the researcher sharing this world and similarly navigating it as photographer and ethnographer (Gómez Cruz 2011). Likewise, Eve Forrest (Forrest 2012), whose ethnography was undertaken in Sunderland and Newcastle, UK, worked with Flickr photographers, here not participating as a photographer, but using alternative walk-through methods and engaging with participants as they went online to explore their online contexts with them. Generally we are starting to see how different photographic technologies and web platforms bring the online and the offline together, linking production and dissemination of images in new ways and, moreover, newly situating photographers socially, digitally and in terms of the places and environments of which they are a part. A further example is that of locative media or camera phone photography (Pink and Hjorth 2012) where, similarly we see that images are produced and posted online as people move through and experience and make their environments in material and digital contexts simultaneously.

Each of the projects discussed in this section has engaged with research participants through digital photography with different groups and using different visual methods. In common, each of these projects has recognised that if we are to understand what people are doing with digital photography and web platforms then we need to follow them as they move between and/or simultaneously participate in physical localities and digital contexts. This might be because they are using camera phones and are thus very obviously in movement as they photograph, because we wish to follow their movements online and offline, or because we are interested in how they move online – or all of these things. Yet the principle is the same.

Doing video ethnography with the web

Video recordings can be shared online on a number of platforms, of which the most prominent is YouTube. On the one hand such sites become digital archives shaped by the people who contribute to them in relation to the affordances of technologies and software. They can be seen as rich catalogues of emergent and traditional forms of visual culture, newly situated in relation to other videos, and potentially sortable in diverse ways. Media scholars have developed interesting methods for analysis of existing online videos and these might be of interest to visual ethnographers as analyses or surveys of web-based visual cultures, particularly in the context of planning visual ethnography research. However, my interest in this chapter is elsewhere in that my focus is on how we might develop digital video ethnography methods in relation to the web. While this is a field that seems full of potential, in their introduction to a special issue of the journal *Visual Studies*, Connor Graham, Eric Laurier, Vincent O'Brien and Mark Rouncefield have commented on the fact that, while the issue is dominated in favour of work on digital photography 'beneath the apparent domination of digital photography lies a more complex picture involving different mobilities, services and socio-technical assemblies' (Graham et al. 2011: 87). Similarly in reviewing this field, I have also found more reported studies of web-based uses of photography than of video. Yet any brief survey of a video hosting web platform such as YouTube will remind readers that the making and uploading of digital videos is also a common everyday practice, engaged in by many people and in many ways. Ethnographic filmmakers are also making increasing use of the web in the dissemination of their work, as in the case of Zem Moffatt's *Queer Giving* web site which hosts the film *Mirror Mirror* discussed in Chapter 5 and which I comment on further in the context of a discussion of dissemination in Chapter 10. In this section, however, I am interested not so much in how ethnographic filmmakers create and disseminate their work online, but in how we might actually use video and web-based media together in a research process. However, as the discussion here and in Chapter 10 will show, this distinction is not always clear-cut, since in participatory and collaborative digital video research making, co-creating and disseminating work online can become interwoven.

In this section I reflect on two rather different studies of ethnographic video and its online presence. In doing so I aim to outline to readers just some of the possibilities and entry points through which we might begin to study this phenomenon. Simultaneously, however, my aim is to suggest how, from the understandings of web-based video practices we are able to develop, we might further imagine these not simply as visual cultures and practices that we might study but as possible methodologies for web-based visual ethnography practices.

A good example of how different dimensions of online video sharing might become part of a visual ethnographic research project is demonstrated in the work of Elisenda Ardévol and Gemma San Cornelio. Their research which focuses on the production of short videos which are uploaded to the internet combines the filmmaking skills of a more conventional approach to visual ethnography with internet skills and media analysis, thus showing well how expanding visual ethnography practice online can also expand the scope of our research to encompass attention to both the research findings and the media through which they are produced. Ardévol and San Cornelio argue that it is important to not only study prominent and 'successful' YouTube uploads but that to understand the cultural implications of the practices through which such images are shared it is important to develop a study of video practices that 'while they are less successful, can nevertheless direct our attention to the production experiences of users and their expectations of the audiences of their products' (Ardévol and San Cornelio 2007: viii). They also raise questions about how such videos play a part in a process of creating urban space – which reflects the wider theoretical and methodological need I have discussed above – to understand how online visual documents are not separate from the ways that we define offline places, but indeed are part of them in ways that expand beyond their immediate physical localities. Their ethnography, which focused on videos made in the Madrid metro began, like many other ethnographic encounters, in a serendipitous way. This also, as they stress, was part of the way that it became a participatory form of observation (Ardévol and San Cornelio 2007: viii). They write: '...the idea emerged when one of us uploaded a video about the Madrid metro to YouTube, and we realized that other people were doing this too' (Ardévol and San Cornelio 2007: viii).

Ardévol and San Cornelio's research took the existing visual culture as its second starting point. They first analysed a wider sample of online videos that were identified through search terms (2007: x) before narrowing down the focus to examine the production and meaning of two videos in detail. Here, drawing from methods in media studies and in ethnography, they undertook a formal analysis of the narrative structure of the video, and online interviews with the authors 'in relation to the context of filming (how the materials was recorded and edited) and the context of exhibition (what for, who for and use of the web-site's resources)' (2007: xi). Their project demonstrates very well some of the possibilities that an online context offers visual ethnographers and the different methods that we might engage for this, such as: participant video maker; analysis of video narratives; and online interviewer. Yet further to this it gives us insights into, as the authors point out, how the presence of an anticipated audience of YouTube viewers becomes part of the practice of making videos. Moreover, as I have highlighted above, this example needs to be understood in terms of the relationality between the different digital/visual technologies that are engaged in the practices of both the participants in the research and the researcher, and how these are integral in the constitution of places that span material and internet contexts.

Along with new web technologies come new ways of engaging with the camera, and new relationships between camera and computing technologies. The webcam, although little discussed in existing literature to date, has an interesting role in contemporary and emergent digital visual ethnography, particularly as computing becomes increasingly mobile, and thus so does the web cam as it moves with smart phones and tablet computers through environments with researchers or participants in ethnographic projects. These potentialities of the mobile web cam offer exciting ways of thinking about future ethnographies, and they can be informed by considering some of the existing ways that the web cam has been used in ethnographic practice. The cultural anthropologist Michael Wesch has written about YouTube videos through a focus on the web cam and its use in the vlog (or video log). He writes:

> They are videos of people sitting alone in front of their webcams and just talking to anybody and everybody who care to click on their video. These vloggers talk about their day, their problems, their accomplishments, their hopes, dreams, and fears. They represent less than 5% of the videos uploaded to YouTube, yet with YouTube bringing in more than 200,000 videos per day, their numbers are not insignificant, numbering in the thousands every day. (2009: 21)

With fifteen student research assistants Wesch began to research this practice in 2007, taking an ethnographic approach to using the webcam and YouTube as a research site. Their methodology was, in ways parallel to the work of Ardévol and San Cornelio (2007) discussed above, analytical and participatory, he describes their 18 months of participant observation, showing how they were able to work with the potential of the web 2.0 as a type of public archive and as a domain in which ethnographers can participate, create and interact. He reports on how 'we have viewed more than 20,000 videos related to this project, and carefully examined more than 500 personal unaddressed vlogs. We also have interviewed several vloggers through YouTube's private messenger service, email, and sometimes through the video response system. In February 2007, as our attention moved increasingly toward personal, unaddressed vlogs, we began creating our own' (2009: 21). His analysis, which draws on comparative historical research about photography in Melanesia, is also distinctly anthropological. Wesch's reflections on how these vlogs can be interpreted in relation to changing technologies and forms of self awareness in contemporary society show how a participatory digital ethnography of YouTube can bring us to reflect on questions about media and social change more broadly. Yet he is also careful to stress the importance of situating the findings of the research in relation to how self-awareness is experienced on other online platforms as well as offline (2009: 32). The work of Wesch and his students is also visual, and interesting examples can be viewed online on his Digital Ethnography page at http://mediatedcultures.net/. Wesch's discussion therefore starts to show us how the web cam can become a technology that is both part of and extends conventional visual ethnography practice: it enables us to perform a series of conventional research practices in new ways, including the interview, and the analysis of visual materials. Yet it also invites participatory forms of visual ethnography practice that run parallel to the new media forms that have developed through the convergence of YouTube and webcam technologies.

These examples suggest that we can begin to understand the place of web-based video in visual ethnography in several ways. First, it involves an 'ethnographic place' (Pink 2009) that is multisited in that it crosses material localities and web platforms. Production and viewing might take place in diverse physical localities, yet form part of a clustering of persons and technologies that, together with the participation of the researcher, create a context of and for ethnographic research. Second, it can involve multiple methods, including participatory methods, the analysis of visual texts and interviewing (including forms of video elicitation methods). Moreover, video-sharing platforms themselves along with other web platforms offer methods of online sorting and archiving (see also Postill and Pink 2012).

Summary

It is not the right moment to define digital or online visual ethnography in any hard and fast way, and perhaps it never will be. We are working in a field of practice that is emergent, and where there already exists a good number of labels – along with a range of different actual practices involving different types of (emergent) technologies, materialities and visual forms. This context is also characterised by a number of exciting future prospects and possibilities that invite us to speculate about what might be possible and the implications this may have: what, for example, would be the implications and possibilities of the three-dimensional printing that is offered by additive manufacturing technologies for digital visual ethnography? And what do the possibilities of digital online co-creation and collaboration offer to visual ethnography practice? And how will these develop in the future? Rather than attempting to speculate about the future answers to such questions my point is that in a fast changing and emergent technological environment a digital visual ethnography needs to develop in ways that are simultaneously innovative and reflexive. The examples discussed in this chapter show how visual ethnographers have variously begun to engage with the possibilities of and emergent practices associated with web 2.0. They have done so in ways that are continuous with the possibilities afforded by the media, technologies and web platforms that have been part of their research methods and sites, and in doing so have been innovative and adaptive to these possibilities. Their work should not necessarily be regarded as a series of examples of methods that can be replicated, although it does represent successful research practices that others might want to try out. I prefer to see their practice as emblematic of the ways that new media invite us to experiment, to follow the action and follow the participants in what they are doing, and to use the routes they take through the web and through the world to create our own routes to ethnographic knowledge. There are many other possibilities that I have not discussed, such as the potential for developing digital storytelling or photo-voice methods within web-based visual ethnography practice. The visuality of web 2.0 offers researchers an increasing set of opportunities to innovate and appropriate methods in ways that are continuous with the reflexive, participatory, collaborative and ethical principles of visual ethnography practice.

Finally I would stress that we should not regard digital visual ethnography as something different or disconnected with the wider practice of using visual methods and media in research. To start with, digital media tend to become part of most visual ethnography practice in some way or another, and for this reason alone it is important to attend to their affordances and qualities. Yet there are more continuities. Internet ethnography itself grew out of the same era of reflexivity, multisitedness, multivocality and self-interrogation in ethnographic practice (see Chapter 2) which paved the way for visual ethnography in the 1990s. This 'reflexive turn' invited us to attend to the routes through which ethnographers produce knowledge and ways of knowing as well as how people, technologies and inequalities are implicated in this. In a contemporary context the participatory and user-generated content potentials of web 2.0 environments create ways to develop further the participatory and collaborative principles of visual ethnography as outlined in earlier chapters, along with the ethical dimensions of participatory working. As we continue to interrogate and explore our methodologies we can see how the online/offline world that is now part of everyday life can offer us a dynamic route through which to consider contemporary methodological themes such as the relationship of a mobile web to the ways we move with the camera.

Further reading

Ardévol, E. (2012) 'Virtual/visual ethnography: methodological crossroads at the intersection of visual and internet research', in S. Pink (ed.) *Advances in Visual Methodology*. London: SAGE.

Pink, S. (2012) 'Visuality, virtuality and the spatial turn', in Pink, S. (ed.) *Advances in Visual Methodology*. London: SAGE.

Pink, S. and L. Hjorth (2012) 'Emplaced cartographies: reconceptualising camera phone practices in an age of locative media', *MIA* (*Media International Australia*), 145: 145–155.

Additional material is available on the book's companion website: www.uk.sagepub.com/pink3e

7

Making Meanings in Visual Ethnography

The ambiguity of visual images, the subjectivity, innovative practices and imaginations of their producers and viewers and the contingencies through which meanings are made have been central concerns of the previous chapters of this book. In this chapter I take a similar approach to the ways we can hope to interpret, analyse and categorise ethnographic photography and video. The academic meanings that we as ethnographers give to visual images are like those that participants invest in them, contingent, they are made in relation to the contexts of our research as well as through disciplinary priorities, frames and practices and methodological and theoretical agendas. We also cannot but bring to these meanings our own personal experiences, memories and aspirations. This contingency of meaning is inevitable, and while it closes the secure possibility of extracting an objective analysis from the visual ethnography process, it opens the opportunity to develop an in-depth understanding of how photography and video participate in the production of ethnographic knowledge and academic understandings and, importantly, it invites us to focus on the relationality of images to other ways of knowing and understanding that have formed part of the research process. Therefore in this chapter I do not offer a guide to how to analyse and extract meanings from ethnographic images, such an exercise would be incompatible with the principles of doing visual ethnography. Neither is this a practical technical guide to using specific technologies in this process. Practical guides to the use of software are discussed in a range of existing publications, along with some useful reflections on their methodological implications (e.g. Dicks et al. 2005; Parmeggiani 2009). In this chapter, I outline how we might develop a reflexive approach to classifying, analysing and interpreting visual research materials that recognises both the constructedness of social science categories, the contexts and relationships through which research materials are produced and the contingencies and relationalities through which academic meanings are made.

There are points in most research projects when ethnographers need either to use an existing method of organising, categorising and interpreting the visual materials they have accumulated, or to invent their own. While visual sociologists and anthropologists have obviously developed ways of ordering and analysing ethnographic photographs and video, until the beginning of the twenty-first century little was written on the storage and analysis of qualitative visual research materials. While a wider literature concerned with visual analysis now exists, little of it is directly relevant to the contingencies of visual ethnography practice. A reason for this increasing interest is that as digital media became predominant in visual methods research an increasing number of software packages for qualitative data archiving and analysis began to accommodate digital video and photography. There has subsequently been significant discussion of CAQDAS (computer assisted qualitative data analysis software) and its use in visual research. However, often these discussions and the use of such software seems more oriented towards linguistic, semiotic and formal methods of analysis that are not commonly part of approaches to creating meaning in visual ethnography as I conceptualise it here. Yet archiving practices are part of visual ethnography practice. Visual ethnographers might have access to a range of digital editing and archiving software, in some cases using the same technologies as research participants. When we load digital images onto our computers some software offers us readymade archiving and editing options and in any case we may want to label and name files for simple retrieval, therefore even in the simplest form we are likely to begin to develop a digital archiving system for ethnographic photographs and videos. In a web 2.0 context new online archiving possibilities are also available in private or public web domains, with possibilities for sharing materials online with participants and co-researchers. We have already seen in Chapter 6 how the use of online video and photography sharing platforms in research also become ways of using or creating visual archives. Whatever system, technology or software is used it is important to be reflexive about how our use of it also moderates the ways we make meanings with images.

Analysis: a stage or a practice

In some ethnographic research projects the distinction between fieldwork and analysis appears clearly defined. In traditional ethnographic narratives this was achieved either spatially or temporally as researchers returned from a fieldwork location to the place where analysis would take place, or when project schedules dictated that the fieldwork period was over and analysis and writing up must begin. However, as most texts on research methods have emphasised, analysis actually continues throughout the whole process of ethnographic research (see Burgess 1984: 166; Hammersley and Atkinson 1995: 205): 'It begins from the moment a fieldworker selects a problem to study and ends with the last word in the report or the ethnography' (Fetterman 1998: 92). During the 1990s ethnographers began to account for the constructedness of distinctions between ethnographic fieldwork site, home and academic institution, arguing that interdependencies and continuities, as well as differences between these different times and location, should be recognised. Sometimes ethnographers do research at home or write up their work while still in the field (see Amit 2000). In this context it was recognised that a strictly conventional fieldwork narrative whereby researchers go to the field, get the images and then take them home to analyse them was not always appropriate or possible. In a contemporary context where the localities of image storage might be digital and online, when our visual ethnography practice may have a web-based dimension, this point becomes increasingly important. The localities of research, analysis and storage can thus overlap, materially, digitally, socially and temporally.

Therefore, in visual ethnography practice any supposed boundaries between research and analysis are complicated, not least because ethnography and our reflexive analysis of it may be conducted in the same or different locations or time-periods and we may develop insights into the relationship between research experiences, theoretical concepts or comparative examples at any moment in the ethnographic process. Given the multiplicity of forms the relationship between research and analysis may take, reflexivity about how this relationship develops in any single project is helpful. In part, for visual ethnography, this means scrutinising how we make meanings with images at different stages in the research process, how visual meanings are relational to other materials and ways of knowing and how technologies, software and collaborations with participants and other researchers enable and change these meanings.

Like all 'things', as insights from the 1980s already told us (e.g. Appadurai 1986), material and digital images can be thought of as having biographies. As they move between and through new contexts or situations, although their content may remain unaltered, in the new context 'the conditions in which they are viewed are different' (Morphy and Banks 1997: 16). As I have argued elsewhere, we may understand these trajectories or biographies of images as representing their movements forward in and through the world, as part of an ongoing process of movement in which their narratives might become interwoven with those of new viewers and materialities (e.g. Pink and Leder Mackley 2012). We can understand the biographies of images as they travel through the ethnographic research process similarly. Images first produced, discussed and made meaningful during fieldwork will be given new significance in academic culture where they are 'separated from the world of action in which they were meaningful and placed in a world in which they will be interrogated and interpreted from a multiplicity of different perspectives' (Morphy and Banks 1997: 16). Thus, for the visual ethnographer, analysis is not a simple matter of interpreting the visual content of photographs and video, or of studying the actions of the people recorded or photographed and putting these images into categories through which they will be analysed. Rather it also involves examining how different producers and viewers of images give subjective and contingent meanings to images, their content and form. That is, we need to situate images, and this calls for an understanding of the relationality between ethnographic images and other ethnographic materials and the ways of knowing associated with them.

Images and words: the end of hierarchies and beyond

To put the approach discussed here into historical context, it can be seen as a point of departure from the modern project of ethnography, which was largely 'to translate the visual into words' (C. Wright 1998: 20). This approach, which formed the basis of scientific approaches to visual research and developed in the twentieth century, assumed that while ethnographic information may be recorded visually, ethnographic knowledge is produced through the translation and abstraction of this data into written text. For example, Collier and Collier, whose approach is discussed in earlier chapters, saw analysis as a distinct stage of research at which the visual was decoded into the verbal through a process analogous to the translation of art to science or subjectivity to objectivity, writing that this 'involves abstraction of the visual evidence so we can intellectually define what we have recorded and what the visual evidence reveals' (Collier and Collier, 1986: 169–70). Through this procedure, they asserted that images may become 'the basis for *systematic knowledge*' (original italics). Following their approach, images can only ever be 'primary evidence' that has an 'independent authority' and 'authenticity', but that 'may often have no place in the final product of the research, except as occasional illustrations' (1986: 170).

Here I outline an approach based on the premise that the purpose of analysis is not to translate visual evidence into verbal knowledge, but to explore the relationship between visual and other knowledge or ways of knowing. Different types of visual and written representations bear varied relations to theory: some might be informed by theory, and others might seek to advance theoretical argument. In practice, it means that what we might call the analytical process consists not in applying a formal method to the materials, as one might if using approaches such as ethnomethodology, multimodality, semiotic or conversation analysis or similar established techniques. Instead it involves making meaningful links between different research experiences and materials such as photography, video, field diaries, more formal ethnographic writing, participant produced or other relevant written or visual texts, visual and other objects. These different media represent different types of knowledge and ways of knowing that may be understood in relation to one another. For example, when I have worked with visual and written materials from my research about slow living, I have been confronted with a range of different types of knowledge about particular themes of the research. They include notes in my diaries, video recordings, audio recordings and transcripts, my own photographs and those sent to me by participants, promotional literature and web sites, video clips and Facebook posts online (see also Pink 2012c, 2012d). During my fieldwork I have used these different digital and visual media to create, record and represent the stories and narratives of my research encounters in different ways. As I have shown elsewhere (and see also Chapter 3) I have taken with me on fieldwork trips in the past, video, audio and still photography technologies, and more recently a smart phone that can perform all of these tasks, so that I may use the most appropriate medium at each moment. Each medium evokes different

Interwoven fieldwork materials in multiple media in a 'slow city'. © Sarah Pink 2005

Figure 7.1 When researching carnival in Aylsham, a town with Cittàslow status, the first event that helped me to understand what was happening was the Carnival Subcommittee meeting held in the Town Hall. In my notes I wrote how I realised that 'Carnival committee draws together a range of people, their networks and resources to produce a multifaceted event'. I also highlighted what was to become a theme in my research as I wrote how people were coming together and collaborating under the umbrella of this cittàslow event. These observations, as well as listening to discussions about how and where different components of carnival should be placed, alerted me to the social and sensory elements of carnival. The themes continued through my audio-recorded interviews with Mo the Town Clerk (bottom left) and Sue the Aylsham Partnership Officer (bottom right), as they elaborated on the history, official regulations and dramas of producing carnival.

At carnival I photographed and videoed. My images were guided by events as they occurred and by the interviews and notes I had already made. I was keen to photograph aspects of carnival I knew were significant for slow living, such as an ice-cream vendor chosen because he produced his ice-cream locally. I was also especially interested in the activities of a group of teenagers who were fund-raising for a trip to Italy to cook at a slow food festival. As part of my carnival research I videoed the cake stalls and kitchen and spoke with those involved. I wanted to get a sense of both the busy kitchen and the excitement at having raised the funding themselves. The research I did at carnival itself linked with my next interviews with two of the teenagers who had prepared and sold cakes at the event, Katy and Amy. Here they discussed with me their experiences of and feelings about carnival and my interview transcripts thus produced a further layer of data as they situated individual experiences, narratives and memories within the wider context of the event.

elements of my fieldwork experience. Therefore the photographs do not simply illustrate the field notes, and the video is not simply evidence of conversations, interviews or actions. Rather, images and words and movements contextualise each other, forming not a complete record of the research but a set of different but interdependent strands of it.

Working with combinations of diverse types of ethnographic materials in this way does not constitute a new method. Rather it is a matter of making explicit the ways that many researchers already find that video recordings, photographs and other types of knowledge or ways of knowing become interwoven in their projects. Some anthropologists have developed reflexive texts that interrogate the process by which the knowledge represented in written or visual work was produced. Ethnographic hypermedia (discussed extensively in the 2007 edition of *Doing Visual Ethnography*) became popular at the turn of the twenty-first century, but went out of date as web 2.0 technologies emerged and CD and DVD technologies were surpassed. However, its period of use in visual ethnography practice remains a good example of how the reflexive turn could be articulated using this then new technology to make analytical process explicit. Hypermedia texts made using web site development software offered us to create layers and threads between different types of ethnographic materials, connected through hyperlinks which could signify multiple routes of relatedness. Such texts were not simply representations of ethnographic findings or films, but delved 'back' into the research process to show how knowledge was constructed. While DVD and web 1.0 technologies are now being relegated to recent history, some of the principles that experimenting with them taught us remain important in visual ethnography practice because they enabled us to bring together diverse materials and create or signify relationships between them within the same text. As a short-lived precursor to contemporary web 2.0 contexts they offer us two lessons. The first is of the importance of engaging adventurously with digital technologies as they develop because, as we have seen in other recent work changing technologies offer us new frames through which to develop our work and the meanings we produce with it. By enabling us to work in new ways with visual materials and organise their use in new ways, they invite new understandings and forms of knowledge, and as I have argued elsewhere, often new ways of understanding past materials and practices (Pink 2011a). The second lesson however is to be aware that these new technologies may be transient, as for the DVD, which still lingers to some extent in contemporary popular culture, and that they may soon be replaced by new software and hardware, with which we will be able to build new techniques and ways of knowing. In a later section I discuss further the implications of Geographical Information Services (GIS), tagging and contemporary web-based archiving for visual ethnography practice. However, first I focus on the development of an approach to understanding the relationship between the content and context of visual materials and meanings.

Content, context and the contingencies of knowing through images

Historically the way visual meanings were understood was dominated by a scientific-realist approach, through which researchers sought to regulate the context in which images are produced in order that their content should comprise reliable visual evidence of complete contexts and processes. The approach that emerged as increasingly dominant from the reflexive turn of the 1980s and 1990s, in contrast argued that it is impossible to record complete processes, activities or sets of relationships visually, and demanded that attention should be paid to the contexts in which images are produced, thus shifting the interest away from what we might learn from the visual content to how we might understand images as emerging from relationships and intentionalities.

A reflexive approach to visual ethnography frees us up to begin to think about the relationality between different processes, persons and things. It invites us to follow the action and the participants, following emotions and stories, rather than trying to control the visual research process by making it systematic. This is not to say that research designs should not, for example, create processes for undertaking similar research exercises across a sample of participants – the video tour method that is discussed in earlier chapters precisely achieves this (and see Pink and Leder Mackley 2012). Yet, the content of our videos is not systematically controlled through a desire to ensure that all processes and environments are documented in exactly the same way, but rather the shared principle in this method is to explore the same research questions through the camera in ways that are suitable to each participant and their home. This means that our analysis can be comparative, or if directly commensurate categories do not emerge from each tour, then as was the case for my cross-cultural comparison of homes in England and Spain, we can seek comparable categories (Pink 2004b).

However, before discussing the reflexive approach to visual ethnography analysis further I would stress that this does not mean that we need to completely abandon realist uses of photography or video – for example, to represent what something or someone looked like, or to document an event or process that has occurred. While we need to maintain a reflexive awareness that images are constructed, there is also a practical and sensible way that we can make claims that images stand at times for records of what actually happened, the sequential orders that they have happened in, and what a person or thing actually looked like from the perspective of the photographer. For example the photographic stills of the woman bullfighter Cristina Sanchez performing, shown in Figure 4.1, work on different levels. First they represent part of the process of a bullfight. Second, they document a sequence where Cristina was tossed into the air and then recovered. They are, albeit subjectively framed and selected, a set of images of a real event. Simultaneously, the reality that is invested in these images varies immensely according to who is viewing. As the Cardiff University Hypermedia and Qualitative Research team also report, in their work they found that 'We utilised both approaches – finding it necessary to treat our video footage both as realist records (which we coded qualitatively according to broad content themes) and as narratives shaped and generated by the researcher's interactions with specific fieldwork contexts' (http://www.cf.ac.uk/socsi/hyper/p02/findings.html). Indeed, both historically (e.g. John Collier's (1973) visual study of education in Alaska) and recently (e.g. Chalfen and Rich 2007) in multidisciplinary and team-based projects using visual anthropology methods, realist approaches to coding complex visual data offer a crucial means of managing and sharing data and triangulating findings. Realist uses of visual images in research are not absolutely incompatible with approaches that recognise the contingency of visual meanings. Yet they have a practical purpose and moreover can be situated through a reflexive narrative.

Making academic meanings: from fieldwork to scholarship

Ethnographers usually re-think the meanings of photographic and video materials discussed and/or produced during fieldwork in terms of academic discourses. They therefore give them new significance that diverges from or at the very least adds to the meanings invested in them during research encounters or by participants.

For example, in 1994 I returned to England after two years' fieldwork in Spain. This was still in the era of analogue technologies. I brought with me photographs I had taken, printed and discussed with people who had participated in my research, and video footage I was yet to even view on a colour monitor. The visual materials were as important as my field diaries and other bits and pieces of local material culture that I had packed in my suitcases. Now extracted from their Spanish contexts, these images, memories, experiences and artifacts had already become re-situated within my personal narrative, as well as having moved to a new physical location where they would inevitably be made meaningful in relation to new objects, gazes and commentaries. They had been extracted from the cultural context where they were produced, to be viewed and discussed in the context of my personal life and the English speaking academic world. Meanwhile in Spain, copies of some of these photographs and video tapes remained in the collections of my friends and people who had participated in the research, gaining other meanings, and taking on a life that departed from the context where I had been present. Maybe they were used to talk about me and how I had photographed or video recorded them, to discuss the event during which the image had been taken, or as realist representations of their subjects.

However, while the images I had taken home were given new academic and other meanings in new contexts, these meanings did not replace the others previously invested in them during fieldwork. Rather, we might think of the ways that meanings can be invested in images as being layered, so that different meanings may be invested in them over time, building on and perhaps contesting each other, but all of which remain, for the researcher, a part of the cumulative biography of the image as an ethnographic artefact. As such images may represent or refer to diverse persons, activities and emotions that may not obviously or directly form part of their visible content. Photographs alone do not represent, for example, emotions, social relations, relations of power and exploitation, but it is their biographically changing situatedness that makes them invoke these feelings and relationships.

Moreover, the anthropological meanings I gave my photographs were informed by meanings that the people who participated in my research gave to these images. For example, one photograph, 'The Bullfighter's Braid', became a focus of attention during the research. The photograph was published in a local newspaper and won a regional photography prize. Several local people and bullfighting clubs asked for copies. This gave me the opportunity to discuss the photograph and its content with a range of different people who I found fitted it into different narratives. Some discussed it in terms of art and its artistic value. One person commented on its 'natural', unconstructed and 'authentic' appearance. Others used it to publicise a forthcoming event. Through my exploration of the different local

The Bullfighter's Braid. © *Sarah Pink 1993*

Figure 7.2 This photograph of Cristina Sanchez became central to my research. During the research it was exhibited on local television, formed part of the collections of local bars, as well as of local people who had asked for copies. It was also published in a local newspaper (Pink 1993). Once returned to the United Kingdom it was exhibited in an ethnographic photography exhibition, published in book chapters and journal articles and was used for the front cover of my book (Pink 1997a). Not only was the image published in different places, but also it was defined in different ways and given new meanings as it travelled between these different contexts.

meanings the photograph was given, I began to invest my own anthropological meanings in it. When I interpreted the photograph in relation to the conventions of the photographic culture of bullfighting I saw it as an ambiguous image that both imitated and challenged the gendered iconography of 'traditional' bullfight photography. While it copied a standard composition in bullfight photography, the conventional symbolism was broken as the bullfighter's hair braid was long, blonde and feminine, rather than the short thin coiled braid of the male performer (see Pink 1997b). When I analysed this ambiguous symbolism together with people's comments on the photography, I linked this to gender theory. Building on different local meanings given to the photograph I added meanings derived, first, from my understanding of local oral and visual discourses on 'tradition' and, secondly, from anthropological theories of gender. For me, 'The Bullfighter's Braid' is laden with local and academic meanings; the photograph itself represents the point at which these different meanings intersect, thus linking the contexts of research and analysis.

In other contexts, the life of images as they are analysed can be interwoven with participants' lives. For example in Chapters 3 and 6, I discussed how in our research into domestic energy consumption video recordings are shown and details are checked with participants as discussed in Pink and Leder Mackley, 2012. Here indeed, the analysis can be impacted by participant responses as we go along. Likewise in the video tours I undertook as part of my research about Slow Cities, I was struck by how a participant's response to viewing a video recording made me aware of something that had not seemed important before. His comments on how the weather had been very different on the day of the recording might on one level seem part of everyday conversation, yet this feedback was important in that it helped me to think through questions relating to how we experienced the environments we moved through, and what I should be looking for in my analysis.

Images we can't 'take home'

Analysing ethnographic images does not only imply images ethnographers take themselves, take away, and perhaps later take back to participants. For example, the elderly people who participated in Okely's (1994) research discussed in Chapter 4 showed her their photographs, and these images formed part of her experience of their memories and histories. The photographs Okely describes comprise part of her ethnographic knowledge and are indispensable to her discussion and analysis. However, she does not mention having the photographs copied or taking them away for analysis. Images that are materially and visually absent from our field notes still form an important part of the analysis of ethnographic knowledge.

In Spain, I researched the career of Antoñita, a woman ex-bullfighter (see Pink 1997a). Similarly, Antoñita showed me her collection of snapshots that documented moments of development and success in her short career and she lent me a video of her performances that I viewed with a group of her friends. It did not feel appropriate to ask for copies of the prints and tapes. However, these images and her uses of them to criticise her performances and reminisce about old acquaintances and events were central to my analysis of her career and how she represented herself in relation to other individuals, institutions and activities in the local bullfighting world. I also took notes on the event of viewing the video and how Antoñita's friends had used it to discuss her performance, skills and career. My analysis was not only of the visual content of video text, but of how people had used it to speak about the woman bullfighter. In these projects the visual content of the Spanish bullfighting video was relevant to my analysis. However, it was less important to ask for copies of the video itself in order to subject it to a systematic content analysis than it was to analyse how it was used to represent and discuss the themes of my research.

Likewise when researching Slow Cities, I found that at many of the events I attended, visual displays were an important part of the environments that research participants created. Often I was able to photograph these displays as a form of visual note taking, and this enabled me to remember and consider analytically the ways in which Slow City leaders constructed the memories and trajectories of their Slow City identities. However, sometimes the displays were digital, involving slide shows or Powerpoint loops (see Pink 2011e). In these situations my interest was to some extent in the narratives that these displays constructed, but, also taking a non-representational approach, I was concerned analytically in the roles these digitally projected loops of images played in the constitution of these events as wider environments. My analytical task was therefore not one of collecting, capturing and deconstructing the images or their content. Instead I was interested in how these images, which were the outcomes of past events that I had been told about by participants, or in some cases attended myself, became visual strands, which were combined with other elements to create Slow City environments.

As visual ethnographers we often need to confront the challenge that there are things that we cannot take away with us in any tangible or visual form. Yet, because these elements of our experiences of ethnographic encounters will always exist in relation to the notes, diaries, objects and images that we can keep we may use our imaginations and associations to be able to invoke them.

Ordering ethnographic images

Just as research methods are usually shaped by the project they serve and are frequently developed during fieldwork, categorising research materials is often a task that ethnographers need to develop in connection with both the specific research materials they have produced and the questions that they wish to pose of them. Because analysis is an ongoing process however, the ways in which materials are categorised will also depend on the emergent themes that have already begun to be established during the research process. Therefore we should see the ways that images are organised in the process of analysis, instead, as being a rather dynamic, changing and ongoing process, which involves sets of theoretical and ethical principles and should be reflexive.

That archives can be imbued with relations of power, like other classificatory systems, was made clear in the critiques of the modern archive developed notably in the 1980s and 1990s, generating an important layer of reflexive awareness around the question of how meanings are produced through archiving practices (see for example, Edwards 1992; Sekula 1989; Lury 1998; Price and Wells 1997), thus calling for a reflexive appreciation of the connections we construct between and among photographs and other visual and verbal materials. The implication for visual ethnography is that we need to understand how such connections contribute to the production of academic ways of knowing.

There is always some tension between different ways of ordering reality through visual images. For example, when ethnographers organise fieldwork photographs they have to contemplate differences between their own personal and academic ways of ordering reality and the orders by which local people construct their worlds and histories visually. Below I suggest some ways this may be resolved, arguing that this tension should be represented in the way images are organised. Indeed in a digital context new possibilities have moreover developed to make archives open, participatory and collaborative, allowing access to them by the people whose images are included, offering possibilities for the making of connections, annotations, the contestation of meanings and more.

The question of how we organise and order the images that emerge from ethnographic projects depends on a series of questions, including the research questions, the nature of the images and the ethnographic encounters from which they have emerged. For example, during my research in Spain in the 1990s I showed three women my photographs of a bullfight we had attended together. I had kept (and numbered) the photographs in the order in which the printers returned them. However, they soon became reorganised as the women prioritised and selected images that represented the event for them. For example, they categorised the images into those of their favourite bullfighter, those of themselves, and photographs they found aesthetically pleasing but not of documentary significance. Their reorganisation of my photographs represented aspects of their experience of the bullfight, centring on their own participation and their favourite bullfighter's performance. Key images showed him waving to the part of the arena where we sat and highlights of his performance. Therefore for my analysis, the temporal sequence in which I took the photographs was less important than the women's comments on, and arrangement of, them, for this was the moment where their knowledge intersected with my photographs. In my analysis these photographs became visual representations of local and personal knowledge and understandings of a specific bullfight and of particular individuals. Ordered temporally and photographed as a systematic record of the procedure of the event on *my* terms rather than on the terms these women had shown me, the set of images would have been little more than a representation of particular performers working to the usual format of the bullfight.

While the original shooting order should not necessarily pre-determine the narrative of any visual representation, it should not be abandoned as it will help situate the images temporally and spatially within the research process. It is useful to keep note of the shooting order to describe the formal structure of events and activities and reflect on how ethnographers structure visual narratives. Using digital technologies the sequencing and spatiality of image production can, moreover, be tagged on digital maps enabling us to analytically trace the ways that images emerge from specific environmental configurations as they change and move temporally and spatially. However, such sequencing is not the only, or the most authentic, version or narrative, as the example of how my bullfighting photographs were re-ordered shows. Likewise, in a digital context the ways that photographs create meanings in relation to each other can involve jumps in sequencing, as shown by the images of my experiences of touring in Slow Cities in Figures 4.3 and 4.4. As Sean Mack, Liza Mack, Lilian Alessa and Andrew Klilskey show through their project to map and reconstruct an abandoned Alaskan village, Geographical Information Systems (GIS) can also be important in locating buildings shown in old photographs, and routes that were used in the past (Mack et al. 2011).

Dealing with diverse photographic meanings

The same image may simultaneously be given different meanings in different (but often interconnected) situations, each of which has ethnographic significance. This means that our systems of ordering and storing images should account for their ambiguity of meaning and fickle adherence to categories and that acknowledge the arbitrary nature of their interconnected meanings and are not dominated by content-based typologies or temporally determined sequences. Below, by interrogating just one photograph, I demonstrate that to place an image in a single category denies the richness of its potential for facilitating and communicating ethnographic understandings. This example discusses how a single photograph taken during fieldwork in Spain was invested with ethnographic meanings that drew together other resources of knowledge about the photograph's subject and her culture. While the image alone reveals nothing, it is given ethnographic meaning when linked to other types of knowledge through my analysis.

The photograph in Figure 7.3 was taken in 1992 in the afternoon during *feria* in Córdoba. Encarni, my friend who also participated in my research, had dressed up in her *traje corto* especially to meet me for the afternoon, show me around the *feria,* and have a drink. She also wanted to show me her outfit because she thought seeing it would be interesting for me and useful for my research. We were engaged in two different leisure activities. Mine was vacation and tourist leisure, and in part my photography was structured by this. Her leisure was *feria* and time with a friend. Simultaneously, our professional agendas were intertwined: one theme of the outing was my anthropological research; another was her chance to practise the spoken English that she needed to do well in her exams. When we planned to

Figure 7.3 This photograph of Encarni became the subject of my other informants' discussions about the image of a 'traditional woman', it became part of her family and personal photograph collection and it also became a reference point in my own academic work, at a conference and in my book, as shown here (Pink 1997a: 74, Figure 10). The original caption to the photograph was as follows:

> Encarni is an English teacher in a FE college in Spain. She has no interest in bullfighting and does not lead what she considers to be a 'traditional' lifestyle. However she is interested in some traditional music and dance and dresses in her *traje corto* for the *feria*. One day during *feria* she dressed in her *traje* so that I may see her 'traditional' costume and photograph her. Most other informants who saw this image remarked that she looked like a 'typical', 'traditional' *Cordobesa*.

meet she mentioned that I should take my camera to photograph her *traje corto*. This portrait was one of three photographs that we took. It was taken in the *casetta* (temporary open-air bar) of the *Finito de Córdoba* bullfighting club.

When I analysed the photograph and considered how it could represent ethnographic knowledge, I reflected on the context of its production. The afternoon was a special occasion, or at least not a normal occasion, for various reasons. First, we were in *feria* – a context some anthropologists would say is distinct from everyday time. In this sense it was a classic context for an anthropological photograph. Secondly we were in a bullfighting club's *casetta*. Encarni does not usually spend her afternoons drinking in bullfight club *casettas* or in the clubs themselves. She took me to the *casetta* because she thought it was the kind of place I should be researching. Thirdly, the occasion was a photographic moment: it was worth taking a photo because Encarni was wearing her *traje corto*. When someone dresses up in a *traje corto* or gipsy dress it is quite normal that a friend or relative should photograph them. In this sense the photograph simply documents a conventional photographic moment.

These aspects of the context helped me to think through how my and Encarni's intentions had intersected to represent themes of anthropological visual interest, local visual conventions and personal objectives. This enabled me to associate certain anthropological and local meanings to the photographs. However, once the photograph was printed, it was invested with new meanings in Córdoba. These interpretations helped me to link the photograph to other aspects of my research, each time making it more heavily laden with meanings.

The photographs were originally taken as slides. I had two copies of this one printed and gave one to Encarni. A couple of days later she asked me if she could also have a copy for her mother; the photograph had already begun to travel. Leisure is a key theme in family photography (see Chalfen 1987; Slater 1995), thus the photograph fitted into the family collection. While the taking of the photograph was not a family event, dressing up at home in the *traje corto* was. The photograph was also in my research slide collection (ready for a seminar presentation at the university the following year). A print was in my personal collection of photos of friends and of parties I had enjoyed in Spain. During my fieldwork this photograph album also became part of my research. Some Spanish friends who flicked through this album of friends, parties and trips said Encarni looked very traditional, very *Cordobesa*. Wearing her *traje corto*, she represented the beautiful traditional Córdoban woman. My mother, who met Encarni when she visited England with me and stayed with my parents, recognised her friend. Later in England the photograph had further adventures. In my PhD thesis I used the photograph to visualise one of the paradoxes of the notion of tradition in Córdoban identity. Encarni had dressed as a traditional woman for *feria* and other informants had used the photograph to identify her as representing local traditional femininity. However, Encarni did not describe herself as traditional. She has two university degrees and is an English teacher. She said she had learnt a lot about local traditions by helping with my research.

This analysis of the photograph was informed by my understandings of a number of other visual and verbal, individual and cultural narratives, discourses and practices. The focus of the analysis was not so much the content of the photograph, but how the content was given meanings relevant to my project. For example, the photograph of Encarni could be fitted into a temporal sequence of a series of photographs that I took of the *feria* that day, or a series of photographic portraits of traditional costumes. In my book I used it to represent knowledge about changing gender roles and identities in contemporary Andalusia. In the future the same photograph may take on further meanings.

The multiple ways that just one image may be significant implies that classifying sets of hundreds of photographs or hours of video footage could create a complex web of cross-referenced themes and images. For some projects it will be worthwhile to develop systems of coding images. However, this can be time-consuming and the extent to which images can and need to be formally managed in this way may depend on the sheer quantity of images, commentaries and themes involved. In some projects, images can be managed more intuitively. In my own experience, I have found that during fieldwork particular images and sequences of images become the focus of the informants' attention and these have tended also to become the main images in my analysis.

Rather than proposing a formula for organising ethnographic images, my intention is to offer a series of suggestions from which to begin working. Any system of organising and storing ethnographic images should situate them in relation to the multiple meanings and themes of the research. Therefore, for example, the photograph of Encarni would be linked to themes of discourses on family photography, traditional iconography and festivals, and this would connect with a range of other visual and printed materials including field notes, photography, video and local documents. It would entail a way of attempting to map the interconnecting elements of discourse and experience to which each image may refer when used in a specific context. A coding system would also need to account for how any one image may later be invested with new meanings as the project develops and researchers make new interpretations and connections between visual, verbal and written materials.

Organising video footage

Above I suggested how ethnographic photographs may be organised and connected to other elements of ethnographic and theoretical enquiry during analysis. Some of these general principles also apply to video.

First, in Chapter 4, I described some video production scenarios, emphasising the collaborative element of video making and the intersubjectivity between the video makers and participants. These social and wider contexts of video production should be accounted for. Secondly, the different meanings participants and ethnographers invested in the video footage at different times and the discourses to which these meanings are linked should be considered. Different people interpret the same footage differently, giving their own meanings to its content. As my discussions of 'The Bullfighter's Braid' and the portrait of Encarni suggest, local interpretations of images are of equal interest to ethnographers as the visual and verbal content of video. Thirdly, relationships between video footage and other research materials and experiences (including memories, diaries, photographs, notes and artifacts) provide important insights as each medium may represent interrelated but different types of knowledge about the same theme.

Video also differs from photography in that it communicates different types of knowledge and information and has different potentials for representation. Video communicates through moving rather than still images, includes sound, and the information is represented lineally on video (although electronic logging can enable one to identify key sections for analysis). There is not *one* process or method for categorising or analysing ethnographic video that every researcher may follow. Rather, this varies according to researchers' objectives, the content of the tapes and the meanings attached to them. In some cases video recordings are treated as realist representations of specific interactions or activities; in others they are used as symbolic representations, evocative of (for instance) emotions, experiences, power relations or inequalities. In some projects they fulfil both roles simultaneously. First, I briefly describe conventional treatments of videotape, logging visual data and transcribing verbal data, suggesting their implications and proposing appropriate uses.

Above I criticised analytical processes that translate visual images into printed words. Logging and transcribing certainly involve representing visual and verbal representations in printed form. As such they could also be said to define video footage. I am not recommending that printed transcripts and verbal descriptions replace video footage, but that logging and transcription are used to map, and make accessible, visual and verbal knowledge that is otherwise only accessible linearly. This should identify and categorise different parts of the tape according to their content and/or the diverse meanings that can be invested in them, and in relation to the contexts and relationships of their production.

Different projects require that video is logged to different degrees of formality. Especially when there is a limited amount of footage, it may be possible simply to work with these materials visually, without documenting their contents verbally. However, in many cases detailed documentation of visual and verbal knowledge represented on the tapes may facilitate easier access. This is especially the case for projects that involve data-sharing (e.g. Rich et al. 2000: 158–160). For close scrutiny of video this could include producing time-coded log tables with information on camera angles and distances, spoken narrative and visual content. If footage includes significant verbal dialogue or interviews, then these may be transcribed. Ethnographers who are interested in the subtleties of conversation and communication among the subjects of the video (and between the subjects of the video and the video maker) may find that a log of the visual and verbal narratives of such interactions is useful for analysis. Visual logs and written transcripts provide easily accessible versions of the content of video, if they are also time-coded, so that images can be easily located for reviewing. Using different approaches to the same materials can also be helpful. For example the Cardiff University Hypermedia and Qualitative Research team note that from their own experiences of working with ethnographic video 'The multimodality of video footage means that its meaning is produced on a number of levels. We found that coding of video was most useful on the level of categorising footage very broadly into general themes. For more ethnographically-attuned analysis, editing the video material into narrative-governed relationships and scenes produced deeper insights into the interactions between filmed participants (and with the researcher and camera)' (http://www.cf.ac.uk/socsi/hyper/p02/findings.html).

Close scrutiny of video footage should also account for links between the content of the video and other aspects of the ethnography (such as photographs, field diaries and notes). For example in Figures Intro. 2 and 4.4, I discuss my experience of interviewing David and Anne during my research about a community garden project. As part of the research about this project I interviewed and photographed David and Anne and David took me on a video tour of the garden site. I have also been to steering group meetings and interviewed the people responsible for managing the project at other levels. Within this research the video sequence plays a vital role because it enables me to connect the sensory and material dimensions of the garden to the administrative, bureaucratic and even emotional narratives that are drawn out more strongly in the interviews, committee meetings and chats that informed my prior knowledge of it. Simultaneously, without the context provided by these other materials, the video footage of David showing me the garden would be unable to evoke the context of the meetings, the sentiments of 'community' and coming together that were discussed in the interview, and the sets of visual and written printed documentation that were integral to the process by which it was being transformed from a disused site to a community garden. It is often by making connections between different sets of visual and written research materials that a deeper understanding of the materials is possible. Visual methods are rarely used in isolation from other methods and correspondingly, visual materials should be analysed in relation to other research texts.

The specific categories used to organise video footage in any one project also depend on how researchers intend to use video to represent their work. If footage is to be edited into a documentary video or a series of short clips, scenes may be categorised because of their ability to communicate on the terms of video editing conventions, their aesthetic appeal, and the quality of sound recording. A different basis for selection and categorisation might be established if the footage is to be screened as clips as part of a conference presentation (see Chapters 7 and 8).

Where to archive

Digital video and photography can be stored on hard drives, shared file spaces in collaborative projects, and online. To a large extent the ways in which materials are stored will depend on what has been agreed with participants, ethical issues relating to this, who needs to access them as well as security issues relating to data protection. Such issues vary immensely between projects, disciplines and of course the nature and themes of the materials, therefore I do not generalise here.

One possibility is to explore the possibilities offered by Computer Assisted Qualitative Data Analysis Software (CAQDAS). Although, it is worth keeping in mind Christine Barry's (1998) advice that 'Not every piece of software will be relevant to every task and researchers will often be able to achieve their ends using non-technology solutions or simple word processing cut and paste'. Barry encouraged potential users of CAQDAS to get to know the different programmes and their capacities, so that they will know when it might be appropriate to use them. She emphasised that such software should not be used as a matter of principle but advises that 'the individual researcher' should 'take responsibility for deciding how useful the software will be for them, which package they should use, and how they will integrate this into their existing analysis methods' (Barry 1998: 2.11–2.12). In some cases such technologies have been helpful, for instance in work relating to the (Video Intervention/Prevention Assessment) method discussed in Chapter 5 (e.g. Rich et al. 2000: 159). Additionally Amanda Coffey, Beverley Holbrook and Paul Atkinson (1996), and Bella Dicks, Bruce Mason, Coffey and Atkinson (2005) have suggested that CAQDAS with a hypermedia component might be useful for ethnographers as a multilinear device that can include visual images and written text and functions as an analytical as well as representational device. In their book *Qualitative Research and Hypermedia* (2005) Dicks et al. reflect on how they selected CAQDAS and other hypermedia software to analyse sociological multimedia data. Their work is a useful case study of the digital production, analysis and storage of visual and other materials within a specific project. Developments in CAQDAS continue to create further possibilities relating to visual materials and likewise the literature around this is expanding. Recent discussions of this area include the work of Silver and Patashnick (2011) who focus on the concept of 'fidelity' in relation to how software fits with the needs of researchers in the context of using software in audiovisual data analysis.

Where visual ethnography has a public scholarship dimension, and a collaborative dimension, the internet also becomes a place where ethnographers can archive their work. As I noted above, this needs to happen in careful collaboration and negotiation with participants, and might involve limited or public access web spaces. The ethical, consent and participant approval issues around this also need to be carefully considered and negotiated. Public archiving where appropriate enables ethnographers to produce an open and transparent digital trace of their research materials and practices, which might be commented on by participants and other researchers. They can also aggregate works from other archives to make themes that represent their own research interests, and/or link their own work to that of others, through bookmarking software and linking. This might be developed as part of a public visual ethnography and this enables other forms of participatory research and collaboration. There are a number of examples of the ways that ethnographers write up fieldnotes online using, for instance blogging platforms, presenting their work in public as it develops, and inviting research participants, other academics and a broader public to comment on and engage with it. Yet there are fewer examples of this in the context of visual ethnography practice. The work of Christina Lammer (e.g. 2012) offers one interesting example, particularly because Lammer's work includes interdisciplinary engagement with photographic, documentary and arts practice (see http://www.corporealities.org/wordpress/).

Summary

I have suggested a departure from the idea that analysing ethnographic video and photographs entails translating systematically recorded and contextualised visual evidence into written words. Instead, a reflexive approach to analysis should concentrate on how the content of visual images is the result of the specific context of their production and on the diversity of ways that video and photographs are interpreted. Photographs and video may be treated as both realist representations of the reality of fieldwork contexts as ethnographers understand them (as in the realist tradition in documentary photography) but they are always representations of the subjective standpoints of the image producer and other viewers, including research participants. This has implications for how visual archives and categories are conceived and demands that researchers pay attention to the interlinkages between visual and other (verbal, written) knowledge. This approach to visual meanings has implications for how photography and video are used in ethnographic representation.

Further reading

Rich, M., Lamola, S., Gordon, J. and Chalfen, R. (2000) 'Video Intervention/Prevention Assessment: a patient-centered methodology for understanding the adolescent illness experience', *Journal of Adolescent Health*, 27(3): 155–165, <http://www.viaproject.org/VIAMethod.pdf> accessed 12 November 2004, (discusses the analysis of video materials in an interdisciplinary team).

Silver, C. and Patashnick, J. (2011) 'Finding fidelity: advancing audiovisual analysis using software', [88 paragraphs]. *Forum Qualitative Sozialforschung / Forum: Qualitative Social Research*, 12(1), Art. 37, <http://nbn-resolving.de/urn:nbn:de:0114-fqs1101372>.

Additional material is available on the book's companion website: www.uk.sagepub.com/pink3e

PART 3

Representing Visual Ethnography

The production of ethnographic text, whether an undergraduate dissertation, MPhil or PhD thesis, monograph or article, has conventionally been referred to as 'writing up'. In Chapter 7, I criticised the related analytical practice of converting fieldwork experience, notes and images into written words. In Chapters 8, 9 and 10, I question this dominance of written words in ethnographic representation. I suggest that representation of ethnographic knowledge is not just a matter of producing words, but one of situating images, sometimes in relation to written words, but also in relation to other images, spoken words and other sounds. Part 3 therefore discusses the potential of photography and video for ethnographic representation in printed and digital formats.

In making written and visual texts ethnographers are concerned not simply with producing different forms of representation and knowledge, but also with what their readers, viewers and audiences will do with these representations. As James, Hockey and Dawson remind us, 'representations, once made, are open to re-representation, misrepresentation and appropriation' (1997: 13). One concern for contemporary authors of ethnographic representations should be how to create texts that will be engaged with self-consciously and reflexively and not taken 'at face value' as written ethnographic facts and visual illustrations or evidence. The agency of readers/viewers to make ethnographic representations meaningful on their own terms also raises ethical issues. As James, Hockey and Dawson warn, 'once we have committed to words on paper, or to visual representation through film, we may at one and the same time lose control yet be haunted by our representations of others' (1997: 13). Similarly, from their ethnographic filmmaking experience, Barbash and Taylor predict that '(e)thical problems will arise despite your best intentions. They may even emerge after your film is finished and in distribution' (Barbash and Taylor 1997: 49).

As these authors' comments have implied, therefore, it is impossible for us to know exactly how any written or visual texts we produce will be used to make meaning by their audiences. Yet, we can think through these issues with theories of viewing that will enable us to at least respond to the possible ways people will engage with our work. One way to being able to consider this is by taking a cue from anthropological approaches to audience studies. For example Elizabeth Bird notes how in the twenty-first century the concept of practice has been (re)discovered 'as a guiding concept with which to conceptualise media audiences' (2010: 85), which goes beyond the 'audience response' and 'media effects' approaches of the past (2010: 86). In doing so, Bird aligns herself with the media theorist Nick Couldry who has proposed that this turn to practice theory suggests the two questions of 'What types of things do people do in relation to media? And what types of things do people say in relation to media' (Couldry 2010: 41, cited by Bird 2010: 86). To this Bird adds a third question of 'how are media incorporated into everyday communicative and cultural practices?' (2010: 86). These questions, through their focus on practical activity and cultural specificity, begin to invite us to consider similar questions in relation to the photographic and video materials that ethnographers produce and publish. How, we might ask, do ethnographic photography and video become part of our everyday academic or applied intervention practices? What do their audiences 'do' with them? And say about them? How will they employ their own culturally and personally specific knowledge and experiences in interpreting our ethnographies? A focus on practice thus enables us to consider the audiences of ethnographic photography and video as active, as appropriators of our images and as makers of meaning. Yet it does not tell us what people 'do' with images in terms of how they make meaning with them, and how this meaning making is part of wider processes of learning and perception. The work of Tim Ingold offers us some ideas about how to think further on this question in ways that go beyond the idea of images as simply holding representations that can be interpreted, appropriated or misinterpreted by our audiences. Ingold suggests that:

> Perhaps it is the very notion of the image that has to be rethought, away from the idea that images represent, on another plane, the forms of things in the world to the idea that they are place-holders for these things, which travellers watch out for, and from which they take their direction. Could it be that images do not stand for things, but rather help you find them? (Ingold 2010a: 17)

By turning around the question in this way Ingold challenges the way we think about the image, and in doing so he invites us to begin to think differently about how we engage with visual media as ethnographers as well as how we might invite audiences to engage with our work. In earlier chapters I have drawn on Ingold's work to emphasise the idea that we might understand the production and consumption of images as something that happens as we move in and through environments. There I have focused on the question of how we make images in movement as part of the process of being a mobile ethnographer. In the following chapters I shift the focus to ask how audiences might move with the ethnographic images we make as they learn through engaging with our work and move forward with it.

This part of the book is divided into three chapters. Chapters 8 and 9 focus respectively on the ways that photography and video have become part of ethnographic representation. Here my focus encompasses digital formats, in that both media have become part of the current focus on electronic publishing. However, as we will see, digital visual ethnography practice in research is not always translated directly into a similar emphasis on visual media and methods in publishing, and often work produced with innovative visual methods is published in conventional printed forms that in some way encompass the visual. Yet new ways of publishing digital visual ethnography are emerging, and indeed generating new forms of publication, ethics of sharing and genres of representation. Therefore in Chapter 10, I go on to introduce some of these new forms and the principles that underlay them.

8

Photography and Ethnographic Writing

This chapter explores uses of ethnographic photography in relation to academic writing in print and digital forms. Although most ethnographers have cameras, in academic publishing photographs usually form part of texts that are predominantly made up of written words possibly accompanied by other visual depictions, including maps, diagrams or graphs. In many existing publications photography has been incorporated into a structure already established for written ethnography. Therefore, first, I briefly discuss how the recent history of debates about ethnographic writing has shaped the ways that we currently write and understand ethnographic text, before focusing on the potential of photography for the printed text medium and its contemporary extension into digital and web-based publishing.

Understanding contemporary approaches to ethnographic writing

In Chapter 1, I discussed the implications of Clifford's (1986) comparison of ethnographic writing to fiction. These pivotal moments in the discussion of the nature of ethnographic representation informed the development of a contemporary context where most ethnographers would understand ethnographic texts as a subjective, but hopefully loyal, representation of ethnographic encounters and of the people who participated in their research. Subsequently, comment on the constructedness of ethnographic text has become an almost mandatory passage in ethnographic methods textbooks published since the last decade of the twentieth century. This has involved an insistence that careful attention is paid to the literary nature of ethnographic writing, and how ethnographers convince their readers of the authenticity and authority of their accounts. Modern ethnographic writing was criticised for its tendency to describe the people studied in abstract and generalising terms, and in the ethnographer's dominant and objectifying voice. Instead, it was suggested that research participants' voices should also be 'heard' in ethnographic text, and that ethnographers should write reflexively in order to acknowledge the subjectivity and experiences on which their writing is based.

In 1995, therefore, George Marcus argued that ethnographic text should be constructed according to a principle of montage to create ethnographic representations that incorporate the multilinearity of ethnographic research and everyday lives (see Marcus 1995: 41). In contrast to the linear narratives of a conventional ethnographic text, a montage text would recognise that sets of diverse worldviews exist simultaneously and would represent these without necessarily translating them into the academic terms of a social science. In Marcus's words, '(s)imultaneity in ethnographic description' replaces 'discovery of unknown subjects or cultural worlds' (1995: 44). Marcus thus called for a type of written text that would not confer hierarchical superiority on academic discourses and knowledge above the discourses and knowledge of local individuals and cultures. He argued that while it is important to maintain an academic 'objectifying discourse about processes and structure' (1995: 48), this should not be privileged above representations of other discourses. Instead, Marcus insisted that a simultaneous and non-hierarchical representation of different local, personal, academic and other epistemologies, each coherent in themselves, should be developed within the same text. Therefore ethnographic text becomes a context where ethnographers/authors can create or represent continuities between these 'diverse worlds, voices or experiences', and describe or imply points in the research at which they met or collided.

An earlier example is Paul Stoller's book, *Sensuous Scholarship* (1997), which demonstrates how representations of diverse realities might coherently intersect in the same text. Stoller proposes a 'sensuous scholarship' that accounts for how ethnographic knowledge is created not just through the observation of visible phenomena, but through other sensory experiences, such as physical pain and taste. For Stoller, the 'flexible agency of the sensuous scholar is key. This combines the 'sensible and intelligible, denotative and evocative' and the 'ability to make intellectual leaps to bridge gaps forged by the illusion of disparateness' (1997: xviii), in his terms 'to tack between the analytical and the sensible' (1997: xv). A flexible representation 'underscores the linkages of experience and reality, imagination and reason, difference and commonality' (1997: 92). To achieve this, he combines a range of different textual styles, including a mystical Sufi story, poetry, autobiographical accounts, academic writing, photographs and a discussion of both performance and ethnographic film.

Text that allows academic, local and individual narratives to co-exist, implying no hierarchical relationship between either the discourses that are represented or their medium of representation certainly offers a temptingly democratic model. However, it should not be used naively or without caution. As James, Hockey and Dawson have warned, the question of how to represent multivocality should not be approached in isolation from a consideration of its political and ethical implications. While the ideals and intentions of multivocality are important, the question of 'whether such democratic representations are in the end possible, or even desirable, remains' (James et al. 1997: 12). Moreover, Josephides has questioned the possibility of a democratic multivocality as 'letting the people speak for themselves, or allowing them agency as actors with their own theoretical perspectives still may not escape the suspicion that the ethnographer is using them for her own ends' (Josephides 1997: 29). She questions whether ethnographers' strategies, apparently intended to bring the reader closer to the informants' subjectivity, really only constitute ethnographers' uses of informants' words to make their own points. Textual practices that are designed to give the subjects of the research a voice (such as printing, recording, or keying in *their* stories, perspectives, words, narratives or photographs) may constitute only a new textual construction in which the narrative of the ethnographer is just as dominant and those of the subjects subordinate. In this sense then we should recognise that as authors our authorial voices might frame and shape the ways other people's stories are told. Different texts will inevitably develop different balances of authority and voice. This will also vary according to the different theoretical, applied or other aims of the text, making it important for us to ensure that we maintain a reflexive awareness of how these relationships are played out.

In the 1990s this attention to the qualities of written text as a medium led to a large literature that discussed these issues in detail from theoretical perspectives (e.g. Clifford and Marcus 1986; James et al. 1997; Nencel and Pels 1991; Stoller 1997) and in methodology texts (e.g. Ellen 1984; Hammersley and Atkinson 1995; Walsh 1998). Just as ethnographic fieldwork practice has continued to be explored in recent texts (e.g. Harris 2007; Halstead et al. 2008; Melhuus et al. 2009) so has the writing of ethnography (eg Van Maanen 2011). Although a good amount of contemporary ethnographic writing remains rather conventional, the reflexive writing of ethnography is increasingly established in contemporary works and the inclusion of photographs in written texts is becoming more commonplace. An increasing number of authors have developed books with accompanying web sites where additional visual materials and links may be included, and as new and conventional forms of online publishing develop we are also seeing an increasing number of digital journals where photography, writing and other visual media might be combined. I do not review all of these in this chapter, but discuss selected examples that are of particular interest for the discussion here.

In this chapter I suggest an approach to combining photographic and written text that responds to the demands of the reflexive ethnography outlined above. I do not aim to advocate an abrupt break with contemporary forms of ethnographic representation, but to demonstrate how the incorporation of photography in printed and online publications offers new opportunities for creating meanings and developing arguments.

Photography and claims to ethnographic authority

The introduction to *Writing Culture* (probably the best-known critical text on ethnographic representation) begins with a passage in which Clifford describes the photograph featured on the book's cover. In this photograph, he tells us, 'the ethnographer hovers at the edge of the frame – faceless, almost extraterrestrial, a hand that writes' (1986: 1). Clifford does not discuss the reality of the specific ethnographic experience represented in the photograph, but uses his written words to invest meanings, relevant to the theme of the book, in the photograph. After this brief demonstration of the ambiguity and arbitrariness of photographic meaning, and the potential of photographs for producing 'fictional' accounts, the contributors to *Writing Culture* do not return to the role of images in creating the 'ethnographic fictions' and partial truths of ethnographic writing (see Clifford 1986: 19). However, in the 1990s other anthropologists began to examine how photography had been used to create particular types of ethnographic knowledge in existing texts. Much of this work focused on historical texts. For example, Edwards's two edited works (1992, 1997b) interrogated (mainly) colonial uses of photographic representation. John Hutnyk's (1990) analysis of Evans-Pritchard's use of photographs in his Nuer texts likewise revealed the power relations and classificatory schemas in which uses of photographs were embedded (see also Pink 2006, Chapter 2 and Edwards 2011). Below, I discuss how others have analysed the way photographs are situated in twentieth-century ethnographies, commenting on the implications of this for the production of ethnographic meanings and understanding other cultures.

Deconstruction of how ethnographers/authors go about convincing their readers of the authenticity of their representations has been central to discussions of ethnographic writing. This has included a critical perspective on how grammatical tenses have been used to situate the subjects of research temporally within ethnographic texts (e.g. Fabian 1983; Pratt 1986). Conventionally, ethnography has been written largely in the present tense, the 'ethnographic present', and some research methods texts (e.g. Fetterman 1998: 124) have recommended this to students. However, this convention is not without its problems as Pratt (drawing on Fabian 1983: 33) demonstrated. Her critical deconstruction of the use of the 'ethnographic present', led her to argue that 'the famous "ethnographic present" locates the other in a time order different from that of the speaking subject', thus abstracting and objectifying the 'other' (Pratt 1986: 33). In contrast, descriptions of the research experience itself would locate 'both self and other in the same temporal order', usually represented in the form of personal subjective narrative and written in the past tense. This inserts 'into the ethnographic text the authority of the personal experience out of which the ethnography was made' (1986: 33). Thus, while writing in the present tense has abstracted and objectified the subjects of research, writing in the past tense has constituted the ethnographer's claim to authority and authenticity.

John Davis interrogated ethnographic uses of photography in a similar way. Drawing on Barthes's comment that the claim of the photographer is that he or she 'had to be there', he points out that in ethnographic texts photographs are often used in the past tense, as the ethnographer's proof that 'I was there' (Davis 1992: 209). As such, photographs have been used to support ethnographers' strategic claims of authenticity and authority to speak as a person with first-hand experience of the ethnographic situation, and as a source of privileged knowledge. Stanley Brandes noted a similar use of photographic portraits in his analysis of photography in existing twentieth century ethnographies of Spain. Here, in Julian Pitt-Rivers's (1954) and Irwin Press's (1979) ethnographies, photographic portraits were used to represent 'evidence' of 'considerable trust between subject and photographer' and to contribute 'to the authenticity of the anthropological study' (Brandes 1997: 10). In this way photographs were part of a strategy to convince the reader and to position the ethnographer as an authoritative voice within the text.

Davis also pointed out that, as part of another textual strategy, ethnographers often situated photographs and maps in the present tense to indicate that 'these kinds of artefact ... are permanent and continuous. Anyone can see them and comment appropriately in the present tense' (Davis 1992: 208). In this way photographs were incorporated in what has been called the 'literary illusion' of the 'ethnographic present' that represents 'a slice of life – a motionless image' (see Fetterman 1998: 124–5), thus becoming part of an objectifying practice. Although, as Pratt (1986: 33) and Davis (1992: 214) have shown, in fact, ethnographers have tended to mix past and present tenses in their writings to particular effect. More recently Narmala Halstead has proposed that we reconceptualise the 'ethnographic present' from a perspective that recognises its processual nature, arguing that 'how we come to know is also about how we experience and question what is given: the ethnographic present emerges in this process and is produced as continual' (2008: 17). This understanding helps us to think of the ethnographic present beyond being simply something that is statically situated in the past and from which we might garner our authority as ethnographers to write of through textual strategies. It rather invites us to acknowledge how we are inventing an ethnographic present in which ethnographic experience, fieldwork materials and academic debates intersect. In this sense it is important that as ethnographic writers and photographers we are aware of the implications of the conventions and strategies of writing and using photographs in ethnographic representations as discussed above, as well as finding ways to acknowledge the processual nature of the ethnographies that they stand for. To demonstrate some of these issues I examine how they are manifested in my photographic ethnography of women and bullfighting.

When a photograph is situated in the present tense and is treated as a realist representation, a particular relationship between the text, the image and the ethnographic context is constructed. The specificity of the photographic moment, set in the past, is lost and instead the photograph is situated in a continuous present. It becomes a photograph that could be taken any time, a generalised representation of an activity or type of person. Such uses tend to present images as evidence of an objective reality that exists independently of the text, yet can be brought into it through the image. In contrast, by situating a photograph in the past, the content of the image may be interpreted as the product of a specific 'photographic moment'. As such it enables us to acknowledge the contingencies of the ways in which photographs are produced and the unique configurations of things that have needed to come together to create this. This approach which also allows ethnographers to locate photographs within the research reflexively, can be seen in the relationship between some photographs and captions developed in my book *Women and Bullfighting*. For example on one image page (Pink 1997a: 102) two photographs show two different uses of photography in ethnographic representation. The first photograph, taken of me with the woman bullfighter by a research participant indeed provides evidence of my presence when she came to the city I was living in. However, it is intended to function differently from the more traditional 'I was there claim' of an ethnographer photographed in the field with his or her informants. Instead, it is intended to represent the process by which my knowledge about local photographic collections and aspirations is linked to representations of self-identity in the bullfighting world (as discussed in Chapter 3). To achieve this it is captioned in a way that refers reflexively to the 'photographic moment' as: 'This photograph of me with Cristina Sanchez was taken when an informant requested my camera to provide me with an appropriate visual image'. The second photograph, of the woman bullfighter signing a photograph for one of her fans, is presented as a realist image, captioned in the ethnographic present as 'Cristina Sanchez signing a copy of *The Bullfighter's Braid* that had been reproduced on the back cover of a bullfighting journal ...'. It is a specific image of something that actually happened, and that refers to the relationship of my own photograph 'The Bullfighter's Braid' to the local context of my research. It is simultaneously intended to be an example of a common local practice – the autographing of photographs by local celebrities. Other good examples of uses of photography that are situated temporally in terms of the moment and context in which they were produced are found in David Sutton's excellent ethnographic monograph on food and memory and Greece. Here, for example, Sutton situates a series of three photographs taken by the anthropologist Vassiliki Yiakoumaki at an EU sponsored seminar on cooking in Greece. He then uses the visual content of the images as a reference point through which to highlight themes and issues related to his research (Sutton 2001: 62–3).

Images, captions, narratives and critical departures

Historical and contemporary uses of photographs in sociological and anthropological texts have tended to use captions or references in a main body of written text to situate photographs (for a detailed review, see Chaplin 1994: 197–274). Below I discuss how the relationship between word and image contributes to the production of ethnographic meanings. First, I outline relevant critiques of the way this developed in earlier ethnographic texts.

In conventional ethnographies photographic captions have tended to make photographic meaning contingent on written text. In Elizabeth Chaplin's interpretation this subordinates photography to the written word since when a photograph is captioned by text, 'it loses its autonomy as a photograph and thus any claim to make a contribution in its own right' (Chaplin 1994: 207). As Chaplin concedes, captioning is not always inappropriate: used correctly photographs and words can work together to produce the desired ethnographic meanings. However, in other contexts photographs need more autonomy. Chaplin proposes that to achieve this, photographs should be separated from written text (1994: 207). As an example of this, Chaplin cites Gregory Bateson and Margaret Mead's *Balinese Character* (1942), in which a series of images are printed on one side of a page and opposite the extended captions are printed. This arrangement creates a subtle separation of image and text, thus allowing some autonomy to the images and permitting the viewer to interpret them in relation to one another rather than connecting each image primarily with its written caption.

Different ways of combining written words and photographs in ethnographic texts are informed by particular theories of photographic meaning. For example, a realist approach to photography would be associated with a text that uses photographs as evidence, to support and illustrate written points. For example, as Chaplin (1994: 232) shows, while making innovative uses of word and image in Bateson and Mead's *Balinese Character* (1942) and in Goffman's *Gender Advertisements* (1979), photographs are treated as ethnographic evidence and displayed in terms of 'scientific categories'. Brandes's (1997) survey of photography in the ethnographies of Spain during the period 1954 to 1988 shows how photographs were used to illustrate abstract versions of social and cultural life of towns and villages that were often given false names, and of informants whose identities were 'hidden'. For example, Brandes claims that the photographs in Pitt-Rivers's *The People of the Sierra* (1954) both distance the village from 'reader's direct experience' (1997: 7) and 'impart an image of the Other' living in a 'rural, poor, religious, superstitious, technologically-backward Spain' (1997: 8). Brandes argues that Pitt-Rivers's use of photography created a problematically primitivising representation of rural Spain.

In the past such social scientific uses of ethnographic photography to represent generalised cultural characteristics and specific categories of activity, or artifacts, overlooked its wider potential for ethnographic representation. This was due, first, to a lack of engagement with photography as a medium and, second, to a neglect of the role of readers/viewers in the construction of ethnographic meanings.

Texts that explicitly challenge conventional scientific formats because they are constructed in novel ways, or contain subjective prose or images, invite new ways of viewing/reading. Good examples of this are still found in the work of John Berger and Jean Mohr (see also Chaplin 1994). Their series of uncaptioned images show how photographic narratives can emphasise the ambiguity of visual meanings, giving viewers/readers greater scope to self-consciously develop their own interpretations of photographs (see especially *Another Way of Telling* (Berger and Mohr 1982)). For instance, in *A Fortunate Man* (Berger and Mohr 1967), visual and written narratives are interwoven in the text but do not explicitly cross-reference one another. The photographs form a visual narrative or story that may be interpreted in relation to the written text, but are not illustrations of it nor explicitly captioned by it. Berger and Mohr's work is not ethnographic, in the sense that they do not intentionally and explicitly work to the academic agenda of ethnographic research or representation. Nevertheless, their texts demonstrate the potential of photography for ethnographic representation. In *Another Way of Telling,* they address the question of viewers' participation in the creation of knowledge and meaning from text, seeing photographs as 'a meeting place where the interests of the photographer, the photographed, the viewer and those who are using the photograph are often contradictory' (1982: 7). The photo-essay 'If each time' (in *Another Way of Telling)* is both an exploration in photographic theory and an exercise in offering agency to the viewer. The authors' introduction emphasises the ambiguity of the images as well as the viewers' role in interpreting them:

> *We are far from wanting to mystify. Yet it is impossible for us to give a verbal key or storyline to this sequence of photographs. To do so would be to impose a single verbal meaning upon appearances and thus to inhibit or deny their own language.* (1982: 133, original italics)

As they note, 'There is no single "correct" interpretation of this sequence of images'. Here Berger and Mohr beg that readers take a self-conscious and reflexive approach to inventing their own storylines or interpretations of the photographic narrative, and are aware that theirs is one 'single' understanding, among many possible others. Berger and Mohr emphasise that the photographs are 'ambiguous', and ought not to be taken at 'face-value'. If this approach is applied to photographs published in ethnographic texts, it invites readers/viewers of photographic representations to participate in producing ethnographic meanings. Berger and Mohr's texts present a strong contrast to conventional social scientific texts in their uses of words and images. However, some social scientists have recognised the value of learning from such examples.

In the 1990s Elizabeth Edwards suggested that ethnographers respond to the possibilities and challenges of photography by looking 'across the boundaries' of the disciplines that 'traditionally' use ethnography to engage with photographic theory (Edwards 1997a: 53). This, Edwards proposed, would be similar to 'literary awareness' in ethnographic writing where 'creative texts expressive of culture, such as novels, diaries, short stories and autobiography', have been incorporated alongside more conventional 'objective' texts. She argued that, similarly, two categories of photography may be used in ethnographic text: on the one hand, 'creative' or 'expressive' photography (which parallels the use of novels, diaries, short stories and autobiography) and on the other, 'realist' images, that treat photography as 'the documenting tool' (which parallels 'objective' written text). Used within the same text, these categories of photography 'might be complementary rather than mutually exclusive' (1997a: 57). These uses of photography in ethnographic representation would challenge the approach 'in which photographic contribution to scientific knowledge depended on the accumulation of visual facts' (1997a: 57) and 'the photograph is intended to function as a *record* rather than an *interpretation*'

(Wright 1999: 41, original italics). Edwards's ideas suggested a new potential for photography in ethnographic representation. Her approach also implied a non-hierarchical use of different types of image and knowledge within the same text, in this case the two categories of 'realist' and 'expressive' photography. As opposed to realist photography, expressive photography (like Berger and Mohr's photographs) exploits the potential of the medium 'to question, arouse curiosity, tell in different voices or see through different eyes' (Edwards 1997a: 54). It breaks the conventions of realist ethnographic photography by, for example, ambiguously representing fragments and details, and acknowledging the constructedness of images. Like expressionism in documentary photography, it 'aims to present a subjective reality' and 'the symbolic value of the image may be more important than straightforward denotation' (T. Wright 1999: 44). Edwards argued that such photography has a place in ethnographic representation because, 'there are components of culture which require a more evocative, multidimensional, even ambiguous expression than the realist documentary paradigm permits' (Edwards 1997a: 54). She indicated how expressive and realist photographs may work together, as metaphors for different types of knowledge. Expressive photographs, she suggested, are hard to comprehend since '[t]hey do not slip easily into preconceived notions of reading culture' (1997a: 69) and because 'expressive' imagery belies 'the *inevitability* of not comprehending everything' – it challenges the claim to authority and 'truth' that is embedded in the 'realist' approach (Edwards 1997a: 75, original italics). Therefore, by begging that readers/viewers do not take photographs 'at face value', expressive photography would encourage a self-conscious and reflexive approach to viewing and producing meaning from photographs. If expressive photographs are published alongside realist photographs in ethnographic text, they may question readers'/viewers' assumptions about the truthfulness and completeness of the realist photographs, and in doing so challenge conventional ways of reading/viewing realist images.

These 1990s discussions thus set the ground for further innovation and freedom in the ways ethnographers might use photography in their written work. In the following sections I discuss examples of how this has developed. However, to add to this I would remind readers of the idea that photographs are produced and consumed in movement, developed in Chapter 6. We should keep in mind that any photograph we take in an ethnographic project and include in a written text (whether with a realist or expressive intention) is the outcome of our own movement through the world. This means considering how the questions of what was above, below and behind the camera are implicated in the image, and how our written words might situate photographs as such.

Photographs in texts of words

Above I noted how ethnographers and publishers are becoming increasingly willing to include photographs in printed academic texts. Nevertheless, even now, in the twenty-first century, it is still not unusual to find an ethnographic monograph or edited collection that contains no photographs at all. Moreover, those ethnographic texts that do include photographs tend to have a dominant written narrative at their core and to use photographs mainly as evidence or illustration. In other cases, even in work that is rooted in visual methods few or no images might be included. Therefore while some ethnographers have experimented with novel arrangements of images and text, most contemporary ethnographic representation does not confer equal importance or space to photographic and written text. In this section I discuss uses of photographs in ethnographic texts where written words form the dominant narrative. There are multiple ways that ethnographic texts could be constructed with different arrangements of photographs and words, and it would be impossible to cover all of these possibilities in this chapter. Here I discuss a series of works that have stood out to me as interesting and inspiring examples. It will be in the practice of researchers and students of ethnography who build on existing work to produce their own visual and written representations that further uses are developed.

The academic journal *Visual Studies* (formerly *Visual Sociology*) regularly publishes articles with a high content of photographs. These take a variety of forms, such as photo-essays with various different contents and arrangements of photographs and text, captioned photographs, and use photography in a variety of ways. Many articles that have been published in *Visual Studies* (*Visual Sociology*) are informed by scientific and realist approaches to ethnography and photography (e.g. Pauwels 1996; Reiger 1996). However (especially more recently), others develop visual and textual narratives that combine realist approaches to photography with an acknowledgement of the arbitrariness of photographic meanings. An earlier example is Deborah Barndt's (1997) essay which combines her own documentary photography with commercial images, interview transcripts, academic discussions of globalisation, and descriptive and reflexive passages. In one section of her text she interlinks photographs and an interview transcript produced on the same day of her research to form a photo-essay in which interview transcripts caption corresponding photographs. In doing so Barndt uses the words of a Mexican tomato worker, Teresa, and the photographs to construct a story related to themes of women's labour and globalisation. While Teresa's voice is represented in the text, it becomes one narrative interlinked with others that is used for the purposes of the researcher's wider project. However, this photo-essay itself becomes a subnarrative in the author's wider, layered story as she later describes how her other informant, Susan, a Canadian cashier who sells the tomatoes, made the representations of Teresa meaningful in terms of her own reality. Barndt's essay takes a step towards multivocality and offers an evocative example of how images and text might work together.

In the articles discussed above, visual images and written texts are laid out alongside each other according to different narratives throughout the text. In others, written and visual parts of the text are separated to produce related narratives (e.g. Goldfine and Goldfine 2003; Harper et al. 2005). In the example discussed here the written text precedes the photographic text. Douglas Harper, Caroline Knowles and Pauline Leonard's essay (2005) focuses on the biographical experiences of Jack, who is an elderly British war veteran living with his Chinese wife in Hong Kong. The first part of the text describes his everyday life and biographical experiences of being a prisoner of war in Japanese camps, showing how the former is still shaped by the latter. This is followed by a series of seven photographs taken by Harper that, by showing Jack at his everyday work at the World War II Veterans' Association and in the war cemetery that he often visits, represent the material signifiers of his practices and memories.

There are many different ways in which photographs may be set within written texts, and vice versa. In the current context of social scientific thesis presentation and academic publishing it appears that the format of including photographs within a written text still dominates in much work. Yet photographs can still be used in novel and provoking ways in book-length written texts. For example, in my monograph *Women and Bullfighting* (Pink, 1997a), wherever possible I tried to use photographs to represent more than simply their content. For example, I captioned images of a bullfighter performing with written details of the technical equipment I had used to take the photograph in order to present my photographs as representations of what amateur photographers may achieve under those circumstances (1997a: 97–8). Other images were captioned in a realist stance (see 1997a: 102) and sometimes I made explicit references between images and the main written text. In one case (1997a: 74), I treat the photograph of Encarni (see Figure 7.3) as a realist representation, but its extended caption reflects on the subjectivity of both the context of its production and of the gazes of other informants who spoke about it. The caption aims to provoke readers to question their interpretations of the photograph and recognise the different ways in which the photograph, and the 'traditional' symbols it represents, may be interpreted. In more recent monographs innovative uses of photography, that go beyond illustration, have been developed in a range of ways. For example, Sarah Buckler divides her book *Fire in the Dark: Telling Gypsyness in North East England* (2007) into three parts. The first two parts are prefaced with two pages showing a combination of captioned photographs and poetry that work together to invite the reader to imagine elements of the contexts she writes about. Photographs can also be effectively used in written ethnographies to help to tell stories, for instance in his monograph *Localizing the Internet* John Postill (2011) introduces the key participants in his research through a written and photographic essay which recounts, in the past tense, an event that he attended. Using a series of photographs taken at a local event that most of these participants attended he interweaves their photographic and written descriptive portraits with the narrative of the dinner. In this text the photographs are effective in stressing the importance of the roles of these individual actors in both the research and in the local field of internet politics that the book focuses on. Significantly, for a book about the internet, they focus on a face-to-face encounter, bringing the materialities and socialities that are essential to electronic governance to the fore.

Finally, the innovative digital documentary artist Rod Coover (whose online work I discuss in Chapter 10) has also represented his work in printed form and his essays offer inspiring examples of how visual and written text can be combined. A more recent innovative essay is Rod Coover's discussion of using digital media in cross-cultural work (see also Chapter 10). Here Coover reflects on his own hypermedia practice, drawing from his *Cultures in Webs* CD-ROM (2003). Rather than simply supporting his written discussion with separate web page captures as has become a convention in social science writing about hypermedia representations (see for example Pink 2006, Chapter 6, and this book Chapter 10), Coover has used the designs from the hypermedia pages of *Cultures in Webs* as a basis for the page layout of his article. In doing so he aims to evoke 'the hypermedia reading experience by interweaving photographs, texts, interview excerpts and proverbs to suggest how relationships between visual and verbal referents evolve in the cultural imaginary' (Coover 2004: 7). His conventional written academic narrative is embedded within, and thus both framed by and part of the multimedia context. In creating this montage Coover succeeds in subverting the relationship between images and words to some degree because whereas usually in academic text images, quotations, proverbs, and similar are usually set in an academic written frame, here the relationship is reversed. Indeed the making of images with images offers an interesting way in which to construct representations of process and of what matters in ethnographic contexts. Other good examples of this include the making of composite images, which can be used to bring together different sets of, for instance, temporal, spatial and perspectival elements. An example of this is Dawn Lyon's development of a composite image to represent embodied work processes in her ethnography of a renovation building project (Lyon 2013: 36). As Lyon comments 'Making a montage of several photographs of Colin at work taken from a similar viewpoint but with some variation in distance and proximity brings adjacent moments (in time and space) into the same moment of seeing (now)' (2013: 36). Another example is shown in the work of Suzanne Goopy, David Lloyd, William Hatherell and Angela Blakely discussed below and reproduced in Figures 8.1 and 8.2.

The photo-essay in ethnography

The photo-essay, although a relatively well-known genre, is infrequently used for ethnographic representation. The main exceptions include articles published in journals such as *Visual Sociology* (now *Visual Studies*) (e.g. Bergamaschi and Francesconi 1996; Gold 1995; Harper 1994; Nuemann 1992; Suchar 1993; Van Mierlo 1994).

Photographs and written text cannot be expected to represent the same knowledge, experience or arguments in the same way. If photographs are thought of as a substitute for written words, and expected to achieve the same ends, then a comparison of the two is bound to conclude that written words do the job better. Rather, photo-essays are appropriate for representing certain types of ethnographic knowledge. Therefore, the definition of a photo-essay I use here is not one solely of photographs, but an essay (book, chapter, article or other text) that is composed predominantly of photographs. Sometimes the photographs are captioned or will be accompanied by other short texts. Some books or articles are divided into two sections – one photographic, one written – each representing ethnographic knowledge in ways that the two media best lend themselves. This interpretation of the photographic essay invokes the question of what written words can express that photographs cannot, and vice versa. Some have argued that ethnographic photo-essays (and film) cannot offer structural, theoretical or critical analysis. Certainly, photographs cannot represent social structures, words spoken in interpersonal interactions or conventional theoretical and critical responses to existing academic discourses in the *same* way that written texts can. Nevertheless photographs can be used in realist or expressive modes to represent, for example, the corporeal experience and facial expressions of people interacting with one another or their material environment, or people who stand for institutions and occupy particular places in power structures. They can also be used to create direct comparisons, and thus evoke difference. For example in an article that has a written text followed by a photo-essay, Rebecca Goldfine and Olivia Goldfine (2003) compare two neighbours, one of whom is a hunter and the other an animal rights campaigner. The visual component of this text places side by side photographs that represent comparable aspects of their lives and serve to emphasise their differences. For instance, in one pair of photographs the hunter stands opposite his wall-mounted stuffed deer's head, while the animal rights campaigner holds her living cat in her arms (2003: 104–5).

Photographs may also be used as critical representations, either with or without written text. Chaplin cites Pollock's (1988) photo-essay of portraits of women, to suggest that 'image-text presentations can make an important contribution to critique' (Chaplin 1994: 97). Schwartz's (1993) Minneapolis Superbowl project is another example of a critical visual essay. In this project Schwartz and other ethnographic photographers worked as 'participant observers' with a team of press photographers. Their project was to produce critical photographic representations that would 'examine the manufacture of the appearance of reality' presented through the iconography of the Superbowl – itself a 'repackaged visual event' (1993: 23). By using novel camera angles they produced photographs the content of which represented 'conventional' aspects of Superbowl iconography arranged in 'unconventional' ways. By 'representing representation itself' (Schwartz 1993: 33) in this way, the photographs represent the Superbowl iconography from alternative, and critical, perspectives, making explicit power relations that were not implied in conventional Superbowl photography. Their photographs are supported by provoking captions and a reflexive text about the context in which they were taken. Thus the photographs form the dominant part of the critique of the way the Superbowl spectacle was manufactured.

In Chapter 5 and above, I introduced Suzanne Goopy and David Lloyd's photographic research about the quality of life of ageing Italo-Australians. I noted that, based on photographs already produced by their research participants and on interviews with them, the researchers and participants then collaborated to create a photomontage that represented the key elements that they associated with quality of life. To represent this work visually Suzanne Goopy, David Lloyd, William Hatherell and Angela Blakely have developed a photo-essay that combines their own introduction to the work followed by a series of plates that use text of varying font sizes to represent the words of their informants, and both single and composite photographs (see Figures 8.1 and 8.2).

Photographs can be used to create representations that express experiences and ideas in ways that written words cannot. This is not to say that one medium is superior to the other, but to seek the most appropriate way to represent different aspects of ethnographic experience and theoretical and critical ideas, and, perhaps most importantly, be prepared to explore how photography can make a significant contribution to this.

Ethical issues in photographic representation

In Chapter 2, I outlined some standard conventions for respecting research participants' rights to anonymity and for demonstrating a commitment to protect their identities and interests. I suggested that the idea of protecting research participants is sometimes overly paternalistic and that by adopting a collaborative approach, whereby the subjects of the photography participate in producing and selecting the photographs that represent them, some of these issues may be avoided. Most of the examples discussed in this chapter reflect this approach. Nevertheless, whatever the role of research participants in the photographic production and representation, ethnographers/authors, in negotiation with publishers, are usually responsible for final editorial decisions relating to those photographs. These decisions should be informed not solely by the willingness of research participants/subjects for their photographs to be published, but also by ethnographers' knowledge of the social, cultural and political contexts in which the published photographs will be viewed and interpreted. As James, Hockey and Dawson stress, ethnographers should not only take an academic approach to ethnographic texts that acknowledges they are constructed 'fictions' or 'partial truths', but should also recognise that their representations can have political implications, and may be appropriated and used by policy makers or other powerful bodies (James et al. 1997: 12). When ethnographers use photographs to make academic points they should also consider the personal, social and political implications of the publication of these images for their subjects.

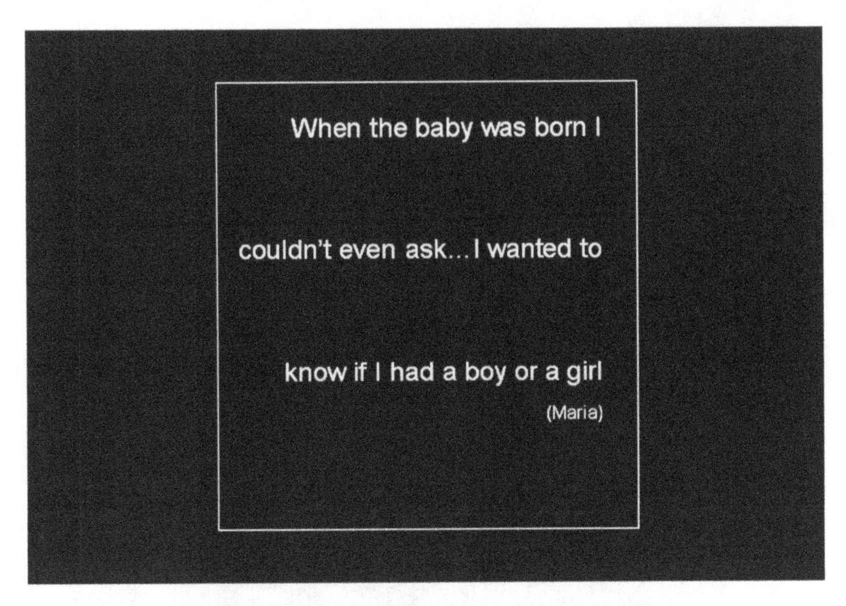

Figure 8.1 Suzanne Goopy, David Lloyd and Angela Blakely have developed an innovative series of images based on visual ethnographic research about quality of life, with older Italo-Australians. Here a quotation from a participant in the ethnography is placed next to a photograph taken to evoke meanings that emphasise how biographical and emotional sentiments can be invested in everyday practices and objects.

Figure 8.2 Here in another example from the work of Suzanne Goopy and her colleagues' (see Figure 8.2) composite images map the domestic space of their Italo-Australian participants, drawing attention to elements of the material environment and social relationships that are important to their self-identities and quality of life. One of a series of composite photographs by Angela Blakely and David Lloyd

When ethical considerations rule out using some photographs, specific visual representations of ethnographic knowledge or theoretical ideas have to be sacrificed or expressed in other ways. Particularly when working with children, researchers might find they are unable to publish photographs. In other cases the intimate nature of the research topic, or issues related to the status of the research participants, or to relationships they are involved in will mean that they do not want to be identified. In some cases identities can be concealed. Another way of protecting research subjects from public exposure while still using images of them in academic publications is by digitally blurring or covering their faces. Lomax and Casey (1998) and Dant and Bowles (2003) have successfully used this technique to publish video stills that guarantee a certain amount of anonymity. However, this practice is uncommon in ethnographic work and can be difficult to reconcile with the idea of using photography *because of* its specificity, yet it provides a route through which to invite readers and viewers to imagine the reality as photographed. Likewise, developments in software have enabled researchers to reproduce photographs that anonymise research subjects and localities by refiguring them in ways resembling line drawings. Examples can be found in the work of Hindmarsh and Tutt (2012) and Tutt et al. (2013: 47–8).

When publishing photographs ethnographers will also need to work with copyright, consent and permissions processes relating to ownership of images and to the people represented. These can vary according to national and legal contexts and therefore no specific guidance is given here, rather it should be determined in context. It is, however, good practice to always secure permissions on an ongoing basis and in a collaborative way as outlined in Chapter 3, rather than retrospectively at the point when one wishes to publish.

In some cases issues around ethics, consent, responsibility of the ethnographer, copyright and permissions might lead to the decision not to include photographs in an article or book. This should not be seen as a limitation or frustration, but rather it can be used to make interesting points precisely through visual absence. These might relate to moralities and research ethics or to the situation of the people whose images are not shown. Absence in such cases can be equally evocative as visual presence. A good example of this is Andrew Irving's powerful essay (2007) in which his unpublished photographs are represented by blank pages.

Summary

In this chapter I have proposed a reflexive approach to constructing texts that combine photographs and words. Authors of ethnography should pay careful attention to the theoretical issues, experiential knowledge and textual strategies that inform their practices of representation. This demands attention to captioning and use of tense, and awareness of how different textual strategies imply particular meanings within texts. Meanings do not, however, reside solely in texts, but ethnographic texts are interpreted and given meanings by readers on *their own* terms. Ethnographers should therefore consider how their texts will be situated and made meaningful in terms of other discourses and other texts. Novel textual strategies that combine photographs and written words to use reflexive, subjective or expressive texts or images alongside objectifying, realist texts may challenge conventional approaches. To read or create such texts reflexively ethnographers should account for how photographs interact with, cross-reference and produce meaning in relation to other elements in the text, and how these connections are given meaning by discourses and gazes that exist outside the text.

Further reading

Coover, R. (2011) 'Interactive media representation', in E. Margolis and L. Pauwels (eds), *The SAGE Handbook of Visual Methods*, London: SAGE.

Irving, A. (2007) 'Ethnography, art and death', *Journal of the Royal Anthropological Institute*, 13(1): 185–208.

O'Neill, M. (2012) 'ethno-mimesis and participatory arts', in S. Pink (ed.) *Advances in Visual Methodology*. London: SAGE.

Visual Studies (formerly *Visual Sociology*). (This journal publishes essays with visual images and photo-essays and is worth checking regularly for new work in addition to the examples discussed in this chapter.)

Additional material is available on the book's companion website: www.uk.sagepub.com/pink3e

9

Video in Ethnographic Representation

In Chapter 5, I argued that video is not simply a data collecting tool but a technology that participates in the negotiation of social relationships and a medium through which ethnographic knowledge is produced. Here I discuss how video may subsequently be used to represent ethnographic knowledge and knowing.

Historically, anthropological filmmakers led the way in using moving images for ethnographic representation, conventionally producing edited ethnographic documentary films or videos (see for example, Durington and Ruby 2011, for a recent discussion of ethnographic film). Successful ethnographic documentaries were screened at ethnographic film festivals, are used for teaching or are broadcast on television. This often remains the practice of visual anthropologists and the aspiration of postgraduates, although ethnographic documentaries are now increasingly published and available online. However, this chapter is not a hands-on guide to ethnographic video production; Masters degree programmes across the world provide practical training in camera, sound and editing skills, as well as ethnographic film theory. Ethnographic documentary production is a vast and detailed topic and is covered in depth in other texts (e.g. Barbash and Taylor 1997) written by practitioners with years of ethnographic filmmaking experience. Such existing texts are excellent sources of reference and I do not repeat their work here. Rather, drawing from the well-established field of anthropological film criticism and theory as well as recent commentaries on the use of video in ethnographic work, I take a different focus. Not all students and researchers who use video in their research aspire to produce ethnographic documentaries, or have video footage of the appropriate technical or visual format or quality to do so. Here I explore other possible uses of video in ethnographic representation, including using video footage and stills in conference presentations and/or printed text.

Ethnographic video: the legacy of visual anthropology

Over 20 years ago, Peter Crawford (1992: 74) listed 'Ethnographic *footage*' as the first of seven categories of ethnographic film, the others being: research films (for academic audiences); ethnographic documentaries; ethnographic television documentaries; education and information films; other non-fiction films; and fiction films. Here I use the term 'ethnographic video', similarly in its broadest sense, to refer to any video footage that is of ethnographic interest or is used to represent ethnographic knowledge. From this perspective ethnographic video does not need to conform to specific film styles or conventions. Rather, it becomes ethnographic when it is used as such. Therefore video representations of any length or style that are used to represent ethnographic knowledge may be referred to as ethnographic video. While video (or film), such as fiction, home movies, or television documentaries may be used ethnographically and might be ethnographic in that they are of interest to ethnographers (see Crawford 1992: 74), they are not discussed here. This chapter is about how video recorded as part of ethnographic research might be used to represent knowledge about or emerging from that research.

The history of and debates over ethnographic film have been well rehearsed (e.g. Heider 1976; Rollwagen 1988; Crawford and Turton 1992; Loizos 1993; Devereaux and Hillman 1995; Banks and Morphy 1997; Ruby 2000a; Grimshaw 2001; Henley, 2004; MacDougall 1998, 2005; Pink 2006; Durington and Ruby 2011; Henley 2010). A detailed analysis of them is not my concern, but is a necessary background for any aspiring ethnographic documentary maker. To briefly summarise this context as a point for departure, early ethnographic film theory and practice suggested ethnographic film should represent whole cultures and, to ensure its scientific value, ethnographic film styles should (among other things) avoid close-ups and attempt to film whole contexts, activities and action, as well as be minimally edited and use only original synchronous sound (e.g. Heider 1976). These approaches intended to avoid subjectivity and specificity and insisted that ethnographic concerns should be prioritised above cinematic strategies. In the 1980s, responses to these initial approaches suggested new theoretical perspectives that put new demands on film styles. For example, Rollwagen argued that anthropological film should be informed by existing anthropological theory and structured according to anthropological demands (1988). Ruby, one of the first visual anthropologists to engage with notions of reflexivity in the early 1980s, argued for a reflexive approach to ethnographic filmmaking that would break down the art/science dichotomy that had dominated social science (1982). Then, by the 1990s David MacDougall (e.g. 1997) had proposed that ethnographic documentary film should be used to challenge objectifying approaches in anthropology to emphasise the experiential and individual nature of social life and develop its potential to represent individuals and specific aspects of experience. This approach, which remains influential, informs a style of filmmaking that focuses on individuals rather than whole cultures and the subjectivities of both filmmakers and subjects. Since the late 1990s, when high quality digital video, smaller cameras and editing on a standard PC or laptop computer became available, further shifts in the practice of and approaches to ethnographic documentary making have emerged. David MacDougall (2001) drew from his own experiences of using digital video to make his *Doon School* films in India to comment on how both the filmmaking process and the sorts of films that he can produce then departed from those associated with the older technologies. As MacDougall (2005: 121–3) and Ruby (2000) have both indicated, freed from the obligations derived from making films financed by television broadcast companies, digital ethnographic documentary makers were able to work alone and in closer collaboration with film subjects, to follow serendipitous narratives during video fieldwork and represent topics or issues that serve both the academic discipline and the film subjects (rather than the agendas of broadcast television). In a contemporary context ethnographic video-making practice is shifting further. There is a growing interest in collaborative and participatory filmmaking, along with continuing discussion of the historical legacy that informs such approaches from the work of Jean Rouch (see Flores 2007; Ten Brink 2007; Henley 2010). Other recent works include those that continue discussions of indigenous media and ethnographic film (e.g. Ginsburg 2011) and experimental film (e.g. Ramey 2011; Schneider 2011).

The relationship between video research and video representation

In Chapter 5, I discussed how researchers may combine video with still photography, tape recording, note taking and other methods in projects in which video making was not the main objective. Then, in Chapter 7, I suggested how video materials might be analysed alongside and in relation to other research materials. Likewise, when video recordings which are already interlinked with other ethnographic media this relationship might be acknowledged.

Historically the relationship between what has been called research footage and documentary film footage was controversial. Some rightly argued that the same footage may participate in more than one category. For instance, Crawford defines 'Ethnographic *footage* ... [as] ... unedited film material, which may be used in its unedited form for research purposes or eventually be edited into a film' (1992: 74). However, subsequent approaches treated research and documentary footage as two distinct types filmed with different intentions. Barbash and Taylor argue that while documentary footage, filmed with an intentionally creative narrative, would be edited into ethnographic film, 'the essential point of research footage is that it be as unselective and unstructured as possible – in other words that it provide less *discourse about* social life than an *objective record* of it' (Barbash and Taylor 1997: 78). In research, '[t]he camera is deployed as an impartial instrument in the service of science, fixing all that is fleeting for infinite future analysis' (1997: 78). In this scenario research footage has no place in ethnographic representation; it would be translated into words. According to Barbash and Taylor, it would be unsuitable for finished films since good observational documentary differs from research footage as 'in its pursuit of objectivity, research filming tends to lack that engagement with human affairs that makes them, to their participants, real. The desire to be impartial tends to make the filming unselective, and so the footage may seem unstructured to anyone not already in the know' (1997: 78). Barbash and Taylor were right to insist that ethnographic documentary footage is selectively and carefully shot to correspond with structural and stylistic demands of documentary making. However, by using an art/science dichotomy to associate artistic, subjective and selective creativity with representation, and scientific, objective and systematic recording with research, they not only ignored the inevitable subjectivity research involves but by defining research footage so narrowly ruled out its potential for ethnographic representation. They delimited video research and video representation as two essentially different projects and in doing so restricted the potential of video representations for reflexive engagement with the research context. The relationship between video research and video representation needs to be explored in terms that go beyond this focus on the question of either producing ethnographic videos or translating of video recordings into verbal knowledge.

David MacDougall's discussions of the making of his *Doon School* films offer one example of how this might be achieved within documentary making practice (2005: 120–144). Rather than simply making a film he 'began to think about a long-term study of the school using a video camera as a means of inquiry'. Through this process, he produced a series of five related films, which had not been 'pre-planned' (2005: 122). Newer work in documentary research practice has created bridges between using video as a research process, something for participants, and part of documentary making. Rebecca Savage's documentary *900 Frames Between Us* (Savage 2011) is a good example. Savage's project focused on how 'event videos' sent to migrants from their place of origin in Mexico to the USA became 'agents in a form of "filmic emplacement" as their produce and consumption bring into being imagined places and selves' (as described online at http://www.docwest.co.uk/projects/rebecca-savage/). Her documentary combines participants' 'event video' materials along with researcher-produced video. It is described as using 'the juxtaposition of ontologically diverse images and sounds to provide an audiovisual evocation of this "filmic home"' (http://www.docwest.co.uk/projects/rebecca-savage/).

Beyond documentary filmmaking, visual ethnographers are starting to share and draw from ethnographic filmmaking styles as part of their methodology for exploring other people's everyday realities. Existing examples include Jayasinhji Jhala's discussion of how he has used a method based on David MacDougall's camera work in his film *Lorang's Way* (1979) that follows the film subject as she/he walks through his dwelling area showing it to the filmmaker and talking to camera (Jhala 2004: 62). In my own video tour method I use a similar technique, which also draws from established ethnographic documentary-making practice and was based on my MA training in observational documentary at the Granada Centre for Visual Anthropology (Manchester, UK). In my own work, as discussed in Chapter 5, video is treated as a medium that can record a trace of our movement through the world. Ethnographic video research and documentary techniques are thus sharing methodology and practice in a way that suggests they can no longer be viably thought of as separate practices.

The ways ethnographers intend to represent their research inevitably inform how they approach their projects, the technologies used, their relationships with participants, and the experiences and knowledge they produce. These relationships, technologies and experiences might also be reflected in their representations. When video plays a key role in the research it seems appropriate to incorporate video in its representation. This does not necessarily mean editing a documentary ethnographic video, but, for example, using video clips, stills or transcripts in conference presentations or hypermedia texts, or with written descriptions in printed publications. Below I suggest some ways in which researchers may experiment with ethnographic video representations. First, however, I discuss video as a medium for ethnographic representation, its difference from and similarities to other media and the theories attached to its use.

Video as a reflexive route to representation

As Edwards has argued for photography (see Chapter 4), use of video for ethnographic representation should be informed by an understanding of the nature of video as a medium, and the type of knowledge it best represents. In the twentieth century, visual anthropologists developed an extensive debate about the relationship between written text and ethnographic film, which forms a relevant background for discussing ethnographic uses of video. More recent work in visual anthropology practice also offers important insights into the potential of video in representation (e.g. in Pink, Kürti and Afonso 2004; Grimshaw and Ravetz 2004; MacDougall 2005; Pink 2006, 2011d).

During the 1980s and 1990s the art/science distinction that had made ethnographic film so problematic for the social sciences was increasingly dissolved. During this period the demand for reflexivity in ethnographic writing increased and some ethnographers began to characterise their representations as inevitably selective constructions, partial truths and ultimately literary works – fictions. It was argued that the scientific objectivity that had been assumed for written text, and that artistic film could not achieve, was in fact unattainable. Written text was therefore potentially equally as subjective and artistic as film. Jay Ruby suggested that reflexivity also had a place in film, arguing that anthropological filmmakers should ensure their audiences were made aware of the differences between reality and film as a constructed representation. He proposed that more artistic, expressive forms had a space in anthropology (Ruby 1982: 130) and that 'since film allows us to tell stories with pictures, its potential becomes enhanced within a reflexive and narrative anthropology' (1982: 131, see also Ruby 2000a). By this time reflexivity had begun to develop in ethnographic filmmaking (especially in Jean Rouch's and David and Judith MacDougall's films), during a period of technical and epistemological innovation which increased 'the ability of the filmmakers to be increasingly explicit about how the films were made, and the whys and for-whoms of their making' (Loizos 1993: 171). However, during the 1990s anthropologists still differed in their conclusions about where these differences. For instance, Hastrup argued that the reflexivity that helps contextualise meanings and differences in ethnographic writing cannot be achieved in ethnographic film because the iconographic visual communication of film is 'taken at face-value' and cannot invoke the degree of reflexivity and self-conscious knowledge that written text does (Hastrup 1992: 21). In contrast, the ethnographic films and theoretical written work of MacDougall demonstrated that reflexivity is not a unique characteristic of written text, but may also be represented visually. Other visual anthropologists compared anthropological film and text on a different basis. Barbash and Taylor claimed ethnographic writing is not concerned so much with reflexivity since 'anthropological texts tend to be ... (although of course by no means exclusively) concerned with non-intuitive abstractions like social structure or population statistics', whereas '[f]ilm is a quintessentially phenomenological medium, and it may have a different orientation to social life than anthropological monographs. It has a unique capacity to evoke human experience, what it feels like to actually be-in-the world' (1997: 74–5). Leslie Devereaux similarly argued that 'the camera's special virtue ... is its direct relation to the personal and the particular', pointing out that whether or not ethnographic film can represent 'reality', its 'ties to the specific' cannot be denied. In contrast, suggesting that 'academic writing, flees the particular and takes hold of the abstract, that enemy of experience', suggesting 'The expository project, extrapolating from the particular, sticking close explaining, is not impossible in documentary film. But sticking with the particular, sticking close to experience, is, if anything, more possible in anthropological film than in writing' (Devereaux and Hillman 1995: 71–2). Moving images and written text certainly bear different relationships to experience and the particular and subsequently represent these differently. However, Barbash and Taylor's and Devereaux's almost binary distinctions seem to ignore the fact that many ethnographers have written texts that go beyond structures and statistics to contend with subjectivity and the evocation of experience (see also Pink 2006). I would also dispute the idea that the abstract has to be the 'enemy' (Devereaux and Hillman, above) of experience. It would seem more reasonable to suggest that the particular and abstract are in fact interdependent ways of representing experience and making it culturally meaningful. A possibly more fruitful way forward is to consider what ethnographers are using video and written representations to achieve. To examine this I look briefly at a currently dominant issue in ethnographic representation: the relationship between the specific and the general and the question of how to represent other people's experiences.

Coping with the relationship between the specificity of human experience and the social scientific practice of producing generalisations is fundamental to academic work. In the 1990s, MacDougall's comparison of ethnographic film and writing focused on how anthropologists have struggled with the 'problem of the individual'. The individual, he wrote, had been the 'raw unit of anthropological study' but ironically had not conventionally been an acceptable element of ethnographic representation. MacDougall suggested that while 'ethnographic writing can more easily elide' this contradiction, in ethnographic film the individual 'is sometimes felt to claim altogether too much of their [ethnographic filmmakers'] attention' (1995: 220–1). Therefore written text can subdue the individual, whereas film cannot. While conventionally ethnographic texts in the twentieth century tended to the abstract, ethnographers are now writing an increasing number of texts that have both incorporated the drive towards reflexivity of the 1980s and 1990s and also seek new ways to come closer to individual experience and the specific in social life. A good example is Robert Desjarlais's (2003) monograph that analyses the biographical experiences of two ageing Yolmo Buddhists in Nepal. The individual is in fact now a current concern for some ethnographic writers as well as for filmmakers. Nevertheless, moving images and written words do have the potential to specialise in different elements of the general and specific and thus represent different types of ethnographic experience and theory. They should not therefore be expected to represent these themes in the same way, as their differences in fact allow ethnographers to broach key issues in different ways. In common, moving-image and written representations form part of ethnographers' projects to represent relationships between different elements (individual, specific, abstract, general, between theory and experience). Ethnographic filmmakers have claimed that video has a special potential to represent the inevitably embodied and multisensory experience of ethnographic fieldwork and evoke other people's sensory experience to an audience/reader. MacDougall suggests video would support this since audiovisual media allows us to produce new understandings of '"sensory" knowledge' concerning 'how people perceive their material environment and interact with it' (2005: 269). Grimshaw asks how 'If one of the foundational principles of anthropological knowledge is experience, understanding emerging from the sensory immersion of "being there", how can it be given form that does not involve translating it into a different register?' (2004: 23). She suggests that observational cinema (the dominant style in ethnographic documentary), if rethought as a subjective art form and following Taussig (1993) as 'a very particular form of mimetic practice' (2004: 26) could achieve this. The direct and immediate audiovisual representation of video is capable of evoking empathetic response in audiences in ways writing cannot. Nevertheless this does not mean written prose cannot also evoke other people's sensory embodied experiences to readers. In written ethnography this can be achieved in ways that are culturally situated and theoretically framed (Pink 2006). Video and writing play different and complementary roles in ethnographic representation. But, *both* are involved in representing individual experience.

One way to comprehend the way video records and represents experience is through a focus on movement, as I have outlined in Chapter 5. Such a theory of what video actually stands for invites us to think of a video recording as being played forward to re-run the route through which it was created. By conceptualising video as such, I wish to subsequently conceptualise the role of the viewer as one of accompanying and learning from the video as they continue to move forward with it (Pink 2011d; Pink and Leder Mackley 2012). I return to this point below in discussing how I have used these ideas to consider video screenings of footage in presentations, as well as in Chapter 10 where I discuss how it can inform online viewing.

My own view is that we need to seek ways to make ethnographic video representations both accessible and relevant to academic debate. There seems to me to be little point in producing ethnographic video that will only be viewed by other ethnographic documentary makers at film festivals. Below I suggest a reflexive approach that takes advantage of the different ways video, photography, and written text can represent sensory embodied ethnographic experience, theory and critique. By combining media and practices in this way it is possible to produce texts and presentations that draw from both arts practice and conventional social science practice. As such, researchers can represent their work by juxtaposing different types of knowledge, subjectivity, epistemology, experience and voice in ways that complement one another. However, the types of creative innovation and reflexivity that this type of representation implies do not exist only within the text. In Chapter 6, I noted how new types of text demand new forms of readership. Therefore, first, I discuss video and reflexive viewing.

Ethnographic video audiences

While there is an existing literature on ethnographic film audiences, to my knowledge audience responses to ethnographic video footage have not been systematically analysed (with the exception of some discussions of screening video for research participants). Indeed, little is known about the viewing practices of ethnographic documentary film audiences (with some exceptions e.g. Martinez 1992; Pack, discussed in Ruby 2000a). Since the 1990s the 'media ethnography' method (see Crawford and Hafsteinsson 1996), which takes an ethnographic approach to studying audiences, has become increasingly developed (e.g. see Levine 2007). It can moreover be argued that audience research is a moral issue and is part of the ethnographers' duty to be able to inform and 'protect' film subjects and participants in relation to the possible consequences of showing video clips or documentaries in which they appear. Even if film subjects agree to footage of them being presented publicly, they may not understand the full implications of such public exposure. As Braun points out in his video *Passing Girl, Riverside: An Essay on Camera Work* (1998), when a Ghanaian village chief agreed to Braun showing video images of his village in North America, did he really understand the implications of this? Consent is one thing, the extent to which it is really informed, or by what it is informed is another.

Ethnographic texts, be they books, videos or photographs, are not usually released for public consumption without some consideration of how they communicate.

It is advisable to research audience responses to video representation before disseminating it in the public domain. Different viewers might offer different types of response, and visual ethnographers might need to weigh up which are the most important for their work. This may include for instance, professional guidance on the content, stylistic and technical matters, comments from academic colleagues and from the ethnographic video subjects – as well as gaining approval from them before the final version is defined (see also Chapter 3). Sometimes research participants can anticipate how certain other viewers may interpret the video and can comment on this. However, it is difficult to predict precisely how video texts will be made meaningful as once they are available in a public domain they are subject to diverse (mis)understandings.

Anthropological filmmakers have been intensely aware of the politics of representation in ethnographic film. Therefore, keeping up to date with discussions and experiences from this context can be useful for informing video representation practices within and beyond ethnographic documentary making. For example David MacDougall has highlighted the complexity of viewers' relationships to film. Drawing from the ideas of film critics, he pointed out the multiplicity of ways that film may act on viewers: 'the conventions of filming and editing do not simply direct us to different visual points of view in a film but orchestrate a set of overlapping codes of position, narrative, metaphor and moral attitude' (1995: 223). MacDougall has also emphasised the specificity of the relationships individuals develop with texts:

> Our reading of a film, and our feelings about it, are at every moment the result of how we experience the complex fields this orchestration creates – partly dependent again upon who we are and what we bring to the film. This complexity extends to our relationship to different modes of cinematic address. (1995: 223)

These points can be applied not only to documentary ethnographic film, but also to other types of video representation. Differently constructed videos will both act on and be acted on by different viewers in their own individual ways.

Video representations of ethnography

There are various options for using video in ethnographic representation that go beyond documentary filmmaking. These include showing clips in conference presentations, video installations in exhibitions or online (see Chapter 10), combining moving and still images, voiceover and text in edited documentaries, or printing video stills and transcripts alongside descriptive passages in books or journals. Some of these are discussed below.

(Edited) clips

Footage of activities, actions, events, interviews, landscapes, artifacts, or other visual aspects of culture can be carefully edited or simply selected as unedited footage.

While a set of clips may not fit together coherently as a full-length documentary narrative, they may be combined with written or spoken words, sound or stills to tell another story. Each clip may itself represent a short story, demonstrate an activity, or represent a research participant's spoken narrative or visual self-representation. Some clips may be realist references to actions and events that respect the order these occurred in. Others might be edited to represent 'real' sequences of events that divert from the original chronology of the footage. There are multiple options, depending on what researchers intend video clips to represent and how clips are situated in relation to other texts that represent aspects of the same ethnographic project.

Each such set of video clips that tells its own ethnographic story may also be part of a larger representation. This wider narrative might include still images, sound and different styles of written text. Rather than photographs and videos serving as illustrations to the written or spoken text, it may be led by any of these media. The same set of video clips may also be used to represent the work in different ways. For example, from my collaborative video tours in one of my research projects about the home I produced about 40 hours of videotape. I used clips selected from these videos to present the work in different ways, including CD ROM projects. I showed clips of the videos of participants who had agreed that I might do, when presenting my work in more public academic contexts as part of seminar papers that I gave in academic departments and at conferences. These showings gave me an opportunity to hear other academics' comments and feedback on both my written and visual materials. Within these presentations I used video in both realist and expressive ways. For example, on one level they were intended to be realist representations of individuals and their material homes. They also portrayed people performing domestic tasks in their homes, which could be interpreted as (my) representations of (their) domestic performances. Because the video tours also recorded the interaction between researcher and participant, the clips also function as reflexive texts that reveal the relationships and processes through which the research produced ethnographic knowledge. Some clips I have shown have been selected specifically for this purpose. As evocative texts, the video clips are also intended to communicate something of the materiality of specific homes and of people's sensory and embodied experiences of them. Finally, I have used the clips to give the research participants a voice – to enable them to express themselves directly to an audience through words and actions (although of course mediated by my camera work, selection and editing of clips).

Likewise our screenings of video re-enactments of bedtime and morning time routines and of parts of video tours of homes as part of the LEEDR project have enabled our ethnographic research team to bring to conference contexts embodied performances of how participants actually show their daily routines in their homes. This enables us to invite audiences to empathise with our own positions as researchers and to scrutinise the materials for their own interpretations. It also means we can show those parts of our research that could not be expressed in spoken or written words, instead using the videos in relation to the spoken parts of our presentations.

THE SENSORY HOME:

AN ANTHROPOLOGICAL APPROACH

Sarah Pink

Loughborough University
s.pink@lboro.ac.uk

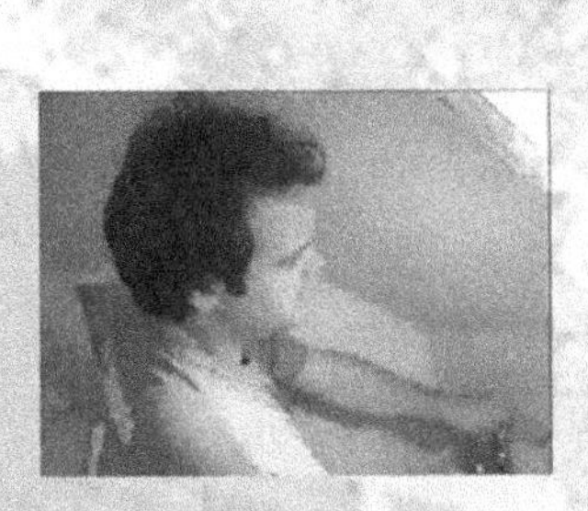

A friend of his had considered moving in to share the flat with him but, he told me:

'very tricky… [because] …you have to stand like this and bend your knees which means you don't want to stand here for too long'.

'she said she wouldn't do that because of the kitchen sink. The kitchen sink was the thing that stopped it in the end. It was the clincher but she wasn't sure anyway'.

(Continued)

(Continued)

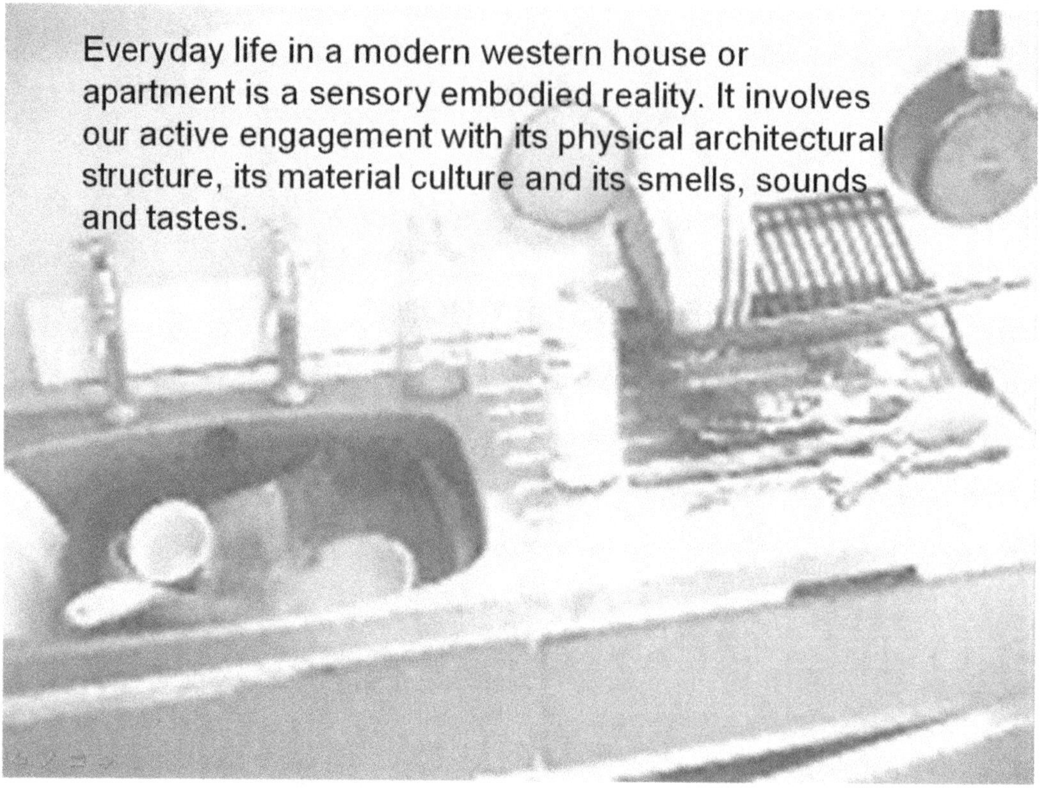

Figure 9.1 When I presented a paper at the Interior Insights symposium at the Royal College of Art (2005) I used a PowerPoint presentation to combine video, photographs and written text. I was not alone in this, as several of the other speakers also used the same range of different media in their own PowerPoint presentations. In the slides reproduced here I show how I used close-up photographs of the textures of home (slide 1) and a video still background foregrounded with a video clip, contextualizng words and quotations from the video transcript (slide 2) and a video still of an everyday domestic reality overlaid with academic writing (slide 3).

During the presentations an interesting ethical issue arose: some of the members of the audience were practising a form of visual note-taking during the presentations. They were photographing the slides from the speakers' presentations as they were screened. This raises another layer of issues relating to consent. A research participant may have agreed that a specific researcher may show a video clip of her or him in public, but not that another individual may subsequently copy it by photographing or video recording the presentation. I asked these members of the audience not to photograph during my presentation.

As I have analysed in detail elsewhere (Pink 2004b, 2006), video clips have some ethnographic documentary video qualities and would not conform to Barbash and Taylor's definition of research footage (1997, see above). Yet neither are they ethnographic documentary; they tell only very short stories that need to be situated in a wider more informative ethnographic context to be meaningful. These video clips sit between realist and expressive representations since they are short visual documents that form part of the constructed ethnographic narratives where they are situated by spoken or written words and other clips. By using video clips in this way I have been able to avoid having to use spoken and written words to describe visual knowledge.

Whereas books, journal articles, and documentary films offer more permanent ways of making statements about ethnographic experiences and theoretical concerns, conference and seminar presentations are also an important part of academic work and offer opportunities to present ideas to wider audiences. Conferences and seminars are also ideal situations for presenting short video clips in combination with other images and texts. Moving images (and sound) can become part of lively evocative presentations that engage audiences audiovisually, as well as verbally, inviting them to participate in interpreting visual knowledge and view images that were part of the research experience. Video clips can also be used in ethnographic exhibitions where they may be set alongside written texts, photographs or other artistic installations. When planning video and/or powerpoint presentations it is important to ensure in advance that appropriate video screening, compatible computing facilities and projection facilities are available.

Description, transcripts and video stills

Some would predict that in the near future print publishing will be superseded by the ever-increasing online publishing. Nevertheless, at the beginning of the twenty-first century, book and journal publishing is still the dominant medium for disseminating ethnography as well as for advancing academic careers, thus obliging researchers to represent their work in written words. For some researchers who work extensively with video, publishing their work in printed form can be understandably frustrating. Here, in this section, I discuss how video may form part of printed ethnography as written description, transcripts of video conversations, and captured video stills. In contrast to the idea that visual knowledge should be interpreted and translated into written words, this approach emphasises the presence of video in research and representation. While written description, transcription and stills do not act on the reader of written text in the same way that screening ethnographic video can, they allow the visual and spoken knowledge of video to become part of ethnographic representation. Existing printed texts that use video stills or transcripts tend to reflect on the role of video in the research and make the process of analysis and the relationship between research and representation explicit.

In Chapter 4, I described Lomax and Casey's use of video in research about midwives' home visits. This work is published in an online article that embeds video transcripts, digitised sound tracks and video stills in the written text. Lomax and Casey take a realist approach, arguing that '[v]ideo generated data is an ideal resource ... as it can provide a faithful record of the process as an aspect of the naturally occurring interaction that comprises the research topic' (1998: 1). Their sociological approach incorporates a response to anticipated criticisms from 'traditional' sociology (as do Prosser and other visual sociologists discussed in Chapter 1) that suggests that greater reflexivity can be achieved by including video in the text. Justifying their use of video against 'scientific' sociological opposition they argue that: 'Far from being a distraction or unimportant a reflexive analysis of the research process can contribute to an understanding of the phenomenon under investigation' (1998: 6). In addition to video materials, Lomax and Casey also provide lengthy quotations from field notes where the use of video was discussed, thus situating video within the wider research process. Each line of their transcribed conversations is numbered and submitted to a conversation analysis method by which the transcripts and digitised sound presented in the text are analysed. By presenting field notes, video transcripts and stills in the same text, the processes of research and analysis are evoked in the text. Lomax and Casey also make good use of video stills to discuss how midwives and their clients managed the camera during examinations of genitalia and other personal body parts by either switching it off or using their bodies to obstruct its view. The authors also participate in this strategy of concealment by blurring their informants' faces to guard their privacy. Lomax and Casey succeed in representing the visual and verbal qualities of video without including moving video images themselves in the text. Tim Dant (2004) has also used video stills to represent aspects of work practices. In his study video recording was used extensively to research the everyday practices of car mechanics working in garages. To represent this work he combines video stills and written descriptions of the activity visually and aurally represented on the video recording (which reference the stills included in the text) and sections of transcriptions of the spoken interactions that are recorded on the video (between mechanics and between mechanics and researcher). Dant complains that 'when still images are used to illustrate text, the crucial flow of action is lost (hands gesturing, holding the wiper as it moves)', but suggests that one quotation technique would be to 'use series of still "frames" in sequence that show how non-verbal forms of communication are integrated within talk' (2004: 58). In Chapter 6, I have discussed Vaike Fors' work. Another method of representing the action and talk of video is by using similar cartoon strip texts to those that Fors develops, shown in Figure 6.1.

In Chapter 4, I discussed Ferrándiz's use of video in his research with a Venezuelan spirit cult. In his (1998) essay about using video in this research, Ferrándiz includes descriptive passages about the video footage, sometimes quoting words spoken by the video's subjects and including still images captured from the video. Ferrándiz attempts to evoke the *experience* of video research in his text in a different way to the more realist approaches employed in the examples discussed in the previous paragraph. The article begins with the following text alongside a video still of a fingerprint and the handwritten name 'ELOY':

> 'What is this fellow doing?'
>
> 'He is filming, *compadre*'
>
> 'Filming what, a paper or something?'
>
> 'Yes'
>
> 'Find me a feather, and ink, and all that stuff, so I can also film. Let me show you how I film, *carajito*'
>
> (Ferrándiz 1998: 19)

Having attended a presentation of this project, accompanied by a screening of some 20 minutes of the footage that Ferrándiz describes (at a conference organised by the *Taller de Antropologia Visual* in Madrid, in 1996), my own reading of the article was inevitably influenced by my experience of seeing the footage. However, even without an accompanying screening, the text succeeds in interlinking a narrative that represents the experiential elements of video production and viewing with theoretical and ethnographic narratives about the visual and spirit possession. Ferrándiz includes twelve still images from the videotapes. In one section of the article, where he describes how his informants used and interacted with the technology when being filmed by him and when filming one another, he includes a series of video stills from footage shot by himself and different informants. These are either captioned with quotes from tapes in which video subjects addressed the camera verbally, or with Ferrándiz's descriptions. For example, an image of a woman videoed by 'Ruben' is captioned: 'Ruben as cinematographer, interacting with Carmencita la Canelita (possessing Teresa) through the camera' (1998: 28). In this project video images and technology became a medium of communication and representation between and among researcher and informants. As video was so important to Ferrándiz's research narrative his written text would be incomplete without it: the video images could not be translated into words. The video stills are not merely 'I was there' images or realist recordings, but fragments of the video images through which meanings were created and communicated in the research. These video stills play at the edge of realism and fiction. They challenge the idea of visual truth as, in the case of the caption I have quoted above, some of the stills are of people who are not there, but whose bodies are possessed by spirits and are therefore someone else.

Further uses of video stills may include constructing visual narratives, as in a photo-essay (see Chapter 6), montage images, or poster presentations. Photographic narratives or montage might be composed, for example, of video stills that represent a series of points or themes from the research. Arranged together in the same montage image or as a series of captioned images, stills can create expressive representations that interlink different moments and themes in the research.

Presented in this way, stills can also allow people to view a visual research narrative differently, without demanding that it is viewed in a linear video narrative. Expressive montage images and poster presentations offer possibilities for further creativity – montage or posters may combine video stills, photographs and other depictions, interview quotations and academic commentaries.

Video stills and transcripts may be used in printed text as both realist and expressive representations. As the examples I have discussed demonstrate, ethnographers have used stills as evidential data, claims of the ethnographer's authority, as well as symbolic or evocative images of the context in which they were produced, the social relationships this involved and the knowledge associated with it.

Collaboration

As Barbash and Taylor point out, 'Documentary filmmaking is by nature collaborative. Quite simply, it's impossible to make a film about other people completely on your own' (1997: 74). Video research is equally collaborative. However, the final stages of making finished ethnographic representations tend to involve less collaboration and, as Barbash and Taylor note for film, there is a danger 'the film maker will remain the real author, with the participants simply being brought in to legitimate a collaborative rubber stamp' (1997: 89). Indeed, in the case of documentary films made for television, and using broadcast practices, control of the editing process is usually the domain of the film company, even if film subjects are invited to comment on or have some input into the editing. As Garry Marvin has put it: 'Here what is generally required is that those who participate in a documentary must sign a "release form" that allows the producers of the film to use the person's voice and image in any way, within the limits of the law, they chose' (2005: 199). Ethnographic documentaries made by academic researchers, however, tend to work according to more collaborative methods, which might involve the people who appear in the video participating, editing or commenting and feeding back on how they and their cultures are represented. Such practices have developed and persisted since the twentieth century, with the example of the work of Prelorian, Prelorian and Saravino (1992) where Zulay, the protagonist of the film *Zulay Frente al Siglo XXI* travels from Eucador to the USA to participate in the editing of the film. More recently the Spanish *A Buen Común* ethnographic documentary-making team (Camas et al. 2004) describe how their collaborative approach revealed that one of their film's protagonists was not comfortable with the edited version. Their videos are developed through a process of constant feedback from both informants and team members. They describe how when making their documentary *La Piel del Monte*,

> We were surprised to discover that one of the main protagonists was not satisfied with the final video. After watching and discussing the film with him we concluded that he did not like how he came across and, worse still, he was worried about the repercussions his words could have on his public image in a community of less than 1,000 inhabitants. (Camas et al. 2004: 138)

In this work the video subjects had the right to 'paralyse the editing process and eliminate the fragments that were most compromising for them' (2004: 138). Thus giving them significant control over how they would be represented in the final film product. In Figure 3.2, I discussed Zemirah Moffat's work, another example of an ethnographic documentary project in which the film's protagonists (one of which is the filmmaker herself) comment on the process of representation. Here, in the film making process and in the film itself, the question of trust and the relationship the filmmaker develops with the other people in the film is brought to the surface at the outset. Further examples include the applied visual anthropology projects of Matthew Durington (2007) and Carlos Flores (2007) (and see Pink 2007b).

Often, though, ethnographers might find that they have to edit their video clips or documentary and write up their texts alone or with the support of technical specialists. Particularly for students and unfunded researchers, it could be costly to return to a distant research site, or to host informants at home after returning, thus making it difficult to show people how they are represented and receive their impressions of rough-cuts. Researchers who work in areas close to their own homes might have more opportunities to collaborate with informants, whose participation may not only let them influence how they are represented in the public domain, but may also increase the researcher's understanding of them. In some cases, however, I have found that people I have video recorded have told me that they do not mind me editing and showing images of them and they do not wish to see these before they are screened in public. While this allows me freedom to work as I like with the materials, my own experience is that because the burden of judging whether a representation is appropriate then falls completely on me as the video maker then my position is one in which I must take total responsibility for getting it right. Therefore the burden is greater.

A final form of collaboration in the representation of ethnographic video is when the video subjects, or protagonists, are also involved in the public presentation of the video. In some cases ethnographic filmmakers have been able to source funding to bring the people who are in their documentaries to the film festivals where they are screened. The benefit of this is that they can also participate in introducing the film and in the sessions where questions are asked about the film and its production (see for example Camas et al. 2004: 136).

The examples discussed in this section have referred mainly to work that has been produced as part of edited ethnographic documentary films. However, the issues raised apply equally to using short edited or unedited clips or video stills.

Ethics

General ethical concerns were discussed in Chapter 2. In this chapter the examples I have discussed above have highlighted some ethical issues specific to using video in ethnographic representation and demonstrate how these were dealt with in existing projects. For example, Lomax and Casey (1998) have blurred their informants' faces to conceal their identities and Braun's (1998) video raised the question of whether, when people consent to be filmed, they are really 'informed' about how they will be represented and how others will interpret this. As I noted for photography in Chapter 6, using consent or release forms can help clarify intentions in some contexts but they do not necessarily resolve the ethical issues that ethnographers are confronted with at the point of representing others on video. Some ethnographers have tried to resolve this by showing their video footage to the people represented in it, inviting them to participate in the process of editing and representation. Additionally, making consent an ongoing process to be re-negotiated over time, rather than a one-off moment of form-signing, can be considered good ethical practice. Yet while including video images can communicate in ways words do not, there may be situations where we do not wish to include them. For example, in my book *Home Truths* (Pink 2004b) for several reasons, including those relating to the privacy of participants, I decided not to include video images. As I noted in Chapter 2, an ethical approach also involves attempting to anticipate how one's representations will be interpreted by a range of other individual, institutional, political and moral subjectivities.

Summary

In this chapter I explored some of the issues and potentials of video for ethnographic representation. As I have demonstrated, there are many more possibilities for video representation than simply ethnographic documentary production. Nevertheless, while I have departed from the emphasis on finished ethnographic documentary videos or films, the debates surrounding ethnographic documentary provide a background for understanding video in ethnographic representation. These existing debates will inevitably inform how other academics receive video representations of ethnography. Moreover, the theory that informs discussions of contemporary ethnographic documentary is well developed and can inform other video representations. Producers of video representations can also learn from the attention ethnographic filmmakers and critics have recently begun to pay to the audiences of their representations.

Further reading

Barbash, I. and Taylor, L. (1997) *Cross Cultural Filmmaking: A Handbook for Making Documentary and Ethnographic Films and Video.* London: University of California Press. (A practical guide to ethnographic filmmaking.)

Camas, V., Martínez, A., Muñoz, R. and Ortiz, M. (2004) 'Revealing the hidden: making anthropological documentaries', in S. Pink, L. Kürti and A. Afonso (eds), *Working Images.* London: Routledge. (An example of collaborative filmmaking practice.)

MacDougall, D. (2005) *The Corporeal Image.* Princeton: Princeton University Press. (Includes a useful discussion of MacDougall's 'Doon School' project.)

Marvin, G. (2005) 'Research, representations and responsibilities: An anthropologist in the contested world of fox hunting', in S. Pink (ed.) *Applications of Anthropology.* Oxford: Berghahn. (A useful discussion of ethical issues in the context of the making of a television documentary based on the author's work.)

Additional material is available on the book's companion website: www.uk.sagepub.com/pink3e

10

Making Visual Ethnography Public Online/Digitally

In the last two chapters I have outlined how photography and video might become part of the ways that ethnography is disseminated in conventional publishing and face-to-face conference presenting. I have discussed these practices of ethnographic representation separately from digital online forms because in this final chapter my emphasis is on how web contexts and platforms are enabling some shifts away from the practices that characterise printed and public screening formats. These shifts include new forms of digital (audio)visual content, but also in some cases alternative conceptualisations of access and distribution, including open source and creative commons licences and alternative publishing rhythms. Yet, I stress that the departures from conventional forms need to be considered not simply as changes, but as involving continuities and common reference points.

In this final brief chapter I discuss some of the contemporary and emerging forms of online visual ethnography dissemination and formal publishing. Where relevant I also draw on other qualitative uses of video that might not be seen as strictly ethnographic, but that offer interesting examples of the potential of the web for visual ethnography practice. While some online journals discussed below are well established, in recent years rapid technological changes have brought new web-based possibilities to visual ethnography publishing and dissemination. This has created a shift from the focus on what was referred to as hypermedia in the 1990s and early 2000s involving first CD and DVD multimedia publishing and then online developments (e.g. Coover 2003, Ruby 2004 and see Pink 2006), to what is at the time of writing a web 2.0 context where online publishing takes on new possibilities. Writing the second edition of this book in 2007, I still referred to this hypermedia context as an emergent process. Yet as recent developments have shown this era of excitement about the possibilities of hypermedia, as well as the scholarly development of multilinearity and researcher-authored types of multivocality that developed around it have now been surpassed by possibilities for participatory, open and collaborative forms. This is not to say that such authored forms have ceased to exist, and as we will see from the examples discussed, conventional forms are part of these new developments. Indeed in this sense, as was the case for Chapter 6, the discussion in this chapter remains tentative, it outlines how contemporary developments are taking shape, identifies those that appear to be more maturely established in terms of their online presence, and is written in recognition that these current forms will continue to shape and be shaped by future developments in online visual ethnography publishing and dissemination.

Finally, before discussing examples of online dissemination of visual ethnography a note on the context of their viewing is needed. The second edition of *Doing Visual Ethnography* was published in 2007, the same year that the iPhone was released. Since then we have seen the uptake of tablet computers, increasingly lightweight laptops and a proliferation in the range of smart phones and locative media. Clearly not only are the technologies that we use to do visual ethnography research changing, but also the possibilities through which we might view and read them. In a context of increasingly mobile media, touchscreens, and more, the ways that digital visual ethnography presented online can be experienced, shared and interpreted are also changing.

The online journal

In the preceding chapters of this book I have emphasised how digital, analogue and material forms of photographic and video practice are not separate fields of activity or visual form, but in fact tend to get entangled and inter-reference each other. The same applies to ethnographic representation. The perhaps most obvious continuity is between conventional printed publishing and digital online versions of the same journal articles. Here we find that journal article publishing, increasingly available in e-journal versions as well as the conventional print version, is both changing the ways that we access journals and also in some cases offering slightly different visual forms – for instance in the case of journals such as *Visual Studies* where one might find online photographs presented in colour whereas their print version counterparts are in black and white. In some cases we also find online supplements to print versions are supplied too. E-journals are also participating in the constitution of new temporalities of publishing, some journals having an 'online first' publishing policy whereby articles are available online before they are printed. However, we should note that access to online journals, or e-journals, that correspond to print journals is often through individual or library subscription, therefore maintaining them in this sense as part of a conventional publishing business.

Yet online journal publishing is also developing in new ways and formats that shift away from the conventional forms of print journals and in some cases produce open access and/or copyright free editions. One obvious visual difference can be seen in the layout formats of journals such as *Sociological Research on-line* (@ http://www.socresonline.org.uk/) and *Forum Qualitative Sozialforschung/Forum:*

Qualitative Social Research (FQS) (@ http://www.qualitative-research.net/index.php/fqs/index) where, for instance, page numbering is replaced by paragraph numbering and videos can be accessed through links. Reminding ourselves that writing is also a form of visual representation, we can also think in terms of how these layouts offer us new ways to reference and access written texts. However, my main reason for referring to these two journals here is to comment on the potentials they offer for the publication of visual ethnography. Indeed, both journals have had special issues in recent years with a focus on visual materials that I have contributed to. They offer exciting possibilities for working with text, still and moving images in relation to each other, and I reflect further on these below. *Sociological Research Online* and *FQS* (see above) are established online journals that publish predominantly written texts. Such journals also offer us possibilities to develop more conventional written arguments in a context where we can also engage visual materials in these works. This is an important opportunity to keep in mind because it enables us to stretch existing and established ways of doing scholarly work into new directions but without forsaking the possibility of simultaneously directly engaging in written form with the issues and debates of academic scholarship as they have developed, and continue to develop, in that format. Below I discuss a series of examples that show how video interviewing, researcher produced video and participant produced video have been introduced in these contexts.

One online journal project that has promoted uses of visual materials is a special issue of *Sociological Research On-line* edited by Susan Halford and Caroline Knowles, focusing on visual research. This special issue aims to go beyond written text, and seeing photography and video as ways to represent the performative nature of everyday life, the editors characterise it as a text 'in which the authors use visual imagery in a variety of ways, captures a live sociology of performances that is not possible without photography and video' (Halford and Knowles 2005: 1.3). They are also conscious of the role of the reader/viewer of sociological text and make it clear that underlying its production was the assumption that its users would also experience it and participate in the creation of meanings from it in new ways. The essays, they write, ' ... also seek to transform sociological participation, drawing the audience "inside": engaging us, as embodied, sensual beings in the living details of the thing we seek to understand' (Halford and Knowles 2005: 1.9). The different articles included in the issue develop this to different degrees, some simply using the capacity of electronic publication to include an extended number of colour photographs and other scanned images framed by a written argument (e.g. Chaplin 2005; Farrar 2005). However, the article that expands the possibilities of hypermedia most creatively is Monika Büscher's 'Social life under the microscope?' (@ http://www.socresonline.org.uk/10/1/buscher.html) which discusses both the embodied work practices of designers and the use of video to research these. Büscher points out that 'Design sessions ... draw to our attention that formulating is not restricted to talk, as drawing, gesturing, enactments, and embodied reference to images, plans or features in the surroundings can all reflexively formulate the imagined object and the scenic intelligibility of the activity' (Büscher 2005: 3.3).

Here the ability of video to represent the embodied and sensory nature of human practice and experience is key. Büscher makes interesting and extensive use of the potential of online publishing to include video, still images and composite images within a written narrative. Her text in many ways follows the conventional structure of a written essay. It is produced in a linear form and divided into sections, following the established style of *Sociological Research Online*. However, linked to this written narrative, in a way that is acutely aware that 'Neither video nor microscopes can provide a way of seeing through to an independent natural or social reality' (2005: 11.1), she uses video, animations, photographs and other images (e.g. maps, examples of design drawings) both as realist images of what is done and what actually happened and to bring examples of her data into the text and make aspects of her analysis explicit. The introduction of so much of the visual data into the text also invites the viewer to several possibilities, including: to engage with the experiences of the people represented on a personal and empathetic level; to re-analyse the data her or himself; to reflect not only on the design process as it is represented in the text, but also on the research process as it is embedded in the video data. In addition to video clips, Büscher also makes creative and interesting uses of video transcripts and still images to represent aspects of the design process. In these representations that combine writing and image she is able to emphasise aspects of the design process in ways that would not be achievable by simply playing a video clip online. Because Büscher's article follows existing conventions established for written online articles, it is easily accessible to mainstream academics. It does not demand that the reader/viewer's initial form of engagement with the text involves vastly unfamiliar practices. Nevertheless, within this familiar frame it invites new forms of engagement and allows the reader/viewer access to forms of knowledge that could not be evoked in conventional printed text. This work provides an excellent example of how we might extend and enhance the capabilities of existing publishing conventions without challenging existing practices of academic communication.

More recent works have shown a series of new forms of integrating audiovisual media into online publishing. Interviewing is often seen as being an ethnographic method and in the previous chapters I have considered interviews, such as the photo-elicitation interview, to be part of the range of visual ethnography methods. In recent years, digital video cameras have become increasingly part of the tool-kit of the ethnographer as well as that of other qualitative researchers and their use in place of the audio-recorder in interviewing has become increasingly prevalent. Thus, for example Pearse, Goodman and Roseware, write of a research project that they represent online with the inclusion of thematically edited video-recorded interviews as 'digital ethnography' (@ http://epress.lib.uts.edu.au/journals/index.php/mcs/article/view/1794/1875). Such projects enable researchers to bring participants' voices and bodies more clearly into their work, thus achieving something of the multivocality that the emphasis on reflexivity developed in the 1990s called for (e.g. see Marcus 1995), in forms that were perhaps unimagined at that point. The use of the interview in such ways in journal articles certainly creates challenges, given the length of interviews, and the question of how best to interweave what might stand as an alternative to simply quoting the interviewee in the text (as is conventional) in the article.

In Chapter 6, I discussed the video diary method as it has been used in visual ethnography projects to generate participant produced video. Below I come back to this topic in relation to project web pages. Participant produced video can also play a role in digital journal publishing. One interesting recent example of the insertion of participants' video diary extracts in a written article narrative can be found in Eldin Fahmy and Simon Pemberton's (2012) *SRO* article, focusing on rural exclusion in the United Kingdom. Here the extended inserts offer rather evocative accounts of the issues faced by participants in this project, thus bringing their voices, and self-reporting on their circumstances, into an arena where they are little heard in such ways. They argue that 'Our research suggests that video research methods offer one fruitful means of promoting this agenda through the development of a more participatory research style which enables participants to convey their stories in ways that break down the barriers between research subjects and research users which constitute people experiencing poverty as "other" and separate from mainstream society' (2012: 6.3). What is interesting about these uses of video diaries and of interviews discussed above is that they are developing ways of adapting existing genres of quoting and giving voice to participants in new ways in a digital context. Another interesting recent intervention in this area has been in the inclusion of participant produced videos of family Christmas celebrations in an *SRO* journal article by Muir and Mason (2012), whose work I have already mentioned in Chapter 5. Here they include a series of video sequences that research participants produced for them during the events of their family Christmas.

Researcher-produced video is arguably still the mainstay of much visual ethnography practice, especially as it relates to documentary making and, as I have discussed earlier, is the main way in which I have focused on exploring people's everyday lives in their homes with them. In a recent article published in *SRO* with Kerstin Leder Mackley (2012) we have included a series of video clips I recorded of one of the participants in our research about domestic digital media and energy consumption. Our use of video offers a contrasting example to observational approaches. Here we use the clips for two purposes: to show our research process and to invite viewers to engage, as we did, with the ways these participants enact and describe their homes and lives in them. As we argue there, 'The video tour is not simply a recording of the home and people in it but a recording of the researcher's body moving forward through a multisensory and social environment. This includes, for instance, moving through changes in temperature, sound levels, smells and textures' (2012; 4.4) and it is this, in part, we are seeking to include in the article by including video clips. However, we have also developed this text as an experiment in audienceship. We invite the audience to engage with the videos in a particular way (while recognising that they might wish to engage on other terms). We write:

> We propose that the video clips should be understood as the outcomes of routes through a multisensory environment that the researcher and camera moved forward through. In this sense, when viewing the video clips we ask viewers to think of them as clips taken from the movement of the camera forward through the home, rather than as distanced images of the home. Therefore we think of playing video *forward* as a way to invite the viewer to travel forward with it, and to add their own empathetic interpretations to the trace of the route through the home it stands for (2012: 4.5).

Such experiments in presenting and viewing video footage are a new move in online visual ethnography publishing, which will develop and indeed to which I hope we will see responses from other writers and video ethnographers.

More recently, however, further journals formats have been developed that focus more specifically on the work of visual scholars, and critical media and arts practice. Such journals, which tend to be open access, offer new possibilities for innovation in digital media practice and scholarship, and within this, opportunities for innovation in visual ethnography practice which engages with these potentials. One existing online example is *Sensate*, an 'issueless journal' which states 'Our mission is to provide a scholarly and artistic forum for experiments in critical media practices that expand academic discourse by taking us beyond the margins of the printed page. Fundamental to this expansion is a re-imagining of what constitutes a work of scholarship or art', online at http://sensatejournal.com. *Sensate* includes 'audiovisual ethnographic research' within its remit and its contributions develop interesting relationships between (audio)visual and written texts in ways that depart significantly from conventional journal and academic writing formats. Moreover, because it is issueless, *Sensate* also participates in the refiguring of the temporalities of journal publishing, replacing the routine and management of issue deadlines, with an ongoingness. While *Sensate* is now established and populated with contributions, other online journals that are of interest are also emerging. For instance, the new open access online journal *Visual Ethnography* (http://www.vejournal.org/) is described as focusing on

> ... the production and the use of images and audiovisual media in the socio-cultural practices; the ethnographic representation through audiovisual media and devices (film, photography, multimedia, etc.); the gaze and the practices where vision is an important item for the construction of the meaning in the social relationships and practices; on the visual dimension of objects, bodies, places and environments. Moreover, the journal reserves a space for articles devoted to reflections on theories and methods of anthropology.

These new developments in journal publishing online also create new possibilities for access to scholarly work. *Sociological Research Online* requires institutional subscriptions but is 'available without charge to individuals accessing it from non-institutional networks' (www.sagepub.com/journals/200794), *Visual Ethnography* is open access and *Sensate* publishes works under a Creative Commons 3.0 Attribution license.

Digital visual ethnography project sites

Another growing trend in online dissemination of visual ethnography practice is the acknowledgement of the ongoingness of this work through project blogs and web sites. In this section I discuss a selection of these types of web presence to give some examples of the range, covering blogs, the dissemination of project work, project web sites, and archives. Elsewhere, in the context of a discussion of the development of applied visual anthropology I review a series of prominent applied audio(visual) anthropology projects which now have web sites or blogs dedicated to their work (see Pink 2011b). These offer interesting examples from a range of different sectors in which anthropologically informed digital visual ethnography materials are posted online. For example in Chapter 5, I discussed the work of Richard Chalfen and Michael Rich (2007) in relation to the use of participant produced video diaries in their Video Intervention/Prevention Assessment (VIA) work. The VIA wider project also has a web site, where a number of materials are presented relating to their work, including some participant-produced videos (http://www.viaproject.org/home/). Other examples include the work of Christina Lammer, again in an applied health context. Lammer has developed both a project web site with a series of visual materials, including video clips from her work with clinicians and patients, and a blog. The blog serves as an ongoing documentation of her project as it develops and can be accessed equally by the different participants in her work, the academics, artists and medical practitioners who she collaborates with and wider academic or other interested audiences. Both genres of online presentation bring work that spans the academic/applied fields into a public domain, yet in different ways. In the field of applied visual anthropology, another example is the work of Patricia Sunderland and Rita Denny (see also Sunderland and Denny 2007). Their work in applied consumer research is rooted in anthropology and involves using video methods. On their web site (http://www.practicagroup.com/pictures_videos.shtml) they include both participant and researcher-produced video clips, which in the context of the web site demonstrate the potential of the work they do, as they describe it: 'Diaries privilege consumers' voices, not ours. We benefit from consumers' in situ perspectives, thoughts, reflections and willingness to explain it all to us – wherever they are and whatever they are doing', and in relation to their ethnographic videos they write that 'We construct our videos in the ethnographic tradition of cinema verité, thereby providing clients with the feel of "life as lived" by their consumers' (http://www.practicagroup.com/anthropology_ethnography.shtml). Other examples beyond applied visual research include the wider body of work of Michael Wesch (2009), which I have touched on in Chapter 6 (http://mediatedcultures.net/about.htm) (and see also Pink 2011f).

These sites are rather different publication venues to the online journals discussed above. They are digital places where research can be publicised, discussed and presented as it develops, and where it can be updated. Indeed they are not expected to be static. These are the places where programmes of research, preliminary findings, video clips that represent project work and more can be presented online. In some contexts this can work towards the development of greater public understanding, in others it can invite research participants to engage with preliminary thoughts and findings on-goingly throughout the research process.

Further examples include the online presentation of documentary films. This is another emergent field, and even so includes different genres and uses. The work of Joana Conill, Manuel Castells and Alex Ruiz, whose documentary *Homenatge a Catalunya II*, which itself has a creative commons licence, is presented online (http://www.homenatgeacatalunyaii.org/enI), offers an interesting example from a number of perspectives. As they note, the documentary, edited from 70 interviews, is itself a stage in a research process, which is 'a tool of research. Not finished, conclusive and closed work' (http://www.homenatgeacatalunyaii.org/en/process) which has been used to generate discussion and debates. In contrast, the work of the documentary maker Zem Moffatt, already discussed in Chapter 6, has an online presence as a completed documentary film at (http://queergiving.co.uk/)

Finally, while most of the discussion in this chapter has focused on digital video online, significant developments are also happening in relation to digital photography. One highly relevant example to visual ethnography practice is a digital archive that has been developed of the work of John Collier Jnr. Collier's work which has been discussed in Chapters 1 and 5 has been highly influential in the development of visual ethnography and is indeed one of the key inspirations for methods that have subsequently developed in new ways and with new theoretical orientations (http://americanimage.unm.edu/).

Digital documentary art, GIS and visual ethnography

Above I mentioned the journal *Sensate*, which publishes innovative works online. A particularly interesting body of work that connects well with visual ethnography is that of Rod Coover. I have already discussed Coover's innovative print publishing initiatives in Chapter 8. His online work is equally interesting and offers an inspiring example to digital visual ethnographers. Here I discuss one example: Coover's *Outside/Inside: Virtual Panoramas of Independence National Historical Park* (2008), a work that he developed during a residency at the Museum of The American Philosophical Society at Philosophical Hall, Philadelphia, as a museum installation which is available online at http://www.unknownterritories.org/APS.html. I recommend that readers view this work in correspondence with reading my discussion of it.

Coover's work is particularly interesting because it resonates theoretically and methodologically with the ideas around movement and viewing practices discussed above and in Chapter 9 in relation to video ethnography practice. Coover's text engages (with) movement in a number of ways. Characteristic of his digital art the user's movement through the text is horizontal rather than vertical as in conventional web design. Given the panoramic format of the long horizontal 'still' image that the viewer scrolls along, in fact the viewer feels located at the centre of the park, looking *around* the environment she/he is in, rather than looking *at* a photograph from outside. The text also has a series of very short documentary videos embedded in the panoramic image which document an exploratory tour of visitors led by a guide and in doing so give a sense of movement in the park as these people move and walk through. For example, the first video clip not only follows the guide but it also takes the viewer up a set of steps. The idea of pathways and the significance of the routes through which we arrive at meaning are also expressed in Coover's written comments printed in a strip at the top of the text along with other quotations. He writes:

> An investigation is often a private and, even lonely experience of searching for answers to a question. Turning evidence in to product – the book, the exhibit, the map – the scientist enters a social sphere where paths of inquiry criss-cross with those of others. The public works form the collective image of a landscape. Its secrets lie in the paths taken to get there. (Coover 2008)

Therefore, this is another example of images that are made *in* environments and that invite the viewer to also traverse and interact with an environment that they might feel they can experience from a visual vantage point that is situated within, seemingly at the centre of the park, rather than looking at it from outside.

A second example of an innovative, although rather different, integration of digital video, photographs and other web-based media is the work of Mack et al. (also mentioned in Chapter 7), who discuss their project to reconstruct the now abandoned Belkofski village in Alaska using 3D-Visualization. These techniques, they point out, have been little used in ethnographic representation (Mack et al. 2011: 456). The project Mack et al. discuss, was intended to lead to an educational DVD, particularly for younger members of the Belkofski tribe (2011: 466) – rather than being a web-based publication. It is an interesting example of the potential of working with 3D-Visualization. In their words, 'with new advances in 3D-modelling and the availability to integrate ethnographic data with a GIS is possible for a wide range of uses' and thus creates potential for its application to ethnographic projects (2011: 466).

While my focus here is on digital work relating to visual ethnography practice, the work of non-fiction artists offers an inspiring context. Further discussions relating to digital editing, interactive documentary and visual research projects are developed by Coover et al. (2012). These provide interesting examples, discussions and potential points of inspiration for the development of digital visual ethnography.

Ethics of digital visual ethnography online publishing

Most of the researchers whose work has been discussed in this chapter have also had something to say about the ethics of digital online publishing of visual materials. As I have stressed, following Clark's (2012) points discussed in Chapter 3, visual ethics are situated and will also vary between different projects. In the case of online publications, where we are seeking to give 'voice' and invite collaborations from research participants, it is often the case that they will be identifiable. Indeed as Fahmy and Pemberton point out 'it is important for researchers to acknowledge participants' "right to be visible" especially where research seeks to challenge wider social processes of disempowerment' (Fahmy and Pemberton 2012: 2.5). Regarding their work about family Christmas discussed above, Muir and Morgan have discussed the efforts they have taken to maintain levels of privacy for their participants. They also make an interesting point when they note how 'whilst we have felt happy to present video clips here in the context of a methodological discussion, we have adopted a different strategy for the presentation of our substantive analysis elsewhere' (2012: 4.14), seeing the presentation of 'video and other data about people's personal lives side by side in a deep and integrated analysis' (2012: 4.13) as being more problematic.

Therefore in these and other cases, as always, informed consent is an important element of this process. Fahmy and Pemberton also stress 'the importance of informing participants of the purposes of data collection and the contexts within which visually identifiable data will be disseminated, as well as offering participants an opportunity to retract evidence at the post-data collection stage' (Fahmy and Pemberton 2012: 2.6). Ongoing processes of negotiating consent are also significant in such forms of publication, and indeed can remain ongoing in that once published online a video or photograph can be removed. This will not change any earlier uses, or downloads of it, and these types of issues should also be accounted for when informed consent is negotiated, but it does offer some possibilities for limiting its dissemination in ways that were not possible in print publishing.

Video and photographic publishing online indeed raises issues beyond simple viewing, but also about downloading, copyrights and permissions for further use of the visual materials by others. Other issues relate to the possibility of online texts going 'viral' and thus becoming part of contexts which go beyond their intended audiences (see for example, Pink 2011f (pp. 209–11), for a discussion of this). The technological issues around these uses of web platforms and software are complex and should be discussed in any context where there are concerns with experts in this area. Ways of informing participants about the possible consequences and (unauthorised) re-uses of the materials should be part of such conversations. However, these might also be mediated in relation to the possible likelihood and interest there might be in this happening. These are indeed complex issues to navigate and will in the future be informed further by both experiences of online publishing and by developments in internet technologies.

Future digital visual ethnography places

As I have discovered in this third writing of *Doing Visual Ethnography*, when we write, think and make images in this field, we do not ever arrive at an end. We instead end in a moment, a temporary configuration which is of course over by the time our work is published or otherwise disseminated. *Doing Visual Ethnography* is not a method – not something that is 'done' but something that is happening in the doing, and the doing is ongoing as technology, theory, practice and life move forward in new ways. There are many web platforms, social media, emergent technologies through which we might speculate about future digital ethnography practice and representation. Many lessons can, however, be learned from reflecting on those which already exist, they are here for us to base our own points of departure in while at the same time new ideas and research techniques and activities may emerge from connections with other fields of research, media and technological practice. New and emergent technologies are changing the contexts in which visual ethnography can be produced and consumed; the types of screens upon which it is shown and projected; the relationships in which they are embedded; and the localities in which we can access these.

While more generally fields of scholarship and research practice and technology are constantly changing and shifting, in writing the third edition of this book I have felt that we are presently at a pivotal moment in the development of visual research methods. We are working in a context where a series of themes – movement, participation, mappings, and sensoriality are increasingly represented in the ways we theorise, approach, actually perform and represent digital visual ethnography in practice. Yet I do not wish to predetermine how connections will be made between them, to put them in a 'system' or turn them into a method. Rather, I suggest them and the potential relationships between them as departures for a digital visual ethnography.

Further reading/viewing

Whereas for other chapters, lists of relevant texts for further reading have been compiled, in the case of this final chapter my recommendation is that readers follow the links that have been given in the text above to explore the web-based materials that I have discussed.

Additional material is available on the book's companion website: www.uk.sagepub.com/pink3e

References

Amit, V. (2000) (ed.) *Constructing the Field*. London: Routledge.

Appadurai, A. (1986) 'Introduction: commodities and the politics of value', in A. Appadurai (ed.), *The Social Life of Things: Commodities in Cultural Perspective*. Cambridge: Cambridge University Press.

Ardévol, E. (2012) 'Virtual/visual ethnography: methodological crossroads at the intersection of visual and internet research', in S. Pink (ed.) *Advances in Visual Methodology*. London: SAGE.

Ardévol, E. and San Cornelio, G. (2007) 'Si quieres vernos en acción: YouTube.com'. Prácticas mediáticas y autoproducción en Internet' *Revista Chilena de Antropología Visual* 10(3), available online at http://www.antropologiavisual.cl/ardevol_&_san_cornelio.htm.

Askew, K. and Wilk, R. (eds) (2002) *The Anthropology of Media: a reader*. Oxford: Blackwells.

Back, L. (1998) 'Reading and writing research', in C. Seale (ed.), *Researching Culture and Society*. London: SAGE.

Banks, M. (1992) 'Which films are the ethnographic films?', in P. I. Crawford and D. Turton (eds), *Film as Ethnography*. Manchester: University of Manchester Press.

Banks, M. (n.d.) 'Visual research methods', in *Social Research Update*. <http://www.soc.surrey.ac.uk/sru/SRU11 /SRU11.html>.

Banks, M. (2001) *Visual Methods in Social Research*. London: SAGE.

Banks, M. and H. Morphy (1997) *Rethinking Visual Anthropology*. London: Yale University Press.

Banks, M. and Ruby, J. (2011) *Made to Be Seen: Perspectives on the History of Visual Anthropology*. Chicago: University of Chicago Press.

Barbash, I. and Taylor, L. (1997) *Cross Cultural Filmmaking: A Handbook for Making Documentary and Ethnographic Films and Video*. London: University of California Press.

Barndt, D. (1997) 'Zooming out/zooming in: visualizing globalisation', *Visual Sociology*, 12(2): 5–32.

Barnes, D. B., Taylor-Brown, S. and Weiner, L. (1997) '"I didn't leave y'all on purpose": HIV-infected mothers' videotaped legacies for their children', in S. J. Gold (ed.), *Visual Methods in Sociological Analysis*, special issue of *Qualitative Sociology*, 20(1).

Barone, F. (2010) *Urban Firewalls: Place, Space and New Technologies in Figueres, Catalonia*. PhD Thesis. United Kingdom: University of Kent, Canterbury.

Barassi, V. and Treré, E. (2012) 'Does Web 3.0 follow Web 2.0? deconstructing theoretical assumptions through practice', *New Media and Society* 14(8): 1269–1285.

Barry, C. A. (1998) 'Choosing Qualitative Data Analysis Software: Atlas/ti and Nudist compared', *Sociological Research Online,* 3(3). <http://www.socresonline.org.uk/socresonline/3/3/4.html>.

Bateson, G. and Mead, M. (1942) *Balinese Character: A Photographic Analysis*. New York: New York Academy of the Sciences.

Baym, N. (2010) *Personal Connections in the Digital Age*. Oxford: Polity.

Becker, H. (1986) 'Photography and sociology', in *Doing Things Together.* Evanston, IL: North Western Press.

Becker, H. (1995) 'Visual sociology, documentary photography or photojournalism (almost) all a matter of context', *Visual Sociology,* 10 (1–2): 5–14.

Bell, D., Caplan, P. and Jahan Karim, W. (1993) *Gendered Fields: Women, Men and Ethnography.* London: Routledge.

Bergamaschi, M. and Francesconi, C. (1996) 'Urban homelessness: the negotiation of public spaces', *Visual Sociology,* 11(2): 35–44.

Berger, J. and Mohr, J. (1967) *A Fortunate Man*. Cambridge: Granta Books.

Berger, J. and Mohr, J. (1982) *Another Way of Telling*. Cambridge: Granta Books.

Bird. E. (2010) 'From fan practice to mediated moments: the value of practice theory in understanding media audiences' in B. Brauchler and J. Postill (eds), *Theorising Media and Practice*. Oxford: Berghahn.

Boellstorff, T. 2008. *Coming of Age in Second Life*. Princeton, NJ: Princeton University Press.

Bourdieu, P. (1990 [1965]) *Photography: A Middle-Brow Art*. Oxford: Polity Press.

Bowman, G., Grasseni, C., Hughes-Freeland, F. and Pink, S. (eds) (2007) *The Frontiers of Visual Anthropology*, a guest edited double issue of *Visual Anthropology.*

Brandes, S. (1997) 'Photographic imagery in Spanish ethnography', *Visual Anthropology Review*, 13(1): 1–13.

Bräuchler, B. and J. Postill (2010) *Theorising Media and Practice*. Oxford: Berghahn.

Braun, K. (1998) *Passing Girl, Riverside: An Essay on Camera Work*. Documentary Educational Resources, USA.

Buckler, S. (2007) *Fire in the Dark: Telling Gypsyness in North East England*. Oxford: Berghahn.

Burgess, R. G. (1984) *In the Field*. London: Routledge.

Büscher, M. (2005) 'Social Life Under the Microscope?' *Sociological Research Online,* Volume 10, Issue 1, <http://www.socresonline.org.uk/10/1/buscher.html>.

Camas, V., Martínez, A., Muñoz, R. and Ortiz, M. (2004) 'Revealing the hidden: making anthropological documentaries', in S. Pink, L. Kürti and A. Afonso (eds), *Working Images*. London: Routledge.

Capstick, A. (2011) 'Travels with a Flipcam: bringing the community to people with dementia in a day care setting through visual technology' *Visual Studies* 26(2): 142–147.

Cerezo, M., Martinez, A. and Ranera, P. (1996) 'Tres antropólogos inocentes y an ojo si parpado', in M. Garcia Alonso, A. Martinez, P. Pitarch, P. Ranera and J. Fores (eds), *Antropologia de los Sentidos: La Vista*. Celeste: Ediciones: Madrid.
Chalfen, R. (1987) *Snapshot Versions of Life*. Bowling Green, OH: Popular Press.
Chalfen, R. and Rich, M. (2004) 'Applying visual research: patients teaching physicians about asthma through video diaries', in S. Pink (ed.) *Applied Visual Anthropology*, a guest edited issue of *Visual Anthropology Review*, 20(1): 17–30.
Chalfen, R. and M. Rich (2007) 'Combining the applied, the visual and the medical: patients teaching physicians with visual narratives'. In *Visual Interventions*. S. Pink (ed.), Oxford: Berghahn.
Chaplin, E. (1994) *Sociology and Visual Representations*. London: Routledge.
Chaplin, E. (2005) 'The Photograph in theory', *Sociological Research Online*, Volume 10, Issue 1, <http://www.socresonline.org.uk/10/1/chaplin.html>.
Clark, A. (2012) 'Visual ethics in a contemporary landscape', in S. Pink (ed.) *Advances in Visual Methodology*, London: SAGE.
Clifford, J. (1986) 'Introduction: partial truths', in J. Clifford and G. Marcus (eds), *Writing Culture: the Poetics and Politics of Ethnography*. Berkeley: University of California Press.
Clifford, J. and Marcus, G. (1986) *Writing Culture: the Poetics and Politics of Ethnography*. Berkeley: University of California Press.
Coffey, A., Holbrook, B. and Atkinson, P. (1996) 'Qualitative Data Analysis: technologies and representations', *Sociological Research Online*, 1(1) <http://www.socresonline.org.uk/socresonline/1/1/4.html>.
Cohen, A. (1992) 'Self-conscious anthropology', in J. Okely and H. Callaway (eds), *Anthropology and Autobiography*. London: Routledge.
Cohen, A. and Rapport, N. (1995) *Questions of Consciousness*. Routledge: London.
Collier, J. (1967) *Visual Anthropology: Photography as Research Method*. Albuquerque: University of New Mexico Press.
Collier, J. (1995 [1975]) 'Photography and visual anthropology', in P. Hockings (ed.), *Principles of Visual Anthropology*. Berlin and New York: Mouton de Gruyter.
Collier, J. and Collier, M. (1986) *Visual Anthropology: Photography as a Research Method*. Albuquerque: University of New Mexico Press.
Connell, R. W. (1987) *Gender and Power*. Cambridge: Polity Press.
Cooke, L. and Wollen, P. (eds) (1995) *Visual Display: Culture Beyond Appearances*. Seattle, WA: Bay Press.
Coover, R. (2003) *Cultures in Webs* (CD ROM). Watertown: Eastgate Systems.
Coover, R. (2004a) 'The representation of cultures in digital media', in S. Pink, L. Kürti and A. Afonso (eds), *Working Images*. London: Routledge.
Coover, R. (2004b) 'Using digital media tools in cross-cultural research, analysis and representation', *Visual Studies*, 19(1): 6–25.
Coover, R. (2008) *Outside/Inside: Virtual Panoramas of Independence National Historical Park*, sample online at http://www.unknownterritories.org/APS.html.

Coover, R. with Badani, P., Caviezel, F., Marino, M., Sawhney, N. and Uricchio, W. (2012) 'Digital technologies, visual research and the nonfiction image', in S. Pink (ed.), *Advances in Visual Methodology*. London: SAGE.

Couldry, N. (2010) 'Theorising media as practice', in B. Brauchler and J. Postill (eds), *Theorising Media and Practice*. Oxford: Berghahn.

Crawford, P. I. (1992) 'Film as discourse: the invention of anthropological realities', in P. I. Crawford and D. Turton (eds), *Film as Ethnography*. Manchester: Manchester University Press.

Crawford, P. I. and Hafsteinsson, S. (eds) (1996) *The Construction of the Viewer*. Aarhus: Intervention Press.

Crawford, P. I. and Turton, D. (1992) 'Introduction', in P. I. Crawford and D. Turton (eds), *Film as Ethnography*. Manchester: Manchester University Press.

Crawshaw, C. and Urry, J. (1997) 'Tourism and the photographic eye', in C. Rojek and J. Urry (eds), *Touring Cultures*. London: Routledge.

Crotty, M. (1998) *The Foundations of Social Research: Meaning and Perspective in the Research Process*. London: SAGE.

Dant, T. (2004) 'Recording the "Habitus"', in C. Pole (ed.), *Seeing is Believing?* London: Elsevier.

Dant, T. and Bowles, D. (2003) 'Dealing with dirt: servicing and repairing cars', *Sociological Research Online*, 8(2), <http://www.socresonline.org.uk/8/2/dant.html>.

Da Silva, O. (2000) *In the Net*, exhibition catalogue. Porto, Portugal: Rainho and Neves Lda.

Da Silva, O. and Pink, S. (2004) 'In the Net: ethnographic photography', in S. Pink, L. Kürti and A. Afonso (eds), *Working Images*. London: Routledge.

Davis, J. (1992) 'Tense in ethnography: some practical considerations', in J. Okely and H. Callaway (eds), *Anthropology and Autobiography*. London: Routledge.

Desjarlais, R. (2003) *Sensory Biographies: lives and death among Nepal's Yolmo Buddhists*. London: University of California Press.

Devereaux, L. (1995) 'Experience, representation and film', in L. Devereaux and R. Hillman (eds) (1995) *Fields of Vision: Essays in Film Studies, Visual Anthropology and Photography*. Berkeley: University of California Press.

Devereaux, L. and Hillman, R. (eds) (1995) *Fields of Vision: Essays in Film Studies, Visual Anthropology and Photography*. Berkeley: University of California Press.

Dicks, B., Mason, B., Coffey, A. and Atkinson, P. (2005) *Qualitative Research and Hypermedia: Ethnography for the Digital Age*. London: SAGE.

Driver, F. (2003) 'On Geography as a Visual Discipline' *Antipode* 35(2): 227–231.

Durington, M. (2007) 'The Hunters' Redux: participatory and applied visual anthropology with the Botswana San'. In *Visual Interventions*, Sarah Pink (ed.), Oxford: Berghahn.

Durington, M. and Ruby, J. (2011) 'Ethnographic film', in M. Banks and J. Ruby (eds), *Made to be Seen: Perspectives on the History of Visual Anthropology*, University of Chicago Press.

Edgar, I. (2004) *Guide to Imagework: Imagination-Based Research Methods*, London: Routledge.

Edwards, E. (ed.) (1992) *Anthropology and Photography.* New Haven, CT: Yale University Press.

Edwards, E. (1997a) 'Beyond the Boundary: a consideration of the expressive in photography and anthropology', in M. Banks and H. Morphy (eds), *Rethinking Visual Anthropology.* London: Routledge.

Edwards, E. (ed.) (1997b) Special issue of *History of Photography*, 21(1).

Edwards, E. (2001) *Raw Histories*, Oxford: Berg.

Edwards, E. (2011) 'Tracing Photography', in M. Banks and J. Ruby (eds), *Made to be Seen: Perspectives on the History of Visual Anthropology*. Chicago: University of Chicago Press.

Edwards, E. and K. Bhaumik (2009) (eds) *Visual Sense: A Cultural Reader.* Oxford: Berg.

El Guindi, F. (2004) *Visual Anthropology: Essential Theory and Method.* California: Altamira Press.

Ellen, R. (1984) *Ethnographic Research: a Guide to General Conduct.* London: Academic Press.

Emmel, N. and Clark, A. (2011) 'Learning to use visual methodologies in our research: a dialogue between two researchers', [40 paragraphs]. *Forum Qualitative Sozialforschung/Forum: Qualitative Social Research, 12*(1), Art. 36, <http://nbn-resolving.de/urn:nbn:de:0114-fqs1101360>.

Emmison, M. and Smith, P. (2000) *Researching the Visual*. London: SAGE.

Engelbrecht, B. (1993) *Copper Working in Santa Clara del Cobre.* Goettingen, Germany: IWF.

Engelbrecht, B. (1996) 'For whom do we produce?', in P. I. Crawford and S. B. Hafsteinsson (eds), *The Construction of the Viewer.* Aarhus: Intervention Press.

Evans, J. and Hall, S. (eds) (1999) *Visual Culture: the Reader.* London: SAGE.

Fabian, J. (1983) *Time and the Other: How Anthropology makes its Object.* New York: Columbia University Press.

Fahmy, E. and S. Pemberton (2012) 'A video testimony on rural poverty and social exclusion' *Sociological Research Online,* 17(1)2, http://www.socresonline.org.uk/17/1/2.html.

Farman, J. (2010) 'Mapping the Digital Empire: Google Earth and the process of postmodern cartography', *New Media and Society*,12(6):869–88.

Farrar, M. (2005) 'Photography: making and breaking racialised boundaries: an essay in reflexive, radical, visual sociology', *Sociological Research Online*, Volume 10, Issue 1, <http://www.socresonline.org.uk/10/1/farrar.html>.

Fernandez, J. (1995) 'Amazing grace: meaning deficit, displacement and new consciousness in expressive interaction', in A. Cohen and N. Rapport (eds), *Questions of Consciousness*. London: Routledge.

Ferrándiz, F. (1996) 'Intersubjectividad y vídeo etnográfico. Holguras y textxuras en 1a grabación de ceremonias espiritistas en Venezuela', in M. Garcia, A. Martinez, P. Pitarch, P. Ranera, and J. Fores (eds), *Antropologia de los sentidos: La Vista.* Madrid: Celeste Ediciones.

Ferrándiz, F. (1998) 'A trace of fingerprints: displacements and textures in the use of ethnographic video in Venezuelan spiritism', *Visual Anthropology Review*, 13(2): 19–38.

Fetterman, D. (1998) *Ethnography* (second edition). London: SAGE.

Flores, C. (2004) 'Indigenous video, development and shared anthropology: a collaborative experience with Maya-Q'eqchi' filmmakers in post-war Guatemala', *Visual Anthropology Review*, 20(1): 31–44.

Flores, C. (2007) 'Sharing anthropology: collaborative video experiences among Maya film-makers in post-war Guatemala'. In *Visual Interventions*. S.Pink (ed.), Oxford: Berghahn.

Forrest, E. (2012) *On Photography and Movement: Bodies, Habits and Worlds in Everyday Photographic Practice*. PhD thesis, Centre for Research in Media and Cultural Studies, University of Sunderland.

Fors, V., A. Backstrom and S. Pink (2013) 'Multisensory emplaced learning: resituating situated learning in a moving world' *Mind, Culture, and Activity: An International Journal*, published on-line first at http://www.tandfonline.com/doi/abs/10.1080/10749039.2012.719991

Fortier, A. (1998) 'Gender, ethnicity and fieldwork: a case study', in C. Seale (ed.), *Researching Culture and Society*. London: SAGE.

Garrett, B. L. (2011) 'Videographic geographies: using digital video for geographic research'. *Progress in Human Geography*, 35(4): 521–541.

Geertz, C. (1973) *The Interpretation of Cultures*. New York: Basic Books.

Gilroy, R. and Kellett, P. (2005) 'Picture me: place memory and identity in the lives and names of older people', Paper presented at the AHRC symposium: *Interior Insights, Design, Ethnography and the Home*. Royal College of Art.

Ginsburg, F. (2011) 'Native Intelligence: a short history of debates on indigenous media and ethnographic film', in M. Banks and J. Ruby (eds), *Made to be Seen: Perspectives on the History of Visual Anthropology*. Chicago: University of Chicago Press.

Ginsburg, F., Abu-Lughod, L. and Larkin, B. (eds) (2002) *Media Worlds: anthropology on new terrain*. California: University of California Press.

Goffman, I. (1979) *Gender Advertisements*. London and Basingstoke: Macmillan.

Gold, S. J. (1995) 'New York/LA: a visual comparison of public life in two cities', *Visual Sociology*, 10(1–2): 85–105.

Gold, S. J. (1997) (ed.) 'Visual methods in sociological analysis', special issue, *Qualitative Sociology*, 20(1).

Goldfine, R. and Goldfine, O. (2003) 'Hunters and healers: social change and cultural conflict in rural Maine', *Visual Studies*, 18(2): 96–111.

Gómez Cruz, E. (2011) *De la "cultura Kodak" a la "cultura Flickr": Prácticas de fotografía digital en la vida cotidiana*. PhD Thesis, Open University of Catalonia, Spain.

Gómez Cruz, E. (2012) *Sobre la fotografía (digital). Una etnografía*, Editorial UOC, Barcelona.

Goopy, S. and Lloyd, D. (2005) 'Picturing cosmopolitanism – identity and quality of life among older Italo-Australians', in D. Ellison and I. Woodward (eds), *Sites of Cosmopolitan Citizenship, Aesthetics, Culture,* Centre for Public Culture and Ideas, Griffith University, pp. 133–9.

Grady, J. (1996) 'The scope of visual sociology', *Visual Sociology,* 11(2): 10–24.

Graham, C., Laurier, E., O'Brien, V. and Rouncefield, M. (2011) 'New visual technologies: shifting boundaries, shared moments', *Visual Studies*, 26(2): 87–91.

Grasseni, C. (2004) 'Video and ethnographic knowledge: skilled vision and the practice of breeding', in S. Pink, L. Kürti and A. Afonso (eds), *Working Images.* London: Routledge.

Grasseni, C. (2007) (ed) *Skilled Visions*. Oxford: Berghahn.

Grasseni, C. (2011) 'Skilled visions: toward an ecology of visual inscriptions', in M. Banks and J. Ruby (eds), *Made to be Seen: Perspectives on the History of Visual Anthropology*. Chicago: University of Chicago Press.

Grasseni, C. (2012) 'Community mapping as auto-ethno-cartography', in S. Pink (ed.), *Advances in Visual Methodology*. London: SAGE.

Grimshaw, A. (2001) *The Ethnographer's Eye*. Cambridge: Cambridge University Press.

Grimshaw, A. and Ravetz, A. (2004) *Visualizing Anthropology.* Bristol: Intellect.

Halford, S. and Knowles, C. (2005) (eds) 'More Than Words: Some Reflections on Working Visually', themed issue of *Sociological Research Online,* 10(1) <http://www.socresonline.org.uk/10/1/knowleshalford.html>.

Hall, S. (ed.) (1997) *Representation: Cultural Representations and Signifying Practices.* London: SAGE.

Halstead, N., E. Hirsch and J. Okely (eds) (2008) *Knowing How to Know: Fieldwork and the Ethnographic Present.* Oxford: Berghahn.

Hammersley, M. and Atkinson, P. (1995) *Ethnography: Principles in Practice,* 2nd edition. London: Routledge.

Harper, D. (ed.) (1994) 'Cape Bretton 1952: the photographic vision of Tim Asch', special issue, *Visual Sociology*, 9(2).

Harper, D. (1998a) 'An argument for visual sociology', in J. Prosser (ed.), *Image-based Research: a Sourcebook for Qualitative Researchers*. London: Falmer Press.

Harper, D. (1998b) 'On the authority of the image: visual methods at the crossroads', in N. Denzin and Y. Lincoln (eds), *Collecting and Interpreting Qualitative Materials*. London: SAGE.

Harper, D. (2002) 'Talking about pictures: a case for photo-elicitation', *Visual Studies*, 17(1): 13–26.

Harper, D., Knowles, C. and Leonard, P. (2005) 'Visually narrating post-colonial lives: ghosts of war and empire', *Visual Studies*, 20(1): 4–15.

Harris, M. (2007) 'Introduction: ways of knowing', in *Ways of Knowing: New Approaches in the Anthropology of Experience and Learning,* edited by M. Harris. Oxford: Berghahn, 1–24.

Harvey, P. (1996) *Hybrids of Modernity: Anthropology, the Nation State and the Universal Exhibition*. London: Routledge.

Hastrup, K. (1992) 'Anthropological vision: some notes on visual and textual authority', in P. I. Crawford and D. Turton (eds), *Film as Ethnography.* Manchester: Manchester University Press.

Heider, K. (1976) *Ethnographic Film.* Austin: University of Texas Press.

Henley, P. (1994) *Faces in the Crowd.* Granada Centre Productions (filmmaker Paul Henley, anthropological consultant, Ann Rowbottom).

Henley, P. (1998) 'Filmmaking and ethnographic research', in J. Prosser (ed.), *Image-based Research.* London: Falmer Press.

Henley, P. (2004) 'Beyond observational cinema ...' in S. Pink, L. Kürti and A. Afonso (eds), *Working Images.* London: Routledge.

Henley, P. (2010) *The Adventure of the Real: Jean Rouch and the Craft of Ethnographic Cinema.* Chicago: University of Chicago Press.

Hindmarsh, J. and Tutt, D. (2012) 'Video in Analytic Practice', in S. Pink (ed.) *Advances in Visual Methodology.* London: SAGE.

Hine, C. (2000) *Virtual Ethnography.* London: SAGE.

Hjorth, L. (2010) 'The game of being social: web 2.0, social media, and online games', *Iowa Journal of Communication,* 42(1): 73–92.

Hobart, M. (2010) 'What do we mean by "media practices"'? In *Theorising Media and Practice,* B. Bräuchler and J. Postill (eds), Oxford: Berghann.

Hockings, P. (ed.) (1975) *Principles of Visual Anthropology.* The Hague: Mouton.

Hockings, P. (ed.) (1995) *Principles of Visual Anthropology,* 2nd edition. The Hague: Mouton.

Hogan, S. (2011) 'Images of Broomhall, Sheffield. urban violence and using the arts as a research aid' *Visual Anthropology,* 24(6): 266–280

Hogan, S. and Pink, S. (2012) 'Visualising interior worlds: interdisciplinary routes to knowing', in S. Pink (ed.) *Advances in Visual Methodology.* London: SAGE.

Holliday, R. (2001) 'We've been framed: visualizing methodologies', *Sociological Review* 48 (4): 503–521.

Hoskins, J. (1993) '"Why we cried to see him again": Indonesian villagers' responses to the filmic disruption of time', in J. Rollwagen (ed.), *Anthropological Film and Video in the 1990s.* Brockport, NY: The Institute Inc.

Howes, D. (2005) *Empire of the Senses: The Sensory Culture Reader.* Oxford: Berg.

Hughes-Freeland, F. (ed.) (1997) *Ritual, Performance, Media.* London: Routledge.

Hutnyk, J. (1990) 'Comparative anthropology and Evans-Pritchard's Nuer Photography' *Critique of Anthropology* 10(1): 81–102.

Hutnyk, J. (1996) *The Rumour of Calcutta.* London: Zed Books.

Ingold, T. (2000) *The Perception of the Environment.* London: Routledge.

Ingold, T. (2008a) 'Bindings against boundaries: entanglements of life in an open world', in *Environment and Planning A,* 40: 1796–1810.

Ingold, T. (2008b) 'Anthropology is *not* Ethnography', *Proceedings of the British Academy,* Volume 154.

Ingold, T. (2010a) 'Ways of mind-walking: reading, writing, painting', *Visual Studies,* 25:1, 15–23.

Ingold, T. (2010b) 'Footprints through the weather-world: walking, breathing, knowing', *JRAI* 16, Issue Supplement s1: S121–S139.

Ingold, T. (2011) 'Worlds of sense and sensing the world: a response to Sarah Pink and David Howes', in *Social Anthropology/Anthropologie Sociale,* 19(3): 313–317

Irving, A. (2007) 'Ethnography, art and death', *Journal of the Royal Anthropological Institute,* 13(1): 185–208.

Irving, A. (2010) 'Dangerous substances and visible evidence: tears, blood, alcohol, pills', *Visual Studies,* 25(1): 24–35.

Jacknis, I. (1984) 'Franz Boas and Photography', *Studies in Visual Communication,* 10(1): 2–60.

James, A., Hockey, J. and Dawson, A. (1997) *After Writing Culture: Epistemology and Praxis in Contemporary Anthropology*. London: Routledge.

Jenks, C. (1995) *Visual Cultures*. London: Routledge.

Jhala, J. (2004) 'In a time of fear and terror: seeing, assessing, assisting, understanding and living the reality and consequences of disaster', *Visual Anthropology Review,* 20(1): 59–69.

Josephides, L. (1997) 'Representing the anthropologist's predicament', in W. James, J. Hockey and A. Dawson (eds), *After Writing Culture: Epistemology and Praxis in Contemporary Anthropology.* London: Routledge.

Kirkpatrick, J. (2003) *Transports of Delight: The Ricksha Arts of Bangladesh.* A CD-ROM). University of Indiana Press.

Knowles, C. and Sweetman, P. (2004) (eds) *Picturing the Social Landscape: Visual Methods and the Sociological Imagination*, London: Routledge.

Kozinets, R. (2010) *Netnography*. London: Sage.

Kulick, D. and Willson, M. (eds) (1995) *Taboo: Sex, Identity and Erotic Subjectivity in Anthropological Fieldwork*. London: Routledge.

Kürti, L. (2004) 'Picture Perfect: community and commemoration in postcards', in S. Pink, L. Kürti and A. Afonso (eds), *Working Images*. London: Routledge.

Lammer, C. (2007) 'Bodywork: social somatic interventions in the operating theatres of invasive radiology', S. Pink (ed.), *Visual Interventions*. Oxford: Berghahn.

Lammer, C. (2009) 'Empathographies: using body art related video approaches in the environment of an Austrian teaching hospital', *International Journal of Multiple Research Approaches,* 3: 264–275.

Lammer, C. (2012) 'Healing Mirrors: Body Arts and Ethnographic Methodologies', in S. Pink (ed.), *Advances in Visual Methodology*. London: SAGE.

Lapenta, F. (2011) 'Geomedia: On location-based media, the changing status of collective image production and the emergence of social navigation systems', *Visual Studies*, 26(1): 14–24.

Lapenta, F. (2012) 'Geomedia based methods and visual research. exploring the theoretical tenets of the localization and visualization of mediated social relations with direct visualization techniques', in S. Pink (ed.) *Advances in Visual Methodology*. London: SAGE.

Larson, H. J. (1988) 'Photography that listens', *Visual Anthropology,* 1: 415–32.

Laurier, E., Strebel, I. and Brown, B. (2011) 'The reservations of the editor: the routine work of showing and knowing the film in the edit suite', *Journal of Social Semiotics*, (21)2: 239–257.

Law, J. (2004) *After Method: Mess in Social Science Research*. London: Routledge.

Levine, S. (2007) 'Steps for the future: HIV/AIDS, media activism and applied visual anthropology in Southern Africa' in S. Pink (ed) *Visual Interventions: Applied Visual Anthropology*. Oxford: Berg.

Lister, M. and Wells, L. (2000) 'Seeing beyond belief: cultural studies as an approach to analysing the visual', in T. van Leeuwen and C. Jewitt (eds), *The Handbook of Visual Analysis*. London: SAGE.

Loizos, P. (1993) *Innovation in Ethnographic Film*. Manchester: Manchester University Press.

Lomax, H. and Casey, N. (1998) 'Recording social life: reflexivity and video methodology', *Sociological Research Online*, 3(2), <http://www.socresonline.org.uk/socresonline/3/2/1.html>.

Lorimer, H. (2005) 'Cultural geography: the busyness of being "more than representational"', *Progress in Human Geography*, 29(1): 83–94.

Lury, C. (1998) *Prosthetic Culture: Photography, Memory and Identity*. London: Routledge.

Lyon, D. (2013) 'The labour of refurbishment: space and time, and the building and the body' in S. Pink. D. E Tutt ad A. Dainty (eds), *Ethnographic Research in the Construction Industry*. Oxford: Routledge.

MacDougall, D. and MacDougall, J. (1991) *Photo Wallahs: An Encounter with Photography in Mussorie: a North Indian Hill Station*. Berkeley, CA: Oxhard Film Productions.

MacDougall, D. (1997) 'The visual in anthropology', in M. Banks and H. Morphy (eds), *Rethinking Visual Anthropology*. London: New Haven Press.

MacDougall, D. (1998) *Transcultural Cinema*. Selected essays, edited by Lucien Taylor. Princeton, NJ: Princeton University Press.

MacDougall, D. (2001) 'Renewing ethnographic film: is digital video changing the genre?' *Anthropology Today*, 17(3): 15–21.

MacDougall, D. (2005) *The Corporeal Image*. Princeton: Princeton University Press.

Mack, S., Mack, L., Alessa, L. and Kliskey, A. (2011) 'The integration of digital terrain visualization in ethnography: the historic village of Belofski, Alaska', *Visual Anthropology*, 24(5): 455–476.

Manovich, L. (2011) 'What is visualization', *Visual Studies*, 26(1): 36–49.

Marchand, T. H. (2010), 'Making knowledge: explorations of the indissoluble relation between minds, bodies, and environment'. *Journal of the Royal Anthropological Institute*, 16: S1–S21.

Marcus, G. (1995) 'The modernist sensibility in recent ethnographic writing and the cinematic metaphor of montage', in L. Devereaux and R. Hillman (eds), *Fields of Vision: Essays in Film Studies, Visual Anthropology and Photography.* Berkeley: University of California Press.

Margolis, E. and L. Pauwels (2011) *The SAGE Handbook of Visual Research Methods.* London: SAGE.

Martens, L. (2012) 'The politics and practices of looking: CCTV, video and domestic kitchen practices', in S. Pink (ed.), *Advances in Visual Methodology*. London: SAGE.

Martinez, W. (1992) 'Who constructs anthropological knowledge? toward a theory of ethnographic film spectatorship', in P. I. Crawford and D. Turton (eds), *Film as Ethnography*. Manchester: Manchester University Press.

Marvin, G. (2005) 'Research, representations and responsibilities: an anthropologist in the contested world of fox hunting', in S. Pink (ed.), *Applications of Anthropology: Professional Anthropology in the Twenty First Century*. Oxford: Berghahn.

Massey, D. (2005) *For Space*, London: Sage.

Matless, D. (2003) ' Gestures around the Visual', *Antipode*, 35(2): 222–226.

McGuigan, J. (ed.) (1997) *Cultural Methodologies*. London: SAGE.

Mead, M. (1975) [1995] 'Visual anthropology in a discipline of words', in Hockings (ed.), *Principles of Visual Anthropology*. The Hague: Mouton.

Melhuus, M., Mitchell, J. P. and Wulff, H. (2009) *Ethnographic Practice in the Present.* Oxford: Berghahn.

D. Miller (ed) (1998) *Material Cultures: Why Some Things Matter*. Chicago: University of Chicago Press.

Miller, D. (2001) (ed.) *Home Possessions*. Oxford: Berg.

Miller, D. (2011) *Tales from Facebook*. Oxford: Polity.

Miller, D. and Slater, D. (2000) *The Internet: An Ethnographic Approach.* Oxford: Berg.

Mitchell, C. (2011) *Doing Visual Research*, London: SAGE.

Mitchell, W.J.T. (2002) 'Showing seeing: a critique of visual culture' in N. Mirzeoff (ed) *The Visual Culture Reader*, Second Edition. London: Routledge.

Mitchell, W. J. T. (2005) 'There are no visual media' *Journal of Visual Culture* 4(2): 257–266.

Mizen, P. (2005) 'A little "light work"? Children's images of their labour', in *Visual Studies,* 20(2): 124–139.

Morley, D. (1996) 'The audience, the ethnographer, the postmodernist and their problems', in P. I. Crawford and S. B. Hafsteinsson (eds), *The Construction of the Viewer.* Aarhus: Intervention Press.

Morphy, H. (1996) 'More than mere facts: repositioning Spencer and Gillen in the history of anthropology', in S. R. Morton and D. J. Mulvaney (eds), *Exploring Central Australia: Society, Environment and the Horn Expedition.* Chipping Norton: Surrey Beatty and Sons.

Morphy, H. and M. Banks (1997) 'Introduction: rethinking visual anthropology', in M. Banks and H. Morphy (eds), *Rethinking Visual Anthropology.* London: Routledge.

Muir, S. and J. Mason (2012) 'Capturing Christmas: the sensory potential of data from participant produced video' *Sociological Research Online, 17 (1) 5,* <http://www.socresonline.org.uk/17/1/5.html>.

Murthy, D. (2008) 'Digital Ethnography: An Examination of the Use of New Technologies for Social Research', *Sociology*, 42(5): 837–855.

Murthy, D. (2011) 'Emergent digital ethnographic methods for social research', in S. Nagy Hesse-Biber (ed.), *The Handbook of Emergent Technologies in Social Research*. Oxford: Oxford University press.

Nencel, L. and Pels, P. (1991) *Constructing Knowledge: Authority and Critique in Social Science*. London: SAGE.

Nuemann, M. (1992) 'The travelling eye: photography, tourism and ethnography', *Visual Sociology*, 7(2): 22–38.

Okely, J. (1994) 'Vicarious and sensory knowledge of chronology and change: ageing in rural France', in K. Hastrup and P. Hervik (eds), *Social Experience and Anthropological Knowledge*. London: Routledge.

Okely, J. (1996) *Own or Other Culture*. London: Routledge.

Okely, J. and Callaway, H. (1992) *Anthropology and Autobiography*. London: Routledge.

O'Neill, M. (2002) in association with Giddens, Breatnach, Bagley, Bourne and Judge, *'Renewed Methodologies for social research: ethno-mimesis as performative praxis', Sociological Review*, (50): 1.

O'Neill, M. (2012) 'Ethno-mimesis and participatory arts', in S. Pink (ed.), *Advances in Visual Methodology*. London: SAGE.

O'Neill, M. and P. Hubbard (2010) 'Walking, sensing, belonging: ethno-mimesis as performative praxis', *Visual Studies*, 25(1):46–58.

O'Reilly, K. (2011) *Ethnographic Methods*. 2nd Edition. London: Routledge.

Orobitg, G. (2004) 'Photography in the field: word and image in ethnographic research', in S. Pink, L. Kürti and A. Afonso (eds), *Working Images*. London: Routledge.

Parmeggiani, P. (2009) 'Going digital: using new technologies in visual sociology', *Visual Studies*, 24(1): 71–81.

Pauwels, L. (1996) 'Managing impressions on visually decoding the workplace as a symbolic environment', *Visual Sociology*, 11(2): 62–74.

Pels, P. (1996) *EASA Newsletter*, 18: 18, <http://www.ub.es.easa.netethic.htm>.

Peterson, M. A. (2010) '"But it is my habit to read the *Times*"': metaculture and practice in the reading of Indian newspapers', in B. Bräuchler and J. Postill (eds), *Theorising Media and Practice*. Oxford: Berghahn.

Pink, S. (1993) 'La mujer en el toreo: reflexiones sobre el éxito de una mujer novillero en la temporada de 1993', *La Tribuna*. Spain, December.

Pink, S. (1996) 'Excursiones socio-visuales en el mundo del toro', in M. Garcia, A. Martinez, P. Pitarch, P. Ranera and J. Fores (eds), *Antropologia de los sentidos: La Vista*. Madrid: Celeste Ediciones.

Pink, S. (1997a) *Women and Bullfighting: Gender, Sex and the Consumption of Tradition*. Oxford: Berg.

Pink, S. (1997b) 'Visual histories of success', in E. Edwards (ed.), *History of Photography*. London and Washington, DC: Taylor & Francis.

Pink, S. (1999a) '"Informants" who come "home"', in V. Amit-Talai (ed.), *Constructing the Field*. London: Routledge.

Pink, S. (1999b) 'A woman, a camera and the world of bullfighting: visual culture, experience and the production of anthropological knowledge', *Visual Anthropology*, 13: 71–86.

Pink, S. (2004a) (ed.) *Applied Visual Anthropology*, a guest edited issue of *Visual Anthropology Review*, 20(1).

Pink, S. (2004b) *Home Truths: Gender, Domestic Objects and Everyday Life*. Oxford: Berg.

Pink, S. (2004c) 'Performance, self-representation and narrative: interviewing with video', in C. Pole (ed.), *Seeing is Believing? Approaches to visual research*. Studies in Qualitative Methodology – Volume 7, Elsevier Science.

Pink, S. (2006) *The Future of Visual Anthropology: Engaging the Senses*. London: Routledge.

Pink, S. (2007a) (ed.) *Visual Interventions: Applied Visual Anthropology*. Oxford: Berghahn.

Pink, S. (2007b) 'Walking with Video', *Visual Studies*, 22(3): 240–252.

Pink, S. (2008a) 'An urban tour: the sensory sociality of ethnographic place-making', in *Ethnography*, 9(2): 175–196.

Pink, S. (2008b) 'Mobilising visual ethnography: making routes, making place and making images', in *Forum: Qualitative Research* (*FQS*), <http://www.qualitative-research.net/fqs/fqs-eng.htm>.

Pink, S. (2009) *Doing Sensory Ethnography*. London: SAGE.

Pink, S. (2010) 'The future of the anthropology of the senses', a debate with David Howes in *Social Anthropology*.

Pink, S. (2011a) 'Sensory digital photography: re-thinking 'moving' and the image' *Visual Studies*, 26(1): 4–13.

Pink, S. (2011b) 'Images, senses And applications: engaging visual anthropology', *Visual Anthropology*, 24(5): 437–454.

Pink, S. (2011c) 'Multi-modality and multi-sensoriality and ethnographic knowing: or can social semiotics be reconciled with the phenomenology of perception and knowing in practice', *Qualitative Research*, 11(1): 261–276.

Pink, S. (2011d) 'Drawing with our feet (and trampling the maps): walking with video as a graphic anthropology', in T. Ingold (ed.), *Redrawing Anthropology*. Farnham: Ashgate.

Pink, S. (2011e) 'Amateur documents?: Amateur photographic practice, collective representation and the constitution of place in UK slow cities', *Visual Studies* 26(2): 92–101.

Pink, S. (2011f) 'Digital visual anthropology: potential and challenges', in M. Banks and J. Ruby (eds) *Made to be Seen: Perspectives on the History of Visual Anthropology*. Chicago: University of Chicago Press.

Pink, S. (2011g) 'Ethnography of the invisible: how to "see" domestic and human energy', *Ethnologia Europaea: Journal of European Ethnology*, 117–128.

Pink, S. (2011h) 'The visual and beyond: a multi-sensory approach to visual methods', in L. Pauwels and E. Margolis (eds), *Handbook of Visual Methods*. London: SAGE.

Pink, S. (2012a) (ed.) *Advances in Visual Methodology*. London: SAGE.

Pink, S. (2012b) 'Advances in visual methodology: an introduction', in S. Pink (ed.), *Advances in Visual Methodology*. London: SAGE.

Pink, S. (2012c) 'Visual ethnography and the internet: visuality, virtuality and the spatial turn', in S. Pink (ed.), *Advances in Visual Methodology*. London: SAGE.

Pink, S. (2012d) *Situating Everyday Life: Practices and Places*. London: SAGE.

Pink, S. and L. Hjorth (2012) 'Emplaced cartographies: reconceptualising camera phone practices in an age of locative media', *MIA (Media International Australia)*, 145: 145–155.

Pink, S., Hubbard, P., O'Neill, M. and Radley, A. (2010) 'Walking Across Disciplines', *Visual Studies*, 25(1).

Pink, S., Kürti, L. and Afonso, A. (eds) (2004) *Working Images*. London: Routledge.

Pink, S. and K. Leder Mackley (2012) 'Video as a route to sensing invisible energy', *Sociological Research Online*, February 2012, <http://www.socresonline.org.uk/17/1/3.html>.

Pink, S. K. Leder Mackley, V. Mitchell, C. Escobar-Tello, M. Hanratty, T. Bhamra and R. Morosanu (2013) 'Applying the lens of sensory ethnography to sustainable HCI', *Transactions on Computer-Human Interaction*.

Pink, S., Tutt, D., Dainty, A. and Gibb, A. (2010) 'Ethnographic methodologies for construction research: knowing, practice and interventions', *Building Research and Information*, 38(6): 647–659.

Pinney, C. (1992a) 'Montage, doubling and the mouth of God', in P. I. Crawford and J. K. Simonsen (eds), *Ethnographic Film Aesthetics and Narrative Traditions*. Aarhus: Intervention Press.

Pinney, C. (1992b) 'The parallel histories of anthropology and photography', in E. Edwards (ed.), *Anthropology and Photography*. New Haven, CT: Yale University Press.

Pinney, C. (1997) *Camera Indica: The Social Life of Indian Photographs*. London: Reaktion Books.

Pitt-Rivers, J. (1954) *The People of the Sierra*. New York: Criterion.

Pole, C. (ed.) (2004) 'Seeing is believing? approaches to visual research', *Studies in Qualitative Methodology – Volume 7*. Elsevier Science.

Pollock, G. (1988) *Vision and Difference: Femininity, Feminism and the Histories of Art*. London: Routledge.

Postill, J. (2005) 'A few comments on media and sociation', paper presented to the EASA Media Anthropology Network 'Media, Anthropology, Theory' workshop, at Loughborough University, <http://www.philbu.net/media-anthropology/lboro_postill.pdf>.

Postill, J. (2010) 'Introduction: Theorising media and practice', in B. Bräuchler and J. Postill (eds), *Theorising Media and Practice*. Oxford: Berghahn.

Postill, J. (2011) *Localizing the Internet*, Oxford: Berghahn.

Postill, J. and S. Pink '(2012) 'Social Media ethnography: the digital researcher in a messy web', *MIA (Media International Australia)*, 145: 123–134.

Pratt, M. L. (1986) 'Fieldwork in common places', in J. Clifford and G. Marcus (eds), *Writing Culture*. Berkeley: University of California Press.

Prelorain, J., Prelorain, M. and Saravino, Z. (1992) *Zulay Frente el Siglo XXI*, Department of Film and Television, University of California, Los Angeles.

Press, I. (1979) *The City as Context*. Urbana: University of Illinois Press.

Price, D. and Wells, L. (1997) 'Thinking about photography: debates, historically and now', in L. Wells (ed.), *Photography: a Critical Introduction*. London: Routledge.

Prosser, J. (1996) 'What constitutes an image-based qualitative methodology?', *Visual Sociology*, 11(2): 26–34.

Prosser, J., Clark, A. and Wiles, R. (2008) *Visual Research Ethics at the Crossroads*. NCRM Working Paper. Realities, Morgan Centre, Manchester, UK. <http://eprints.ncrm.ac.uk/535/>.

Prosser, J. and Schwartz, D. (1998) 'Photographs within the sociological research process', in J. Prosser (ed.), *Image-based Research: a Sourcebook for Qualitative Researchers*. London: Falmer Press.

Radley, A. and Taylor, D. (2003a) 'Images of recovery: a photo-elicitation study on the hospital ward', *Qualitative Health Research*, 13(1): 77–99.

Radley, A. and Taylor, D. (2003b) 'Remembering one's stay in hospital: a study in recovery, photography and forgetting', *Health: An Interdisciplinary Journal for the Social Study of Health, Illness and Medicine*, 7(2): 129–159.

Radley, A., Hodgetts, D. and Cullen, A. (2005) 'Visualizing homelessness: a study in photography and estrangement', *Journal of Community and Applied Social Psychology*, 15: 273–295.

Ramey, K. (2011) 'Productive dissonance and sensuous image-making: visual anthropology and experimental film', in M. Banks and J. Ruby (eds), *Made to be Seen: Perspectives on the History of Visual Anthropology*. Chicago: University of Chicago Press.

Ramos, M. J. (2004) 'Drawing the lines: the limitations of cultural *ekphrasis*', in S. Pink, L. Kürti and A. Afonso (eds), *Working Images*. London: Routledge.

Rapport, N. (1997a) *Transcendent Individual: Towards a Literary and Liberal Anthropology*. London: Routledge.

Reiger, J. (1996) 'Photographing social change', *Visual Sociology*, 11(1): 5–49.

Rich, M., Lamola, S., Gordon, J. and Chalfen, R. (2000) 'Video Intervention/Prevention Assessment: a patient-centered methodology for understanding the adolescent illness experience', *Journal of Adolescent Health*, 27(3): 155–165.

Rollwagen, J. (1988) *Anthropological Film making*. New York: Harwood Academic Press.

Rose, G. (2000) *Visual Methodologies*, first edition. London: SAGE.

Rose, G. (2003) 'On the need to ask how, exactly, is geography "visual"?', *Antipode*, 35(2): 212–221.

Rose, G. (2011) *Visual Methodologies*, third edition. London: SAGE.

Rothenbuhler, E. W. and Coman, M. (eds) (2005) *Media Anthropology*. Thousand Oaks, CA: SAGE Publications.

Rowe, J. (2011) 'Legal issues of using images in research', in E. Margolis and L. Pauwels (eds), *The SAGE Handbook of Visual Research Methods*. London: SAGE.

Ruby, J. (1982) 'Ethnography as *Trompe L'Oiel*: film and anthropology', in J. Ruby (ed.), *A Crack in the Mirror: Reflexive Perspectives in Anthropology*. Philadelphia, PA: University of Pennsylvania Press. <http://www.temple.edu./anthro/ruby/trompe.htm>.

Ruby, J. (2000a) *Picturing Culture: Explorations of Film and Anthropology*. Chicago: University of Chicago Press.

Ruby, J. (2004) *The Taylor Family* (CD ROM). Oak Park Stories series. Distributor, Documentary Educational Resources, Watertown, MA, USA.

Ryan, J. (2003) 'Who's afraid of visual culture', *Antipode*, 35(2): 232–237.

Sage, D. (2013) 'Building contacts: the trials, tribulations and translations of an ethnographic researcher in construction' in S. Pink. D. E Tutt ad A. Dainty (eds) *Ethnographic Research in the Construction Industry*. Oxford: Routledge.

Savage, R. (2011) *900,000 Frames Between Us*, documentary video produced as part of R. Savage *Digital Exile Transnational Vernacular Video and Ethnographic Film Making*, PhD thesis, University of Westminster, UK, details available online at http://www.docwest.co.uk/projects/rebecca-savage/

Schneider, A. (2011) 'Expanded visions: rethinking anthropological research and representation through experimental film', in T. Ingold (ed.), *Redrawing Anthropology: Materials, Movements, Lines*. Farnham: Ashgate.

Schneider, A. and Wright, C. (eds) (2005) *Contemporary Art and Anthropology*. Oxford: Berg.

Schneider, A. and Wright, C. (eds) (2010) *Between Art and Anthropology: Contemporary Ethnographic Practice*. Oxford: Berg.

Schwartz, D. (1992) *Waucoma Twilight: Generalizations of the Farm*. Series on Ethnographic Inquiry. Washington DC: Smithsonian Institution Press.

Schwartz, D. (1993) 'Superbowl XXVI: reflections on the manufacture of appearance', *Visual Sociology*, 8(1): 23–33.

Secondulfo, D. (1997) 'The social meaning of things: a working field for visual sociology', *Visual Sociology*, 12(2): 33–46.

Sekula, A. (1982) 'On the invention of photographic meaning', in V. Burgin (ed.), *Thinking Photography*. London: Macmillan.

Sekula, A. (1989) 'The archive and the body', in R. Bolton (ed.), *The Contest of Meaning*. Cambridge, MA: MIT Press.

Shanklin, E. (1979) 'When a good social role is worth a thousand pictures', in J. Wagner (ed.), *Images of Information*. London: SAGE.

Shove, E. and M. Pantzar (2007) 'Recruitment and reproduction: The careers and carriers of digital photography and floorball.' *Human Affairs* 17 (2): 154–67.

Silva, O. and Pink, S. (2004) 'In the Net: ethnographic photography', in S. Pink, L. Kurti and A. Afonso (eds), *Working Images*. London: Routledge.

Silver, C. and Patashnick, J. (2011) 'Finding fidelity: advancing audiovisual analysis using software', [88 paragraphs], *Forum Qualitative Sozialforschung/Forum: Qualitative Social Research*, 12(1), Art. 37, <http://nbn-resolving.de/urn:nbn:de:0114-fqs1101372>.

Slater, D. (1995) 'Domestic photography and digital culture', in M. Lister (ed.), *The Photographic Image in Digital Culture*. London: Routledge.

Spinney, J. (2009) 'Cycling the city: movement, meaning and method', *Geography Compass*, 3: 817–835.

Stafford, B. M. (2006) *Echo Objects: the Cognitive Work of Images*. Chicago: University of Chicago Press.

Stoller, P. (1997) *Sensuous Scholarship*. Philadelphia, PA: University of Pennsylvania Press.

Strecker, I. and Lydall, J. (1995) *Sweet Sorghum*. IWF, Goettingen, Germany.

Suchar, C. (1993) 'The Jordaan: community change and gentrification in Amsterdam', *Visual Sociology*, 8(1): 41–51.

Sunderland, P. and Denny, R. (2007) *Doing Anthropology in Consumer Research*. Left Coast Press Inc.

Sutton, D. (2001) *Remembrance of Repasts*. Oxford: Berg.

Ten Brink, J. (2007) *Building Bridges: The Cinema of Jean Rouch*. Wallflower.

Thrift, N. (2008) *Non-Representational Theory: Space, Politics, Affect*. London: Routledge.

Tutt, D., Pink, S., Dainty, A. and Gibb, A. (2013) 'Our own language', in S. Pink, A. Dainty and D. Tutt (eds), *Ethnographic Research in the Construction Industry*. London: Taylor & Francis.

Uricchio, W. (2011) 'The algorithmic turn: photosynth, augmented reality and the changing implications of the image', *Visual Studies*, 26 (1):25–35.

van Leeuwen, T. and Jewitt, C. (2000) (eds) *Handbook of Visual Analysis*. London: SAGE.

Van Maanen, J. (2011) *Tales of the Field: On Writing Ethnography*, Second Edition. Chicago: University of Chicago Press.

Van Mierlo, M. (1994) 'Touching the invisible', *Visual Sociology*, 9(1): 43–51.

Wagner, J. (1979) 'Avoiding error', in J. Wagner (ed.), *Images of Information*. London: SAGE.

Walsh, D. (1998) 'Doing ethnography', in C. Seale (ed.), *Researching Culture and Society*. London: SAGE.

Wendl, T. and Du Plessis, N. (1998) *Future Remembrance. Video*. IWF, Goettingen, Germany.

Wendl, T. (2001) 'Entangled traditions – photography and the history of media in southern Ghana', *Res, Journal of Anthropology and Aesthetics*, 39: 78–101.

Wesch, M. (2009) 'YouTube and you: experiences of self-awareness in the context collapse of the recording webcam', *Explorations in Media Ecology*, (8)2: 19–34.

White, S. (2003) *Participatory Video: Images that Transform and Empower*. London: SAGE.

Wiles, R., Clark, A. and Prosser, J. (2011) 'Visual research ethics at the crossroads', in E. Margolis and L. Pauwels (eds), *The SAGE Handbook of Visual Research Methods*. London: SAGE.

Wiles, R., Coffey, A., Robison, J. and Prosser, J. (2012) 'Ethical regulation and visual methods: making visual research impossible or developing good practice?', *Sociological Research Online*, 7(1)8, <http://www.socresonline.org.uk/17/1/8.html>.

Wright, C. (1998) 'The third subject: perspectives on visual anthropology', *Anthropology Today*, 14(4): 16–22.

Wright, T. (1999) *The Photography Handbook*. London: Routledge.

Young, M. W. (1998) *Malinowski's Kiriwina: Fieldwork Photography, 1915–1918*, Chicago: University of Chicago Press.

Index

900 Frames Between Us (Savage), 186

Adair, G., 114
Advances in Visual Methodology (Pink), 4, 18
Alessa, L., 153
Another Way of Telling (Berger and Mohr), 172
anthropology
  new ethnography and, 3
  objectives of, 39
  reflexivity and, 42
  See also visual anthropology
Ardèvol, E., 125–126, 128, 135–136, 137
art history, 17
art therapy, 39
Association of Social Anthropologists (ASA), 59
Atkinson, P., 34, 159
audiences, 190–191
authority, 167–170
Aylsham Care Trust (ACT), 91

Balinese Character (Bateson and Mead), 171
Banks, M., 21, 22–23, 49–50, 88, 117
Barassi, V., 22
Barbash, I., 161, 185–186, 188, 194, 198
Barndt, D., 174
Barnes, D. B., 65
Barone, F., 133
Barry, C., 159
Barthes, R., 168
Bateson, G., 73, 171
Baym, N., 124, 125, 131
Becker, H., 19, 74
Berger, J., 171–172, 173
Bhaumik, K., 30
Bird, E., 162
Blakely, A., 177, 178, *179–180*
blogs, 209–210
Boas, F., 73
Boellstorff, T., 127
Bourdieu, P., 43–44
Bowles, D., 181
Brandes, S., 169, 171
Braun, K., 190, 200
British Sociological Association (BSA), 59
Buckler, S., 175
bullfighting culture project
  captions and, 175
  categorising and archiving in, 152–153
  collaborative photography and, 88–89
  ethnographer as subject in, 89–90
  getting started with photography in, 80
  Internet and, 124–125
  meanings of photographs in, 74, 75–76, *77*, 148–150, *149*, 153–156, *154*
  methods and planning, 50–51, 53, *54*
  participant's images in, 150–151
  photo elicitation in, 93–95, *94*, 111
  photography and authority in, 169–170
  public displays and, 100
  realist uses of photography and video in, 147–148
  technology and, 56
Büscher, M., 205–206

Camas, V., 198–199
captions, 170–173, 175
Casey, N., 107, 111, 181, 195–196, 200
Castells, M., 210
Cerezo, M., 108
Chalfen, R., 114–115, 117, 209
Chaplin, E., 25, 41, 170–171, 178
Clarke, A., 61, 83, 212
Cleaning, Homes and Lifestyles project, 111, 112–114, 207–208
Clifford, J., 20–21, 165, 167–168
clips, 191–195, *193–194*
Coffey, A., 159
Cohen, A., 36, 44
collaboration
  vs. covert research, 62
  photography and, 51, 81, 86–89
  video and, 112–114, 198–199
Collier, J. Jr.
  on analysis, 144
  digital archives and, 210
  on photo elicitation, 93
  on photography, 79, 80–81

Collier *cont.*
on video, 103, 105
on visual anthropology, 19–21
Collier, M.
on analysis, 144
on photography, 79, 80–81
on video, 103, 105
on visual anthropology, 19–21
Computer Assisted Qualitative Data Analysis Software (CAQDAS), 142, 159
Conill, J., 210
Coover, R., 176–177, 210–211
Copper Working (film), 68
Couldry, N., 45, 162
covert research, 61–62
Crawford, P.I., 33, 183–184, 185
Cullen, A., 51
cultural studies, 17–18
Cultures in Webs (Coover), 176–177

Dant, T., 106, 181, 196
Davis, J., 168, 169
Dawson, A., 161, 166, 181
Desjarlais, R., 189
Devereaux, L., 188
Dicks, B., 159
digital archives, 210
digital ethnography, 127–128
digital photography, 44–45, 210
Doing Sensory Ethnography (Pink), 4–5, 34, 46–47
Doing Visual Research (Mitchell), 61
Doon School (films), 184–185, 186
Durington, M., 199

Edgar, I., 38
Edwards, E., 21, 30, 73–74, 75, 168, 172–173, 187
Emmel, N., 86
Emmison, M., 25
empowerment, 64–65, 117–119
Engelbrecht, B., 67–68
environment, 80–86, *83–84*, *85–86*
ethics
anxiety and harm to participants and, 62–63
archiving and, 159
informed consent and, 61–62, 212
institutional requirements and, 3–4
overview, 58–61
ownership of research materials and, 68
permission to publish and, *8*, 63–64
photography and, 181–182
video and, 181, *194*, 200
web-based visual ethnography and, 212
ethnographic hypermedia, 146, 203
ethnographic photographs
authority and, 167–170
captions and, 170–173
ethnographic photographs *cont.*
categorising and archiving, 210
collaboration and, 51, 81, 86–89
digital archives and, 210
digital photography and, 44–45, 210
environment and, 80–86, *83–84*, *85–86*
ethical issues and, 181–182
ethnographer as subject in, 89–92, *91*
geography and, 27
Internet and, 132–134
meanings and, 74–76, *77*, 153–156, *154*
overview, 73–78
participant-produced images and, 96–98, *97–98*
photo albums and, 95–96
photo elicitation and, 51, 92–95, *94*, 111
photo essays and, 172, 174, 177–178, *179–180*
public displays and, 99–101
rapport with research participants and, 78–80
realist uses of, 41, 147–148
reflexivity and, 76–78
video stills and, 197–198
walking and, 81–86
written words form as dominant narrative and, 173–177
See also bullfighting culture project
ethnographic present, 168
ethnographic video
audiences and, 190–191
collaboration and, 112–114, 198–199
definition of, 104–107, 184
empowerment and, 117–119
ethical issues in, 181, *194*, 200
geography and, 27
getting started with, 110–111
Internet and, 134–138
meanings and, 156–158
overview, 103–104
participants' relationships with, 107–110
photo elicitation in, 95
realist uses of, 41, 147–148
reflexivity and, 21, 184, 187–190
research and representation in, 185–187
by research participants, 114–117, 207
seeing with, 111–112
technology and, 103–104
transcripts and, 195–198
uses of, 191–198, *193–194*
video stills and, 181, 195–198
viewing with participants, 119–121, *120*, 150
visual anthropology and, 103, 183–185, 191
See also video tour method
ethnographic writing
captions and, 170–173, 175
contemporary approaches to, 165–167

ethnographic writing *cont.*
ethical issues in, 181–182
photo essays and, 172, 174, 177–178, *179–180*, 197
photographs in texts of words, 173–177
photography and authority in, 167–170
video and, 195–198
web-based visual ethnography and, 203–213
ethnography
definition of, 18–19, 34–35
objectives of, 39
See also visual ethnography
Evans, J., 43
exhibitions, 99–101

Faces in the Crowd (film), 95
Fahmy, E., 207, 212
Ferrándiz, F., 110, 116, 119, 196–197
Fire in the Dark (Buckler), 175
flickr culture, 57
Flores, C., 117, 118, 199
Forrest, E., 134
Fors, V., 132–133, 134, 196
A Fortunate Man (Berger and Mohr), 171–172
Forum Qualitative Sozialforschung/Forum: Qualitative Social Research (FQS) (journal), 204–205
The Future of Visual Anthropology (Pink), 22

Gardner, R., 105
Garrett, B. L., 27
Geertz, C., 17
Gender Advertisements (Goffman), 171
geography, 3, 17, 26–29
Gibson, J. J., 31
Gillen, F., 73
Gilroy, R., 99–100
Goffman, I., 171
Gold, S. J., 24
Goldfine, O., 178
Goldfine, R., 178
Gómez Cruz, E., 43, 45, 57, 134
Goopy, S., 97–99, 177, 178, *179–180*
Graham, C., 135
Grasseni, C., 23, 111–112, 113
Grimshaw, A., 189

Haddon, A.C., 73
Halford, S., 25, 205
Hall, S., 29, 43
Hammersley, M., 34
Handbook of Social Research (van Leeuwen and Jewitt), 18
Harper, D., 24–25, 92, 93, 175
Harvey, P., 17
Hastrup, K., 52–53, 188
Hatherell, W., 177, 178
Hatton, P., 76–78
Henley, P., 95
Hindmarsh, J., 181
Hine, C., 127, 128–129
Hjorth, L., 131–132
Hockey, J., 161, 166, 181
Hodgetts, D., 51
Hogan, S., 39, 86
Holbrook, B., 159
Home Truths (Pink), 200
Homenatge a Catalunya II (documentary), 210
Hubbard, P., 86
human geography, 5
Hutnyk, J., 168

informed consent, 61–62, 212
Ingold, T., 23, 30–31, 39, 40, 82, 107, 162
interdisciplinarity, 15–19, *16*
Internet
research planning and, 55
See also web-based visual ethnography
Internet studies, 17
interviews
photo elicitation and, 51, 92–95, *94*, 111
video and, 206–207
iPhone, *86*
Irving, A., 39, 82, 85–86, 182

James, W., 161, 166, 181
Jenks, C., 39–40
Jewitt, C., 18
Jhala, J., 186
Josephides, L., 9–10, 166–167

Kellett, P., 99–100
Kliskey, A., 153
Knowles, C., 25, 175, 205
Kozinets, R., 127
Kürti, L., 100–101

Lammer, C., 16, 25, 92, 117–119, 160, 209
Lapenta, F., 26, 130–131
Laurier, E., 125, 135
Leder Mackley, K., *16*, *67*, 114, 207–208
LEEDR (Lower Effort Energy Demand Reduction) Project
clips and, 193
ethical issues in, *67*
interdisciplinarity and, *16*
permission to publish and, *8*
video tours and, *8*, 114, 150
viewing video with participants in, 121
Leeuwen, T. van, 18
Leonard, P., 175
Lister, M., 29
Lloyd, D., 97–99, 177, 178, *179–180*
Localizing the Internet (Postill), 175
Lomax, H., 107, 111, 181, 195–196, 200
Lorang's Way (film), 186
Lyon, D., 25, 76–78, 177

MacDougall, D.
- attention to the senses and, 46
- on audiences, 191
- *Doon School* films and, 184–185, 186
- on ethnographic images, 40
- on methodology, 9
- *Photo Wallahs* and, 95
- reflexivity and, 21, 187–189

MacDougall, J., 21, 187
Mack, L., 153
Mack, S., 153, 211
Made to be Seen (Banks and Ruby), 22–23
Malinowski, B., 73
Manovich, L., 130
maps and mapping, 28
Marcus, G., 166
Margolis, E., 18
Martinez, A., 108
Marvin, G., 198
Mason, B., 159
Mason, J., 115–116, 207
Massey, D., 28
McCarthy, A., 162
McGuigan, J., 9
Mead, M., 19, 73, 171
meanings
- analysis and, 74–76, *77*, 142–146, 150–151, 153–158, *154*
- categorising and archiving, 151–153, 158–160
- overview, 141–142
- participant's images and, 150–151
- scholarship and, 148–150

media anthropology, 17, 45
media studies, 17
Mirror Mirror (film), 119–121, *120*, 135
Mitchell, C., 61
Mitchell, W. J. T., 30, 33
Moffat, Z., 119–121, *120*, 135, 199, 210
Mohr, J., 171–172, 173
more-than-representational theory, 5, 28
Morphy, H., 21, 49
Muir, S., 115–116, 207, 212
Murthy, D., 127–128

new ethnography, 3, 24–25, 93
non-representational theory, 5, 28, 31, 151

O'Brien, V., 135
Okely, J., 42, 95–96, 100, 150
O'Neill, M., 25, 86
online journals, 204–209
O'Regan, K., 31
Orobitg, G., 55–56
Outside/Inside (Coover), 210–211

Pantzar, M., 44–45
Passing Girl, Riverside (Braun), 190
Patashnick, J., 159
Pauwels, L., 18, 81
Pels, P., 60
Pemberton, S., 207, 212
The People of the Sierra (Pitt-Rivers), 171
photo elicitation, 51, 92–95, *94*, 111
photo essays, 172, 174, 177–178, *179–180*, 197
Photo Wallahs (film), 95
photographs. *See* ethnographic photographs
La Piel del Monte (documentary), 198–199
Pinney, C., 87
Pitt-Rivers, J., 169, 171
Pole, C., 18
Pollock, G., 178
Postill, J., 45, 51, 90–91, 175
postmodernism, 3, 20–21, 36–38, 93
practice theory, 45
Pratt, M. L., 168, 169
Press, I., 169
Prosser, J., 7, 24, 61, 195
public displays, 99–101

Qualitative Research and Hypermedia (Dicks et al.), 159

Radley, A., 51, *97–98*, 99
Ranera, P., 108
Rapport, N., 36, 44
Redrawing Anthropology (Ingold), 23
reflexivity
- anthropology and, 42
- ethnographic photographs and, 76–78
- ethnographic video and, 21, 184, 187–190
- visual ethnography and, 3–4, 36–38, 147

Representation (Hall), 29
research participants
- anxiety and harm to, 62–63
- collaboration with, 51, 62, 86–89, 112–114, 199
- empowerment and, 64–65, 117–119
- as image-makers, 43–46
- participant-produced images and, 96–98, *97–98*
- participant-produced video and, 114–117, 207
- permission to publish and, *8*, 63–64
- photo albums and, 95–96
- public displays and, 99–101
- rapport with, 78–80
- relationships with video, 107–110
- technology and, 56–57
- viewing video with, 119–121, *120*

Rich, M., 114–115, 117, 209
Rollwagen, J., 184
Rose, G., 26–27, 29
Rouch, J., 117, 186, 187–188
Rouncefield, M., 135
Rowes, J., 61
Ruby, J., 19, 22–23, 184, 185, 187

Ruiz, A., 210
Ryan, J., 27

Sage, D., 37
SAGE Handbook of Visual Research Methods (Margolis and Pauwels), 18
San Cornelio, G., 125, 135–136, 137
Savage, R., 186
Schwartz, D., 24, 79, 81, 93, 178
Secondulfo, D., 81
Seeing is Believing (Pole), 18
Sekula, A., 41
Sensate (journal), 208–209
senses
  culture studies and, 30–31
  ethnographic writing and, 166
  geography and, 28
  visual ethnography and, 4–5, 31–32, 46–47
Sensuous Scholarship (Stoller), 166
Servon, L., *86*
Shanklin, E., 79
Shove, E., 44–45
Silva, O. da, *6*
Silver, C., 159
Slow Cities project
  categorising and archiving in, 153
  ethical issues in, *66*
  ethnographer as subject in, 91–92, *91*
  getting started with photography in, 80
  interwoven fieldwork materials in, *145*
  meanings of photographs in, 74–75
  participant's photographs in, 151
  photography and walking in, 81–82, *84*, *85–86*
  public displays and, 101
  reflexivity and, 37
  research participants in, *7*, 80
  technology and, 42, 57
  video and, 109–110
  video tours and, 150, 158
Smith, P., 25
social anthropology, 3
Sociological Research on-line (journal), 204–205, 208
sociology, 3, 17–18, 44–45
Sociology and Visual Representations (Chaplin), 25
Spencer, B., 73
Spinney, J., 27
Stafford, B. M., 30–31
Strecker, I., 42
Strecker, R., 42
Sutton, D., 170
Sweet Sorghum (documentary), 42
Sweetman, P., 25

Taussig, M., 189
Taylor, D., *97–98*, 99
Taylor, L., 161, 185–186, 188, 194, 198
Taylor-Brown, S., 65
transcripts, 195–198
Treré, E., 22
Tutt, D., 89, 181

Uricchio, W., 129–130, 131

video. *See* ethnographic video
video diary method, 112, 115, 207, 209
Video Intervention/Prevention Assessment (VIA), 115, 209
video stills, 181, 195–198
video tour method
  clips and, 192
  collaboration and, 112–114
  organisation and, 158
  participants' relationships with video and, 108–109
  permission to publish and, *8*
  planning and, 50
  research and representation in, 186
  viewing video with participants in, 150
videographic geographies, 27
virtual ethnography, 127–128
vision, 33–34
visual anthropology
  historical development of, 5, 17–18, 19–24
  photography in, 73–74, 88
  video and film in, 103, 183–185, 191
Visual Anthropology (J. Collier and M. Collier), 19–21
visual culture studies, 17–18, 29–31
visual ethnography
  culture studies and, 17–18, 29–31
  ethnographers and research participants as image-makers in, 43–46
  geography and, 3, 17, 26–29
  historical development of, 3–6
  interdisciplinarity and, 15–19, *16*
  invisibility and reality in, 38–41
  methods for, 49–53
  overview, 1–2
  planning and, 53–56
  reflexivity and, 3–4, 36–38, 147
  sensory turn in, 4–5, 31–32, 46–47
  sociology and, 17–18, 24–26
  technology and, 4, 5, 41–43, 56–58, 103–104, 204
  theory, methodology and method in, 7–10
  vision and, 33–34
  See also ethnographic photographs; ethnographic video; web-based visual ethnography
Visual Ethnography (journal), 208–209
Visual Interventions (Pink), 23, 117
Visual Methodologies (Rose), 26

visual sociology, 17–18, 24–26
visual studies, 17
Visual Studies (formerly *Visual Sociology*) (journal), 18, 135, 174, 177, 204

walking, 81–86
Walsh, D., 36
web-based visual ethnography
  archiving and, 159–160
  dissemination and formal publishing, 203–213
  ethical issues and, 212
  Internet as context in, 128–132
  online journals and, 204–209
  overview, 123–128
  photography and, 132–134
web-based visual ethnography *cont.*
  project blog and websites and, 209–210
  video and, 134–138
web-cams, 136–137
websites, 209–210
Weiner, L., 65
Wells, L., 29
Wesch, M., 127, 137, 209
Wiles, R., 61
Women and Bullfighting (Pink), 74, 170, 175
Worth, S., 114
Wright, C., 104
Wright, T., 41, 76, 173
Writing Culture (Clifford), 20, 167–168

Zulay Frente al Siglo XXI (film), 198

CPSIA information can be obtained
at www.ICGtesting.com
Printed in the USA
BVHW060912300720
584600BV00003B/15

9 781446 211175